CIVIL PROCEDURE AND HARMONISATION OF LAW

CIVIL PROCEDURE AND HARMONISATION OF LAW

The Dynamics of EU and International Treaties

Edited by

Anna Nylund
Magne Strandberg

intersentia
Cambridge – Antwerp – Chicago

Intersentia Ltd
Sheraton House | Castle Park
Cambridge | CB3 0AX | United Kingdom
Tel.: +44 1223 370 170 | Fax: +44 1223 370 169
Email: mail@intersentia.co.uk
www.intersentia.com | www.intersentia.co.uk

Distribution for the UK and Ireland:
NBN International
Airport Business Centre, 10 Thornbury Road
Plymouth, PL6 7PP
United Kingdom
Tel.: +44 1752 202 301 | Fax: +44 1752 202 331
Email: orders@nbninternational.com

Distribution for Europe and all other countries:
Intersentia Publishing nv
Groenstraat 31
2640 Mortsel
Belgium
Tel.: +32 3 680 15 50 | Fax: +32 3 658 71 21
Email: mail@intersentia.be

Distribution for the USA and Canada:
Independent Publishers Group
Order Department
814 North Franklin Street
Chicago, IL 60610
USA
Tel.: +1 800 888 4741 (toll free) | Fax: +1 312 337 5985
Email: orders@ipgbook.com

Civil Procedure and Harmonisation of Law. The Dynamics of EU and International Treaties

ISBN 978-1-78068-693-6
D/2019/7849/30
NUR 822

British Library Cataloguing in Publication Data. A catalogue record for this book is available from the British Library.

PREFACE

This book presents the results of a research project that looks at the interplay between national and international civil procedure law. While the project covers many kinds of international law – both soft law and hard law from a number of international institutions – the influence of European Union civil procedure law on national civil procedure forms the heart of the project. The editors of this book, together with Professor Halvard Haukeland Fredriksen, had previously conducted research on the interplay between Norwegian civil procedure and EU law. The interest in EU law in Norway may appear somewhat surprising at first, since Norway is not a member of the Union. However, Norway is part of the single market through its participation in the European Economic Area Agreement. Accordingly, EU law exerts an influence on national civil procedure through the EEA Agreement, voluntary harmonisation, hard law and soft law.

Our previous engagements in comparative projects sparked our curiosity, as we noticed divergent attitudes, practices, policies and outcomes in countries in our geographical neighbourhood. As a result, in 2016, we initiated a research project, drawing on our networks and discussions with Professor Volker Lipp, that focused on the interplay between national and international civil procedure law in north-western Europe. A research workshop was organised in Tromsø in late August and early September 2017, where experts from Germany, the Netherlands, the United Kingdom and the Nordic countries took part. Most of the papers contained in this book are based on the discussions that took place during that workshop.

We would like to express our gratitude to the Faculty of Law at the University of Tromsø – The Arctic University of Norway for its financial contribution, which made both the workshop and the book possible. We also wish to thank Satu Svahn for her review of the English language of the contributions. Harald Hofgaard, a student in Tromsø, provided valuable assistance in preparing the papers for publication. Finally, we are grateful to all of the authors for their participation.

Anna Nylund and Magne Strandberg
Tromsø/Bergen, August 2018

CONTENTS

LIST OF CONTRIBUTORS

Alain Ancery is Legal Counsel for a bank. He has previously worked as a Law Clerk at the Supreme Court of the Netherlands. He obtained his PhD from the University of Groningen in 2012, conducting his research on the subject of the *Ex Officio* Application of EU Law. He regularly publishes on the interface between EU Law and Dutch civil law. alain.ancery@ing.com

Torbjörn Andersson is Professor of Civil and Criminal Procedural Law at Uppsala University. His research is primarily concerned with the fields of Swedish and international civil and criminal procedural law, EU law in general and EU competition law. torbjorn.andersson@jur.uu.se

Ivo Bach is Professor of Civil Law, Medical Law, and European and International Private Law at the University of Göttingen, Germany. ivo.bach@jura.uni-goettingen.de

Laura Ervo is Professor and Excellent Teaching Practitioner at Örebro University School of Law, Psychology and Social Work, Sweden. She is also Adjunct Professor (docent) in procedural law at the University of Turku, the University of Helsinki and the University of Eastern Finland. laura.ervo@oru.se

Halvard Haukeland Fredriksen is Professor of European Law and Civil Procedural Law at the University of Bergen, Norway. He is Co-chair of the Research group of civil procedural law at the Faculty of Law at the University of Bergen. halvard.fredriksen@uib.no

Wolfgang Hau is Professor at the Ludwig-Maximilians-Universität Munich, where he holds the Chair for Private Law and German, International and Comparative Civil Procedure. He is also a Judge at the Oberlandesgericht (Higher Regional Court) in Germany. wolfgang.hau@jura.uni-muenchen.de

Maria Astrup Hjort is Associate Professor at the University of Oslo where she holds the Chair for Civil Procedure. Her teaching and research cover issues in national and comparative civil and criminal procedure, legal history and ethics. m.a.hjort@jus.uio.no

Bart Krans is a Professor at the University of Leiden, the Netherlands, where he holds the Chair of Private Law and Civil Procedure Law. His research mainly concerns civil procedure law and contract law. Two of his areas of interest are the law of evidence in civil cases and the influence of EU law on Dutch civil procedure law. h.b.krans@law.leidenuniv.nl

Volker Lipp is Professor of Civil Law, Civil Procedure, Medical Law and Comparative Law at the Faculty of Law at Georgia Augusta University Göttingen, Germany. vlipp@gwdg.de

Anna Nylund is Professor of Law and Head of the Research group for procedural law and dispute resolution at the University of Tromsø – The Arctic University of Norway. anna.nylund@uit.no

John Sorabji is a Senior Teaching Fellow at University College London and the principal Legal Adviser to the Lord Chief Justice of England and Wales and the Master of the Rolls. He is the author of, amongst other publications, *English Civil Justice after Woolf and Jackson*. j.sorabji@ucl.ac.uk

Eva Storskrubb is Associate Professor (docent) of Procedural Law and researcher at Uppsala University, Sweden. She is also a practicing lawyer holding the title of Dispute Resolution Counsel. She has acted as co-reporter for two working groups in the ongoing ELI-UNIDROIT project on European Rules of Civil Procedure. eva.storskrubb@jur.uu.se

Magne Strandberg is Professor of Civil Procedural Law at the University of Bergen, Norway. He is Co-chair of the Research group of civil procedural law at the Faculty of Law at the University of Bergen. He is also Member of two working groups in the ongoing ELI-UNIDROIT project on European rules of civil procedure. magne.strandberg@uib.no

LIST OF ABBREVIATIONS

AcP	Archiv für die civilistische Praxis
BGBl	Bundesgestetzblatt
CMLR	Common Market Law Review
Ct	Court
DL	Defensor Legis
EC	European Communities
ECHR	European Convention on Human Rights
ECJ	European Court of Justice
ECR	European Court Reports
EEA	European Economic Area
EFTA	European Free Trade Association
ERPL	European Review of Private Law
EU	European Union
EUI	European University Institute
EuZW	Zeitschrift für Europäisches Wirtschaftsrecht
Family	Fam
Int	International
IP	Intellectual Property
J	Journal
JFT	Tidskrift utgiven av Juridiska Föreningen i Finland
JT	Juridisk tidskrift
JuS	Juristische Schulung
JZ	Juristenzeitung
L	Law, Legal
LoR	Lov og Rett
MDR	Monatsschrift für deutsches Recht
MvV	Maandblad voor Vermogensrecht
NJW	Neue Juristische Wochenschrift
NOU	Norske Offentlige Utredninger
OJ	Official Journal
Ot.prp.	Odelstingsproposisjon
Priv	Private
Proc	Procedural
Prop.	Proposisjon til Stortinget (Bill to the Norwegian Parliament)
Q	Quarterly

RabelsZ	Rabels Zeitschrift für ausländisches und internationals Privatrecht/ The Rabel Journal of Comparative and International Private Law
Rep	Report(s)
Rev	Review
RSCAS	Robert Schuman Centre for Advanced Studies
Rt.	Norsk Retstidende
SIEPS	Swedish Institute of European Policy Studies
TCR	Tijdschrift voor Civiele Rechtspleging
TEU	Treaty on the European Union
TFEU	Treaty on the Functioning of the European Union
TfR	Tidskrift for Rettsvitenskap
TRIPS	The Agreement on Trade-Related Aspects of Intellectual Property Rights
UP	University Press
YB	Yearbook
ZEuP	Zeitschrift für Europäisches Privatrecht
ZEuS	Zeitschrift für Europarechtliche Studien
ZRP	Zeitschrift für Rechtspolitik
ZZP	Zeitschrift für Zivilprozess

INTRODUCTION

Anna Nylund and Magne Strandberg

1. MULTIPLE LEVELS OF INTERNATIONAL RULES ON CIVIL PROCEDURE

Although civil procedure law has been traditionally considered to be deeply embedded in national (legal) culture and thus resistant to harmonisation,[1] legislative efforts over the last few decades have given rise to a growing international influence on national civil procedure. While civil procedure law in the nineteenth and twentieth centuries was not free from foreign influences, ideas were mainly transferred from one country to another and not from international law to national law. Although the Brussels Convention of 1968[2] and the European Convention on Human Rights of 1950 marked the early emergence of supranational law of civil procedure, the momentum for extensive regulation was gained only at the turn of the millennium. Today, supranational and international influence on national civil procedure emanates from multiple sources, both binding and non-binding.

During the last couple of decades, a body of international instruments concerning civil procedure has emerged. Most of these emanate from the European Union (EU), but other institutions, such as the United Nations, the European Council, The Hague Conference on Private International Law and UNIDROIT, are also of importance. The current situation regarding

1 R. Marcus, 'Exceptionalism and convergence: form versus content and categorical views of procedure' [2010] *Supreme Court Law Review* 521.
2 Brussels Convention on jurisdiction and the enforcement of judgments in civil and commercial matters [1972] OJ L299/32.

international legal sources on civil procedure is rather complex and not easily comprehensible, but we can identify a number of categories or levels into which most of the international rules on civil procedure law should fit:

- basic human rights;
- general principles of EU law;
- EU secondary law;
- international conventions or treaties on legal co-operation; and
- soft law.

As the first category, at both an overarching and a deep level, we find basic human rights. From the perspective of civil procedure law, the most important human rights are the right to a fair and public hearing found in Article 6 of the European Convention on Human Rights (ECHR), Article 14 of the UN Covenant on Civil and Political Rights, and Article 47 of the European Charter of Fundamental Rights. However, civil procedure law is also influenced by other human rights, such as the right to respect for privacy and family life found in Article 8 ECHR and the right to an effective remedy found in Article 13 ECHR.

At the level of EU principles, we find the principles of effectiveness and equivalence. The principles are not based on any specific EU regulation or directive, but have been developed by the European Court of Justice (ECJ).[3] The principle of effectiveness means that national procedural law cannot make it impossible or excessively difficult to derive rights based on EU law, and the principle of equivalence means that national procedural law cannot be less favourable for rights based on EU law than for any other rights. These principles do not set out specific requirements for national law, but are general minimum standards that the whole system of procedural law must meet.

As a third category, we find a growing EU secondary law on civil procedure. After the emergence of the EU civil procedure law 50 years ago with the Brussels Convention of 1968,[4] several EU regulations and directives now directly and primarily deal with matters of civil procedure law. The rather long list includes, *inter alia*, the Brussels I *bis* Regulation,[5] the Evidence Regulation,[6] the Service Regulation,[7] the Small Claims Regulation,[8] and the Alternative Dispute

---

3 See Storskrubb, in this volume, for further details.

4 Convention of 27 September 1968 on jurisdiction and enforcement of judgments in civil and commercial matters.

5 Regulation (EU) 1215/2012 on jurisdiction and the recognition and enforcement of judgments in civil and commercial matters [2012] OJ L351/1.

6 Regulation (EC) 1206/2001 on co-operation between the courts of the Member States in the taking of evidence in civil and commercial matters [2001] OJ L174/1.

7 Regulation (EC) 1393/2007 on the service in the Member States of judicial and extrajudicial documents in civil or commercial matters (service of documents) [2007] OJ L324/79.

8 Regulation (EC) 861/2007 establishing a European Small Claims Procedure [2007] OJ L1999/1.

Resolution Directive.[9] Other regulations and directives primarily deal with substantive matters, but also contain clauses on civil procedure law. The Directive on damages for infringement of EU competition law,[10] for instance, contains several rules on evidence and proof, though it primarily deals with matters of tort and competition law. Compared to other international instruments that influence civil procedure law, EU hard law is quite technical and detailed. A further characteristic of EU hard law is that it has a limited scope of application, for instance covering only cross-border disputes or disputes concerning one type of substantive law. Therefore, these rules may be difficult to implement in a national procedural system that typically takes a general approach, with one set of rules for all substantive cases. ECJ case law interpreting secondary law has been paramount to ensuring the uniform application of secondary law and the necessary development of EU law in general. The doctrine of *ex officio* application of EU consumer and competition law serves as an example.

As a fourth category, we find different sorts of international conventions and treaties, by which we mean law that neither contains human rights nor can be considered EU law. A few international treaties directly deal with matters of civil procedure, such as the Hague Convention of 1970 on the taking of evidence.[11] Other treaties primarily deal with substantive matters, but nevertheless include some articles on civil procedural matters. An example is the TRIPS Agreement,[12] which mainly deals with substantive rules for intellectual property rights, but also contains, in Article 50, procedural rules on provisional measures and access to information. Such rights to information are also an important aspect of the EU Directive on enforcement of intellectual property rights,[13] which further develops the rights contained in the TRIPS Agreement and is thus an example of the important interplay between global law and EU law. The 2007 Hague Convention on the International Recovery of Child Support and Other Forms of Family Maintenance was drafted in parallel with the EU Maintenance Regulation, and, as a result, EU law is interlaced with international law. EU law may also give rise to the need for specific international treaties reaching beyond the Union. The Lugano Convention,[14] which connects Norway, Iceland and

---

9 Directive (EC) 52/2008 on certain aspects of mediation in civil and commercial matters [2008] OJ L136/3.

10 Directive (EU) 104/2014 on certain rules governing actions for damages under national law for infringements of the competition law provisions of the Member States and of the European Union [2014] OJ L349/1.

11 Convention on the taking of evidence abroad in civil and commercial matters, The Hague, 18 March 1970.

12 Agreement on Trade-Related Aspects of Intellectual Property Rights, annex 1C of the Marrakesh Agreement Establishing the World Trade Organization of 15 April 1994.

13 Directive (EC) 48/2004 on the enforcement of intellectual property rights [2004] OJ L157/2004.

14 Convention of 13 October 2007 on jurisdiction and the recognition and enforcement of judgments in civil and commercial matters (Lugano Convention) [2007] OJ L 339/3.

Switzerland to the Brussels regime, is based on the Brussels Regulation and is normally interpreted in line with the Brussels Convention and its interpretation by the ECJ.

At a fifth level, we find international soft law – that is, non-binding rules or guidelines. A well-known example of soft law is the ambitious project 'From Transnational Principles to European Rules of Civil Procedure', which is a collaboration between the European Law Institute (ELI) and UNIDROIT. The project is an ongoing effort; it takes the ALI-UNIDROIT Principles of Transnational Civil Procedure as its starting point and aims at further development of a concise model law for Europe.[15] Soft law on civil procedure may also be established by an EU recommendation, such as the recommended procedural principles for collective redress.[16]

These instruments serve various goals. Some of them aim primarily at facilitating cross-border proceedings, others at harmonisation or at least approximation of civil procedure, still others at improving the quality of proceedings or enforcement of certain rights, or any combination of these. Some of them are intended as general rules applicable to all kinds of civil and commercial cases, while others are intimately connected to a specific area of substantive law, such as consumer law, competition law or family maintenance. Although the primary goal might not be harmonisation or approximation, these serve as subsidiary goals for many of these instruments. Their impact on national law varies both in strength and form. Some have limited impact, while others have the potential to produce fundamental changes. Much EU legislation is sectoral, aiming at enforcing rights, but this may, by contrast, be at odds with the national emphasis on coherence and structure. The effects of an instrument may also vary between states, with the strength and nature of the influence depending on numerous factors.[17]

2. THE INTERPLAY BETWEEN NATIONAL CIVIL PROCEDURE AND INTERNATIONAL RULES

The relationship between international, supranational and national civil procedure law is complex. There is the potential that the adjustments necessary to meet obligations arising from supranational law may cause trouble. There could be, for instance, tensions between the conceptual framework of national law and

---

15 See Sorabji, 'The ELI-UNIDROIT Project', in this volume.

16 Recommendation 2013/396/EU of 11 June 2013 on common principles for injunctive and compensatory collective redress mechanisms in the Member States concerning violations of rights granted under Union law [2013] OJ L201/60.

17 See e.g. A. Nylund and B. Krans (eds), *The European Union and National Civil Procedure* (Intersentia 2016).

concepts that have to be imported or invented to meet duties under supranational or international law. Some international regulation is sector-specific or limited to cross-border cases only. While sector-specific rules may be beneficial in terms of providing rules tailored to the specific problems encountered in enforcing certain types of substantive law, such as family maintenance or intellectual property rights, they may also result in fragmentation of national rules and lack of coherence. The method of implementation, 'over-implementation', and the content and quality of enacting 'bridge' regulation when connecting international regulation to national regulation, may moderate the potential adverse consequences.

International regulations can also be a source of inspiration for the development of national law. Concepts and solutions from international law may be better – either more accurate or more effective – than those applied nationally. Although soft law is often associated with benchmarking and providing inspiration for national reforms, hard law and case law may also induce us to rethink national rules, concepts and institutions.

International regulation may also be affected by national law, for instance when an international rule picks up concepts and legal instruments developed successfully in one or several states. In practice, the success of international law is also dependent on national law. Several international instruments, both those that primarily concern substantive law and those dealing more directly with procedural law, rely on national judicial systems to ensure efficient enforcement of rights and efficient cross-border proceedings.

International rules seem to influence national civil procedure in various ways and with varying intensity, according to recent studies that also identify several underlying factors that may explain these variations:[18] the degree of similarity between features or concepts in the instruments and in the established national law, the degree of knowledge about the instruments, attitudes towards Europeanisation, quality of the legislation implementing the international instruments or bridging these to national law, and differences in approaches to and methods of implementation.[19] The existing studies are primarily exploratory and tentative in their conclusions, offering some insights into the field of study and serving as a rough sketch for future, more in-depth studies.

---

18 V. Harsagi and M. Kengyel (eds), *Einfluss des Europäischen Zivilverfahrensrechts auf die nationalen Rechtsordnungen* (Nomos 2009); M. Ahrens, V. Lipp and I. Varga (eds), *Europäische Zivilprozessrecht. Einfluss auf Deutschland und Ungarn* (Universitätsverlag Göttingen 2011); X.E. Kramer and C.H. van Rhee (eds), *Civil Litigation in a Globalising Worlds* (Springer 2012); and A. Nylund and B. Krans (eds), *The European Union and National Civil Procedure* (Intersentia 2016).

19 B. Krans and A. Nylund, 'Conclusions and Outlook' in A. Nylund and B. Krans (eds), *The European Union and National Civil Procedure* (Intersentia 2016).

3. MULTI-SPEED INTEGRATION AND CIVIL PROCEDURE

In addition to the various levels of international and supranational law affecting national civil procedure, the varying relationships to the EU and EU law among European countries adds to the complexity by creating multi-speed integration. Norway, Iceland and Liechtenstein take part in the internal market due to their membership of the European Economic Area (EEA) Agreement. There are important differences between EEA membership and full EU membership, and the differences pertaining to civil procedure law are notable.[20] Judicial co-operation does not fall under the scope of the EEA Agreement. Hence, EU directives and regulations that primarily deal with civil procedural matters are not applicable. Moreover, the official Norwegian view is that matters of civil procedure law, as such, are outside the scope of the EEA Agreement, unless a specific article in the Agreement has certain effects on procedural law. According to the official Norwegian view, then, EU hard law that contains a combination of substantive law and procedural law is also not considered to have EEA-relevance. Nevertheless, Norwegian civil procedure law is still affected by EU law. Firstly, Norway is a party to the Lugano Convention, which is, at least in the main, parallel to the Brussels I *bis* Regulation and interpreted in line with the ECJ's interpretations of the that Regulation. Secondly, the general principles of equivalence and effectiveness also apply under the EEA Agreement, which means that even case law developed by the ECJ under these principles is binding for Norwegian law. Thirdly, Norway has voluntarily incorporated into its national law several of the regulations and directives containing rules on civil procedure law, especially those where certain procedural arrangements have been ruled out in order to achieve goals and purposes related to the substantive law in question.[21]

In a similar way, Denmark, Ireland and the United Kingdom have opt-outs from judicial co-operation, which reduces coherence within the EU. While quite a lot of academic attention has been paid to the Europeanisation of civil procedure law, less attention has been paid to how European law, in itself or accompanied by other forms of international law, affects the systems of civil procedure in each jurisdiction. It seems that most of the debates on incorporation of European law concern the effect of one element of EU law on

---

[20] See A. Nylund, 'Norway: An Insider Outside – or an Outsider Inside – European Civil Justice' in A. Nylund and B. Krans (eds), *The European Union and National Civil Procedure* (Intersentia 2016) 101–114; H.H. Fredriksen and M. Strandberg, 'Norwegian Civil Procedure under the Influence of EU Law' in A. Uzelac and C.H. van Rhee (eds), *Transformation of Civil Justice. Unity and Diversity* (Springer 2018) 41–62.

[21] See Hjort, in this volume.

one particular jurisdiction. As a result, the approach is oftentimes piecemeal. Comparative aspects of the implementation of European law and its effects on national law have received less attention. Since the regulations on a European or international level must be implemented and incorporated into national civil procedure law, we may ask whether the effects of European instruments are alike in each jurisdiction or whether there are major differences. Moreover, there may be variation in the reception of different kinds of instruments: some instruments may have a profound impact on national legal systems, while others may have less impact. Thus, comparing categories of instruments may help us uncover the extent to which these produce harmonisation and serve as an impetus for reforms of national law.

4. THE PRESENT STUDY: PURPOSE, SELECTION OF COUNTRIES AND METHODOLOGY

This study grew out of a desire to understand the interplay between national law and various types of international rules within Europe today. Several recently published studies have taken that interplay as (part) of their topic (see especially the research mentioned in section 2 above), so one of our aims is to further develop the understanding of that interplay in greater depth and detail. In order to do so, our study deals with selected aspects of European and international legal instruments, how these instruments have affected a small group of European countries, and the modes of implementation applied by each country in order to cope with the instruments. Narrowing the scope in this way allows us to go into more detail, to compare the impact of one specific (set of) international instrument(s) in the selected countries and to compare the impact of different instruments. Concurrently, our aim is to discuss similarities and differences between the sources of international rules and national law in the selected countries. Perhaps it is the case that EU hard law, for instance, is more powerful or influential in some countries than in others, perhaps some countries are more willing to engage in benchmarking and voluntary 'over-implementation' than others, or perhaps some countries are more or less haphazard in dealing with EU hard law.

We have chosen a small number of north-western European jurisdictions – England and Wales, Finland, Germany, the Netherlands, Norway and Sweden – as the targets of our study. The reasons for choosing these specific countries are that the legal cultural differences between the countries are not very profound and that their civil procedural systems are based on a number of common principles. England is the only exception, as common law has some marked differences to the law of the other countries. However, the societies are fairly similar, and the court culture relies partly on similar ideas and is highly efficient and well-functioning in all the countries studied. Recent decades have also marked a clear approximation among the countries in this study. These countries are bound by more or less the same European rules, are obliged to incorporate these rules into their national legal systems, and are characterised by relatively efficient civil justice systems. On these assumptions, it should be interesting to go deeper into the following questions: How are the respective countries affected by, for instance, a particular EU regulation? Has the regulation resulted in changes to the national law? Are the European rules, or the national rules following from them, often applied in court practice?

Our selection of international instruments has been guided by an ambition of comparing the impact of different types of instruments, how different type of instruments are implemented in a country and how the implementation of an instrument may affect other aspects of civil procedure law than those directly covered by the instrument. Therefore, we have included all sorts of EU hard law that may affect civil procedure law, including both regulations that primarily deal with civil procedure law and regulations that primarily regulate substantive law and only indirectly concern civil procedure law. This approach serves as an invitation to discussion of how these instruments have been implemented into a domestic system of national procedure law, whether the instruments have led to domestic inconsistencies, and whether the instruments play any important role in practice. Furthermore, we have focused in particular on EU consumer law, the procedural requirements developed by the ECJ, and whether or how these instruments have had any influence on the countries studied. Finally, we focus on maintenance cases, which allows us to go deeply into a specific branch of civil procedure law and lets us analyse the interplay between national law, European law and other kinds of international law.

In addition, we wish to explore whether the instruments lead to harmonisation of law by encouraging reassessment or even adaptation of national rules, concepts and doctrines, or by serving as a source of inspiration for national reforms. Although harmonisation is often at least an implicit goal when international civil procedure law is established and developed, several factors may hinder approximation of civil procedure. The quality of EU law has sometimes been cited as a reason for its lack of harmonising effects.[22] The possibility of finding superior solutions in international law may also be overlooked at the national level. Soft law with an outspoken interest in harmonisation could prove to be as efficient as hard law in producing harmonisation of law.

We have taken what could be characterised as a loose, semi-structured approach. Each author was requested to answer a few broad questions to allow for the authors to explore their subject freely. As the field is still nascent, the risk

22 See X.E. Kramer, 'Small claim, simple recovery? The European small claims procedure and its implementation in the member states' [2011] *ERA Forum* 119; and R. Manko, 'European Small Claims Procedure: Legal Analysis of the Commission's Proposal to Remedy Weaknesses in the Current System', European Parliamentary Research Service 2014.

of asking the 'wrong' questions remains high, and an open format allows each author to contribute to posing 'appropriate' questions and offering their views on how the topic is best approached. As a result, the contributions present diverse takes on the same topic, and may reflect, at least partly, the research interests and background of the author. The drawback is the loss of direct comparability that a rigid questionnaire-style would afford. In addition, the technicalities of implementing EU law are bypassed. While purposive sampling allows for more detailed studies, the results may not be representative for all instruments and European countries in general.

This book contains analysis from a variety of perspectives, both broad and narrow in scope. After the European background and its policies, principles and practices are described by Eva Storskrubb in the first chapter, John Sorabji then discusses the content and prospects of the ELI-UNIDROIT project for a future European model law of civil procedure. The next chapters concern the effects of EU hard law in Germany, Sweden, England and Norway, handled by Wolfgang Hau, Laura Ervo, John Sorabji and Maria Hjort, respectively. These quite broad-brush descriptions are followed by more detailed discussions of procedural law in relation to specific substantive matters. Discussions of the influence of ECJ case law on the *ex officio* application of EU consumer law in the Netherlands, Germany, Sweden and Norway are provided by Alain Ancery and Bart Krans, Ivo Bach, Torbjörn Andersson, and Halvard Fredriksen and Magne Strandberg, respectively. The book closes with a focus on maintenance cases: Volker Lipp provides us with the perspective of an insider, while Anna Nylund takes the outsider's perspective in analysing maintenance cases as they are regulated in Norwegian law.

EU CIVIL JUSTICE AT THE HARMONISATION CROSSROADS?

Eva Storskrubb

1. INTRODUCTION

At a conference in 2016, Professor Marcel Storme looked back at the plea he had made over 30 years ago, in 1986, in favour of the unification of civil procedural rules within the EU. He noted that the project that he later headed and that resulted in the so-called Storme Report of 1993 had removed a taboo and opened the doors to civil procedural harmonisation at the EU level.[1] However, despite the time that has passed since Professor Storme's plea and the Storme Report, we have yet to see a comprehensive civil procedural harmonisation project in the EU. At the same conference, Professor Storme eloquently referred to Erasmus of Rotterdam in stating that, 'Indeed, only fools can dream of such a simple approach.'[2] I will in this chapter argue that there are several current developments

1 M. Storme, 'Approximation of Procedural Law in Europe' in B. Hess and X.E. Kramer (eds), *From Common Rules to Best Practices in European Civil Procedure* (Nomos 2017). For the Storme Report see M. Storme (ed), *Approximation of Judiciary Law in the European Union* (Nijhoff 1994).

2 Storme, 'Approximation of Procedural Law in Europe' (n 1) 483.

that indicate we may be closer than ever before to the harmonisation crossroads of EU civil justice.

First, it is pertinent to set out some of the background and context to these current developments in EU civil justice, taking the institutional perspective into account. In depicting the state of play, the various strands of civil justice will first be briefly presented (section 2.1). Next, the results of the institutional positions and regulatory choices made so far will be analysed (section 2.2). These practices and choices have led to the fragmented landscape of EU civil justice that we have today. This fragmentation in itself may be a trigger factor that occasionally calls for further harmonisation. However, there are additional ostensible pressure and trigger factors for harmonisation that will be presented (section 3), namely: (i) mutual trust, (ii) the rule of law, and (iii) soft law. Against this backdrop it will be possible to analyse whether any institutional and regulatory changes are likely to emerge at the potential harmonisation crossroads (section 4).

2. STATE OF PLAY

2.1. STRANDS OF PROCEDURAL DEVELOPMENT

Traditionally, the EU was not considered to have competence in the field of procedural law, and the Member States were considered to have autonomy over national civil procedure. The awareness that the Member States' procedural autonomy is *de facto* limited has emerged gradually, and various developments mean that today the traditional perception is no longer correct.[3] There is, however, at present no specific legal basis that grants the EU the right to generally harmonise procedural rules, even though there has been an ongoing debate as to the feasibility of procedural harmonisation in the EU since the beginning of the 1990s.[4] The debate has resurfaced more recently, and I will return to it below.

That being said, there has been considerable interaction between EU law and domestic procedural law over the decades and the impact of EU law, both on domestic procedural law in general and in domestic courts, can be considered significant. However, the impact so far has been fragmented and disparate. I have previously compared this development to tentacles that find their way

3 See *inter alia* J. Delicostopoulos, 'Towards European Procedural Primacy in National Legal Systems', (2003) 9 *European Law Journal* 599; and C.N. Kakouris, 'Do the Member States Possess Judicial Procedural "Autonomy"?', (1997) 34 *CMLR* 1389.

4 There are some who have argued otherwise, e.g. Storme (ed), *Approximation of Judiciary Law* (n 1). For a review of the historical discussion on the legal basis and of the debate on procedural harmonisation following the Storme Report, see E. Storskrubb, *Civil Procedure and EU Law - A Policy Area Uncovered* (OUP 2008) 19–27. See also below sections 2.2. and 4.1.

into domestic law, at times in perhaps unexpected ways.[5] There is no common method of legal systematisation of the fragmented procedural landscape of the EU today.[6] I have chosen to categorise the development into five separate strands of enacted procedural rules or other types of measures.[7] The five strands are not presented chronologically, but rather divided from a normative perspective into broad groups of legislative and regulatory development. We start with general primary rules and case law principles, before moving to secondary rules of varied scope, and finally to soft forms of regulation.

The first strand constitutes the primary norms. In particular, Article 47 of the EU Charter of Fundamental Rights (the Charter) states that everyone whose rights and freedoms guaranteed by the law of the EU are violated has the right to an effective remedy before a tribunal and is entitled to a fair and public hearing within a reasonable time by an independent and impartial tribunal previously established by law. In addition, Article 19(1) of the Treaty on European Union (TEU) provides that Member States shall provide sufficient remedies to ensure effective legal protection in the fields covered by Union law. These general articles embody the fundamental principle of and right to access to justice in the EU context.

The second strand has been created by the European Court of Justice (CJEU) by imposing from 1976 onwards the requirements and principles of *equivalence* and *efficiency* on national procedural rules.[8] This means, in the words of the Court, that in the absence of any relevant harmonised procedural rules, it is for the domestic legal system to set out detailed procedural rules (principle of the procedural autonomy of the Member States). However, those rules must not be less favourable than those governing similar domestic actions (principle of equivalence), nor may they be framed in such a way as to make it

---

5 E. Storskrubb, 'Några tankar om hur EU-rättens tentakler genomtränger processrätten', in *Festskrift till Dan Frände, JFT* 2–4/2017, 360.

6 For other ways of systematisation see B. Hess, 'Procedural Harmonisation in a European Context' in X.E. Kramer and C.H. van Rhee (eds), *Civil Litigation in a Globalising World* (T.M.C. Asser Press 2012) 159; and B. Krans, 'EU Law and National Civil Procedure Law: An Invisible Pillar', (2015) *European Review of Private Law* 567.

7 I first presented my systematisation in E. Storskrubb, 'Alternative Dispute Resolution in the EU: Regulatory Challenges', (2016) 24(1) *European Review of Private Law* 9.

8 The seminal cases are Case 33/76 *Rewe-Zentralfinanz eG and Rewe-Zentral AG v Lanswitschaftskammer für das Saarland* ECLI:EU:C:1976:188; and Case C-45/76 *Comet BV v Produktschap voor Siergewassen* ECLI:EU:C:1976:191. The case law has dealt with a myriad of domestic procedural and remedial issues, including standing, evidence, legal aid, division of costs, time limits, *ex officio* raising of issues and *res judicata*, and continues to grow and evolve. For a review of the complexities of this case law, see *inter alia* M. Dougan, 'The Vicissitudes of Life at the Coalface: Remedies and Procedures to Enforcing Union Law before National Courts' in P. Craig and G. de Búrca (eds), *The Evolution of European Law* (OUP, 2nd edn 2011). Note that most of the CJEU case law has been in the context of administrative or public law, but its importance for the private law field has been perceived as increasing; see Storskrubb, *Civil Procedure and EU Law* (n 4) 16–17.

virtually impossible or excessively difficult to exercise the rights conferred by Community law (principle of efficiency).[9] Article 19(1) TEU, mentioned as part for the first strand above, is intended to embody these principles. This case law has highlighted the fact that enforcement of substantive rights under EU law is decentralised, meaning that enforcement relies on proceedings in national courts and hence on the national procedural and remedial rules.

The third strand of regulation is the main body of legislation and procedural rules that exists today in the EU. It has been enacted under the policy area of judicial co-operation in civil matters, with Article 81 of the Treaty of the Functioning of the European Union (TFEU) as its legal basis. The policy area was introduced in the Treaty of Amsterdam under the general political project of the Area of Freedom, Security and Justice (AFSJ).[10] Initially, measures enacted in this policy area dealt with traditional aspects of private international law and international procedural co-operation: jurisdiction of courts, applicable law, service of documents, taking of evidence, and enforcement of judgments in cross-border civil disputes.[11] Subsequent measures have gone further in breadth and depth, and have been innovative, either dealing with specific matters, such as insolvency, or creating discrete new European procedures, such as the European Small Claims Procedure or the recent European Account Preservation Order.[12] Commentators have identified different generations of measures.[13]

---

9 See *inter alia* Case C-430/03 *Jeroen van Schijndel and Johannes Nicolaas Cornelis van Veen v Stichting Pensioenfonds voor Fysiotherapeuten* ECLI:EU:C:1995:441, para 17.

10 For the earlier historical and nascent development of civil justice in the EU see STORSKRUBB, *Civil Procedure and EU Law* (n 4) 33–38.

11 See Regulation (EU) 1215/2012 on jurisdiction and the recognition and enforcement of judgments in civil and commercial matters (recast) [2012] OJ L351/1; Regulation (EC) 593/2008 on the law applicable to contractual obligations (Rome I) [2008] OJ L177/6; and Regulation (EC) 864/2007 on the law applicable to non-contractual obligations (Rome II) [2007] OJ L199/40. Note that the policy area also includes separate measures specifically for jurisdiction and choice of law rules in various types of family law matters. In addition, see Regulation (EC) 1393/2007 on the service in the Member States of judicial and extrajudicial documents in civil or commercial matters [2007] OJ L324/79; and Regulation (EC) 1206/2001 on cooperation between the courts of the Member States in the taking of evidence in civil and commercial matters [2001] OJ L174/1. Note that, due to separate Protocols (Nos 21 and 22) to the Lisbon Treaty, measures in the field may not apply to the United Kingdom, Ireland or Denmark.

12 Regulation (EC) 805/2004 creating a European Enforcement Order for uncontested claims [2004] OJ L143/15; Regulation (EC) 1896/2006 creating a European payment procedure [2006] OJ L399/1; Regulation (EC) 1346/2000 on insolvency proceedings [2000] OJ L160/1; Regulation (EC) 861/2007 establishing a European Small Claims Procedure [2007] OJ L199/1; Directive 2002/8/EC to improve access to justice in cross-border disputes by establishing minimum common rules relating to legal aid [2003] OJ L26/41; Directive 2008/52/EC on certain aspects of mediation in civil and commercial matters [2008] OJ L136/3; and Regulation (EU) 655/2014 creating a European Account Preservation Order to facilitate cross-border debt recovery in civil and commercial matters [2014] OJ L189/59.

13 B. HESS, 'The State of the Civil Justice Union' in B. HESS, M. BERGSTRÖM and E. STORSKRUBB (eds), *EU Civil Justice – Current Issues and Future Outlook* (Hart 2016) 3–5.

What currently nevertheless limits the remit of these measures is that they only relate to cross-border disputes.

The fourth strand of regulation is special procedural rules enacted by the EU for specific types of disputes under certain limited substantive policy areas. It is not a new phenomenon that substantive legislative instruments limited to a particular field of EU law may include private international law or even procedural rules, e.g. the insurance directives. Originally, such rules were fairly limited in terms of both their scope and their impact from a procedural point of view. Such rules were often only an ancillary part of a directive that focused on harmonisation of substantive rules or had a narrow procedural scope.[14] However, recent developments have seen a surge of sector-specific initiatives with procedural rules as their only focus. Such developments have taken place in the areas of intellectual property rights, competition law and consumer rights.[15] The specific measures that have been enacted on the legal basis of the internal market are not necessarily limited to cross-border matters. The impact of much of this development has yet to be seen, since many of the new specific procedural rules have only relatively recently entered into force or are not yet applicable.[16]

The fifth and final strand of procedural regulation involves the overarching and supporting measures of a soft law nature, such as networks,[17] judicial

14 See *inter alia* H. Duintjer Tebbens, 'Les règles de conflit contenues dans les instruments de droit dérivé' in A. Fuchs, H. Muir Watt and E. Pataut (eds), *Les conflits de lois et le système juridique communautaire* (Dalloz 2004), in relation to choice-of-law rules. See also *inter alia* T. Andersson, 'Approximation of Procedural Law in Europe' in M. Storme (ed), *Procedural Laws in Europe. Towards Harmonisation* (Maklu 2003) 56–58; and Dougan (n 8) 435–437.

15 In the intellectual property field, see the Agreement on a Unified Patent Court [2013] OJ C175/1. In the competition field, see Directive 2014/104/EU on certain rules governing actions for damage under national law for infringements of the competition law provisions of the Member States of the European Union [2014] OJ L349/1. In the consumer field see Directive 2013/11/EU on alternative dispute resolution for consumer disputes [2013] OJ L 165/63; and Regulation (EU) 524/2013 on online dispute resolution for consumer disputes [2013] OJ L165, 18/1. See E. Storskrubb, 'Civil justice: Constitutional and regulatory issues revisited' in M. Fletcher, E. Herlin-Karnell and C. Matera (eds), *The European Union as an Area of Freedom, Security and Justice* (Routledge 2017) for a further review of development of the sector-specific measures.

16 All of the other measures had deadlines for transposition or entered into force in 2015 and 2016; however, at the time of writing the Unified Patent Court did not have sufficient ratifications to enter into force.

17 Decision 2001/470/EC establishing a European Judicial Network [2001] OJ L174/25; and Decision 2009/568/EC amending Council Decision 2001/470/EC [2009] OJ L168/35. See further *Report on the Functioning of the European Judicial Network*, COM(2006) 203. For a more general presentation of the current networks see A. Molitorisová, 'On Some Aspects of the Current State of Horizontal Judicial Cooperation in the European Union with Special Regard to EU Law Development', (2014) *Europarättslig Tidskrift* 85.

training programmes[18] and e-justice portals.[19] The impact of such regulation is becoming more important as the other strands of civil justice in the EU grow and mature.[20] Further, under this heading we can include the measures that the Commission itself groups together as 'effective justice' measures.[21] These include, first and foremost, the so-called Justice Scoreboards, published annually by the Commission since 2013.[22] The other main steering mechanisms that the Commission includes in promoting 'effective justice' are its measures to protect the rule of law.[23] These will be returned to below in the context of the triggers and ostensible pressures for harmonisation.

2.2. REGULATORY CHOICES AND INSTITUTIONAL POSITIONS

The brief presentation of the five strands above shows that their development has not been linear or chronological and that there are inconsistencies. For example, there is incoherence between the specific development of procedural harmonisation in certain policy areas of the internal market, such as consumer law, and the strict approach of the Member States in limiting general civil justice measures to cross-border disputes. I have previously identified the so-called cross-border limitation, on the legal basis of Article 81 TFEU, as the focal point of the struggle between the EU institutions regarding the potential incursion of the EU into national procedural autonomy. The struggle has concerned whether the scope of EU civil justice should be defined in a restrictive or expansive way, specifically how 'matters having cross-border implications' should be interpreted. The Commission has argued for a broad interpretation, but so far the Council (i.e. the Member States), supported for nearly two decades by the

---

18 Communication from the Commission, *Building Trust in EU-wide Justice – A New Dimension to European Judicial Training*, COM(2011) 551 final, and subsequent Council Conclusions [2011] OJ C361/7. The Commission has set the objective of enabling 700,000 legal practitioners, half of the legal practitioners in the EU, to participate in training activities by 2020. See further <e-justice.europa.eu/content_the_european_judicial_training_policy-121-en.do>.

19 Council Multiannual European e-Justice Action Plan [2014] OJ C182/2. See further E. Storskrubb, 'E-Justice, Innovation and the EU' in B. Hess and X.E. Kramer (eds), *From Common Rules to Best Practices in European Civil Procedure* (Nomos 2017).

20 H. Hartnell, 'EUstitia: Institutionalising Justice in the European Union', (2002) 23 *Northwestern Journal of International Law and Business* 65, was one of the first contributions to realise their impact on civil justice. See also Storskrubb, *Civil Procedure and EU Law* (n 4) 233–258.

21 See <https://ec.europa.eu/info/strategy/justice-and-fundamental-rights/effective-justice_en>.

22 See below section 4.1.

23 See <https://ec.europa.eu/info/strategy/justice-and-fundamental-rights/effective-justice_en>.

European Parliament, has steadfastly refused to enact any general procedural measures that would apply to purely domestic matters.[24]

The first legislative proposal that caused this disagreement was the Legal Aid Directive. In the latest regulation to be enacted in the civil justice field, the European Account Preservation Order Regulation, we can see that the same institutional dynamic is repeated. In addition, in the review of relevant measures both the Council and the Parliament, in relation to the amendment of the Small Claims Regulation, rejected a broadening of the Regulation's cross-border scope.[25] The example of collective redress is a different but also instructive example since the most recent consultation process was not subsequently followed by a legislative process. The Member State responses in the consultation process publicly evidenced the concerns some of them had about expanding the legal basis and the importance they placed on respecting national procedural systems.[26]

It is clear that the Member States in the Council have wanted to keep the development of civil justice limited to cross-border procedures. The limitation has even been called the 'vigorously defended' 'wall of exceptionalism' around the policy area and against its expansion.[27] In contrast, the sector-specific procedural rules are a significant development in the manner in which the EU can impact directly on procedural law in the Member States. These rules can at times even have an impact on disputes that are not cross-border in nature, although each measure is limited to specific types of disputes. This dynamic but disparate development has been called a 'new approach' to procedural harmonisation,[28] 'vertical harmonisation'[29] or the 'invisible pillar of Europeanisation of procedural law'.[30] The measures do not simply provide for new sets of rules but

---

24 See E. Storskrubb, 'Civil justice: The contested nature of the scope of EU legislation' in F. Trauner and A. Ripoll Servent (eds), *Policy Change in the Area of Freedom, Security and Justice* (Routledge 2015) 205–212; and Storskrubb, 'Civil justice: Constitutional and regulatory issues revisited' (n 15) 307–312.

25 See Council Document 15841/14 (24.11.2014) 2; and Parliament Report A8-0140/2015, 10–11.

26 Storskrubb, 'Civil justice: Constitutional and regulatory issues revisited' (n 15) 310–312. See also follow-up report COM(2018) 40 final. The most recent development is that the Commission has proposed a sector specific directive that grants representative actions for the protection of the collective interests of consumers COM(2018) 184 final.

27 C. Crifò, '"Trusted with a Muzzle and Enfranchised with a Clog": The British Approach to European Civil Procedure' in B. Hess, M. Bergström and E. Storskrubb (eds), *EU Civil Justice - Current Issues and Future Outlook* (Hart 2016) 94.

28 B. Hess, 'Procedural Harmonisation in a European Context' in X.E. Kramer and C.H. van Rhee (eds), *Civil Litigation in a Globalising World* (T.M.C. Asser Press 2012) 164.

29 G. Wagner, 'Harmonisation of Civil Procedure: Policy Perspectives' in X.E. Kramer and C.H. van Rhee (eds), *Civil Litigation in a Globalising World* (T.M.C. Asser Press 2012) 101.

30 Krans (n 6) 571.

also introduce considerable structural changes and mechanisms such as online platforms for litigants in the consumer field or the future court system in the intellectual property rights field.

The result of this difference between generic civil procedural regulation and sector-specific procedural regulation is a constitutional incoherence. Linked to the strict constitutional question of competence is an underlying broader tension between a restrictive and an expansive political vision of EU civil justice. The opposing visions relate to how far procedural harmonisation in Europe is considered practically feasible and politically desirable. A debate on such harmonisation took place within the academic community in Europe close to two decades ago, subsequent to the Storme Report.[31] The perspectives put forward in that debate are still highly relevant. However, we already have a wealth of generic civil justice measures enacted. Thus, to some extent, the goalposts have been moved. The current measures are much broader than private international law or even international procedural law in its traditional sense. Although they may be limited to the cross-border realm, many of the reforms of the enacted regulations demonstrate incremental pressures towards deeper integration. In addition, some of the second-generation measures – such as the Small Claims Procedure, Payment Order and Account Preservation Order Regulations – create discrete, alternative and independent supranational procedures.[32] Thus, we are already inevitably dealing with some form of harmonisation, albeit so far limited. In addition, we have the parallel and more recent development of sector-specific rules, which shows that the Member States are willing to proceed with procedural harmonisation in some instances under the guise of effective enforcement of substantive EU civil law.[33]

The persistent resistance of the Member States in the Council to a broad interpretation of the cross-border limitation must, nonetheless, be acknowledged. It demonstrates that civil justice matters are sovereignty-sensitive. Procedural systems are deeply ingrained in society and its fundamental legal structures. Member States' procedural reforms, both completed and ongoing, demonstrate

---

31 For an overview of the subsequent debate see Storskrubb, *Civil Procedure and EU Law* (n 4) 21–25. A few of the voices in the debate include: P.H. Lindblom, 'Harmony of the Legal Spheres: A Swedish View on the Construction of a Unified European Procedural Law', (1997) *European Review of Private Law* 11; Andersson (n 14); J. Niemi-Kiesiläinen, 'International Cooperation and Approximation of Laws in the Field of Civil Procedure' in V. Heiskanen and K. Kulovesi (eds), *Function and Future of European Law* (Forum Iuris 1999); and P. Biavati, 'Is Flexibility a Way to the Harmonization of Civil Procedural Law in Europe?' in F. Carpi and M. Lupoi (eds), *Essays on Transnational and Comparative Civil Procedure* (Giappichelli 2001).

32 X.E. Kramer, 'Harmonisation of Civil Procedure: Interaction with Private International Law' in X.E. Kramer and C.H. van Rhee (eds), *Civil Litigation in a Globalising World* (T.M.C. Asser Press 2012) 127–128.

33 See Hess, 'Procedural Harmonisation in a European Context' (n 28) 164–165.

that quests for efficiency and proportionality are finely tuned and that the effect of any reform needs to be carefully considered in terms of how it impacts the justice system as a whole.[34] If the underlying structural features of the Member State procedural systems differ, for example in relation to the organisation of the relevant actors (*inter alia* courts, bailiffs and the bar), is it at all possible to harmonise? Will any supranational harmonisation attempts harm the carefully balanced equilibrium of national justice systems behind which are broader societal goals and visions, for example in relation to costs or litigiousness?[35] Are we able to say that we have a mutual vision in Europe or should the political will concerning that understanding and vision first be clearly uniform before any harmonisation is attempted? Logically, a mutual vision on justice may be necessary if any such project is to succeed.

In parallel to these issues related to potential further harmonisation, there is existing criticism of the fragmented nature of procedural regulation thus far. There may be valid political arguments for this fragmentary approach, which can also be called a piecemeal or incremental approach. However, several commentators have pointed out that it has its disadvantages. There is a risk of overarching procedural principles being neglected when procedural rules are enacted in discrete policy areas and for specific types of disputes.[36] In addition, an overly narrow specific substantive policy focus and a multitude of different procedural rules and solutions may create complexity that negatively affects user-friendliness and legal certainty, as well as creating a risk of conflicts between different procedural rules. So far, there has been no overall road map or systematic approach in relation to the five strands outlined above.[37] Coordination and coherence have been advocated by many commentators.[38] I have also called for debate on the best regulatory choices and methods, including a discussion on subsidiarity, i.e. the governance level at which it is appropriate to legislate on civil justice matters.

---

34 See *inter alia* A. Uzelac, 'Goals of Civil Justice and Civil Procedure in the Contemporary World' in A. Uzelac (ed), *Goals of Civil Justice and Civil Procedure in Contemporary Justice Systems* (Springer 2014), and the further national contributions in the same volume.

35 C. Hodges, 'Competition Enforcement, Regulation and Civil Justice: What is the Case?', (2006) 43 *CMLR* 1398, 1404 and 1406.

36 See *inter alia* Wagner (n 29) 110–112; M. Storme, 'Harmonisation of Civil Procedure and the Interaction with Substantive Private Law' in X.E. Kramer and C.H. van Rhee (eds), *Civil Litigation in a Globalising World* (T.M.C. Asser Press 2012) 152–154; and Storskrubb, 'Civil justice: Constitutional and regulatory issues revisited' (n 15) 382.

37 Hess, 'The State of the Civil Justice Union' (n 13) 10.

38 See *inter alia* M. Tulibacka, 'Europeanization of Civil Procedures: In Search of a Coherent Approach', (2009) 46 *CMLR* 1533; E. Storskrubb, 'Civil Justice – A Newcomer and an Unstoppable Wave?' in P. Craig and G. de Búrca (eds), *The Evolution of EU Law* (OUP, 2nd edn 2011) 318; and X.E. Kramer, 'Procedure Matters – Construction and Deconstructivism in European Civil Procedure', *Erasmus Law Lectures* (2013) 24–26.

3. OSTENSIBLE HARMONISATION PRESSURES AND TRIGGERS

As noted above, there are within the realm of the current fragmented civil justice regulation several regulatory pressures towards further and deeper integration, even harmonisation. These pressures are a result of the regulatory and constitutional history of the emergence of civil justice as a policy area in the EU. They are also a result of the governance choices so far made by the EU legislator in the evolution of civil justice. Furthermore, commentators have identified an increased constitutionalisation of civil justice with increased focus on the Charter and thus fundamental procedural rights and principles.[39] In addition to these pressures, I have identified three further, more recent and separate developments that may each be potential harmonisation 'pressures' or 'triggers' for civil justice in the EU.

One of the developments has arisen within the civil justice policy area and in the context of the development of its legislative acts and their interpretation by the CJEU, namely the issue of mutual trust in the recognition and enforcement of civil and commercial judgments. The other two developments have emerged adjacent to the civil justice policy area but clearly linked to it. The first has arisen within the EU and encompasses the renewed focus on and efforts linked to the rule of law by the EU institutions. The second is a soft law project called 'Model Rules of European Civil Procedure'. The project is external and developed under the auspices of two independent bodies in co-operation, the European Law Institute (ELI) and UNIDROIT. I will briefly illustrate the main thrust of these three developments below. However, the purpose here is not to describe all the details of these developments, as they have been charted elsewhere. It is rather to explain their potential role as so-called harmonisation pressures or triggers for EU civil justice. It will then be possible to consider tentatively whether any institutional and regulatory changes are likely to emerge at the potential harmonisation crossroads (section 4).

3.1. MUTUAL TRUST

Aside from the above-mentioned criticism that there is a lack of overarching vision for and systematic development of EU civil justice, the issue of mutual trust has in recent years become one of the central and most critical issues

[39] Hess, 'Procedural Harmonisation in a European Context' (n 6). See also E. Storskrubb and A. Wallerman, 'Judicial Cooperation in Civil Matters: Coming of Age' in A. Ripoll Servent and F. Trauner (eds), *The Routledge Handbook of Justice and Home Affairs Research* (Routledge 2018) 290.

for the evolution of EU's AFSJ.[40] In civil justice, the question of mutual trust has been strongly linked to the goal of implementing mutual recognition and direct enforcement of judgments across borders without any intermediate *exequatur* procedure. The principle of mutual recognition underpins most of the legislative measures in the third strand, i.e. measures enacted under the legal basis for judicial co-operation in civil matters.[41] However, there are in many of the measures still so-called grounds for refusal of enforcement and also other safeguards in the form of minimum procedural standards. Mutual trust has thus become an important complement to justify mutual recognition, direct enforcement and the potential further removal of existing safeguards.[42]

In practice, problems may arise in applying direct enforcement. The question may arise in the Member State where enforcement is sought whether judicial proceedings in the original Member State upheld the fundamental rights and principles of a fair trial.[43] In relations to the AFSJ, these issues reached a constitutional level in the tensions arising from the potential accession of the EU to the European Convention on Human Rights. The CJEU went as far as to say that the principle of direct enforcement requires Member States to consider all other Member States to be compliant with the fundamental rights recognised by EU law, save in exceptional circumstances.[44] This presumption has come under criticism, and commentators including the present author have noted

40 For a general introduction see *inter alia* E. Brouwer and D. Gerard (eds), *Mapping Mutual Trust – Understanding and Informing the Role of Mutual Trust in EU Law*, EUI Working Paper MWP 13/2016. See also V. Mitsilegas, 'The Limits of Mutual Trust in Europe's Area of Freedom, Security and Justice: From Automatic Inter-State Cooperation to the Slow Emergence of the Individual', (2012) *YB Eur Law* 319; and the contributions in T. Marguery and T. van den Brink (eds), 'Mutual Recognition and Mutual Trust: Reinforcing EU Integration', *European Papers* (3/2016 and 1/2017). As regards specifically civil justice see *inter alia* M. Weller, 'Mutual Trust: In Search of the Future of European Union Private International Law', (2015) *Journal of Private International Law* 64; M. Weller, 'Mutual trust within judicial cooperation in civil matters: a normative cornerstone – a factual chimera – a constitutional challenge', (2017) 35 *Nederlands International Privaatrecht* 1; and E. Storskrubb, 'Mutual Trust and the Dark Horse of Civil Justice', (2018) *Cambridge YB of Eur Legal Studies* (online version) 1.

41 See Council programme for the implementation of mutual recognition of civil and commercial judgments [2001] OJ C12/1, 5. For a description of the different emanations of the principle in the civil justice legislation see *inter alia* M. Linton, 'Abolition of Exequatur, All in the Name of Mutual Trust!' in B. Hess, M. Bergström and E. Storskrubb (eds), *EU Civil Justice – Current Issues and Future Outlook* (Hart 2016) 257–282; and A Frackowiak-Adamska, 'Time for a European "Full Faith and Credit Clause"', (2015) *CMLR* 191.

42 Storskrubb, 'Mutual Trust and the Dark Horse' (n 40) 3–9.

43 For civil justice see *inter alia* M. Requejo Isidro, 'On the Abolition of the Exequatur' in B. Hess, M. Bergström and E. Storskrubb (eds), *EU Civil Justice – Current Issues and Future Outlook* (Hart 2016); and Weller, 'Mutual Trust: In Search of the Future' (n 40).

44 Opinion 2/13, ECLI:EU:C:2014:2454, paras 191–192. See also the defence of the CJEU by its president, K Lenaerts, 'La vie après l'avis: Exploring the principle of mutual (yet not blind) trust', (2017) 54 *CMLR* 805, 806–808 and 840.

that it is problematic from the perspective of breaches of fundamental rights in individual cases.[45] More recent case law has shown a more nuanced approach and commentators now point to the acceptance of limitations to mutual trust, one of them referring to 'temperate mutual trust' with a new dialectic relationship to the need to protect human rights.[46] The present author has noted that many cases in the civil justice context also demonstrate a balanced approach to mutual trust.[47]

Notwithstanding the above, what is perhaps more relevant at the macro level is that criticism has also been levelled at the choice of mutual recognition and the ancillary and necessary principle of mutual trust as method of governance for justice issues.[48] Mutual recognition as a governance method transposed from the internal market means that the Member States *de facto* relinquish sovereignty to a degree that they were perhaps not originally prepared to do.[49] In addition, since mutual recognition in the internal market has never been unconditional, commentators have noted that there is a difference between blind and binding trust.[50] Proportionate restrictions to protect important national rights and values have always been present in the treaties and also established through case law.[51] In addition, mutual recognition has not been the sole regulatory method; it has been used in parallel with *inter alia* minimum harmonisation and other governance techniques such as administrative co-operation and communication structures.[52] Mutual trust is also not seen as an unconditional principle in the internal market, and it has also affected the regulatory strategy by occasioning a need for harmonised rules, deeper administrative co-operation and increased transparency.[53]

---

45 Storskrubb, 'Mutual Trust and the Dark Horse' (n 40) 10.

46 L. Marin, 'Only You: The Emergence of a Temperate Mutual Trust in the Area of Freedom, Security and Justice and its Underpinning in the European Composite Constitutional Order', (2017) *European Papers* 144.

47 Storskrubb, 'Mutual Trust and the Dark Horse' (n 40) 11–14.

48 See E. Storskrubb, 'Mutual Recognition as a Governance Strategy for Civil Justice' in B. Hess, M. Bergström and E. Storskrubb (eds), *EU Civil Justice – Current Issues and Future Outlook* (Hart 2016) 306–308; see further S.K. Schmidt, 'Mutual Recognition as a New Mode of Governance', (2007) *J of Eur Public Policy* 667.

49 Storskrubb, 'Mutual Recognition' (n 48) 308–310; see further S. Lavenex, 'Mutual Recognition and the Monopoly of Force: Limits of the Single Market Analogy', (2007) *J of Eur Public Policy* 767.

50 Storskrubb, 'Mutual Recognition' (n 48) 310–311, with reference to K. Nicolaïdis, 'Trusting the Poles? Constructing Europe through Mutual Recognition', (2007) *J of Eur Public Policy* 685.

51 See further J. Snell, 'The internal market and philosophies of integration' in C. Barnard and S. Peers (eds), *European Union Law* (OUP 2014).

52 Snell (n 51).

53 S. Prechal, 'Mutual Trust before the Court of Justice of the European Union', (2017) *European Papers* 90; and N. Cambien, 'Mutual Recognition and Mutual Trust in the Internal Market', (2017) *European Papers* 108–109.

Thus, the need for an ever-developing, multi-layered regulatory strategy and the limits of mutual trust have been understood in the internal market.[54] Moreover, the lessons learnt from the internal market also seem to be slowly having an impact on mutual recognition as a regulatory strategy in civil justice, for example in the emphasis on ancillary measures to support mutual recognition.[55] However, the debate on mutual trust and its limits also clearly indicates a further potential regulatory development that has already been prominent in the criminal justice field, namely the potential of legislative harmonisation in civil justice.[56] As noted, harmonisation has been used in other fields to mediate the effects of mutual recognition and support mutual trust.

3.2. THE RULE OF LAW

As is well known, the EU is founded on common values shared by its Member States and set out in Article 2 TEU. These values include the rule of law. Since the Amsterdam Treaty there have also been provisions in the EU treaties regarding sanctions for the breach of the common values, now in Article 7 TEU. The mechanism in Article 7 TEU can be characterised as a political tool. Its first 'preventative' limb constitutes a formal determination or 'warning' issued by the Council, which can include recommendations. The second limb consists of a determination that there has been a persistent breach, which can ultimately lead to sanctions that are political in nature since they relate to the Member States' right to participate in EU decision-making.[57] All decisions under Article 7

---

54 See J. Snell, 'The Single Market: Does Mutual Trust Suffice?' in E. Brouwer and D. Gerard (eds), *Mapping Mutual Trust – Understanding and Informing the Role of Mutual Trust in EU Law*, EUI Working Paper MWP 13/2016, 14; and W-H. Roth, 'Mutual Recognition' in P. Koutrakos and J. Snell (eds), *Research Handbook on the Law of the EU's Internal Market* (Edward Elgar 2017) 460.

55 E. Storskrubb, 'Mutual Trust in Civil Justice Cooperation in the EU' in A. Barkdjieva Engelbrekt et al (eds), *Trust in the European Union in Challenging Times* (Palgrave 2018) 174–175.

56 See *inter alia* V. Mitsilegas, 'Conceptualising Mutual Trust in European Criminal Law. The Evolving Relationship Between Legal Pluralism and Rights-Based Justice in the European Union' in E. Brouwer and D. Gerard (eds), *Mapping Mutual Trust – Understanding and Informing the Role of Mutual Trust in EU Law*, EUI Working Paper MWP 13/2016, 32–34, noting that this development is a paradigm shift in the criminal justice field. For a comparison with civil justice, see M. Requejo Isidro, 'Do we Need to Achieve Harmonious Cooperation? Judicial Cooperation in Criminal Matters as a Testing Field', and M. Hazelhorst, 'Harmonious Judicial Cooperation through Harmonisation: (What) Can We Learn from Criminal Matters?', both in B. Hess and X.E. Kramer (eds), *From Common Rules to Best Practices in European Civil Procedure* (Nomos 2017).

57 See *inter alia* S. Carrera, E. Guild and N. Hernanz, *The Triangular Relationship between Fundamental Rights, Democracy and the Rule of Law in the EU: Towards and EU Copenhagen Mechanism* (CEPS 2013) 5–7 <https://www.ceps.eu/publications/triangular-relationship-between-fundamental-rights-democracy-and-rule-law-eu-towards-eu> for a short description

require a super-majority of Member States in the Council and the European Parliament has to consent. In addition, the decision to activate the second limb with the threat of potential sanctions has to be unanimous in the European Council (excluding the relevant Member State).[58]

In 2010–2012, situations arose in a few Member States that caused general concern within the EU as to the protection of its values in Article 2, including the rule of law. One of the situations related to the make-up of Hungarian courts, occasioned by a new system of early retirement of judges. Despite these concerns, the political sanction mechanism in Article 7 was not activated.[59] Since then, many actors, including Member States, have called for the development of more effective tools to protect the EU's common values.[60] These events also encouraged the EU institutions to take measures to allow more active work on protecting the rule of law. In addition, the events fostered an intense doctrinal debate.[61] The Council now organises an annual rule-of-law dialogue meeting.[62] In addition,

of the mechanism that has never been activated at the time of writing. Note though that 14 Member States decided to independently impose bilateral economic sanctions against Austria in 2000 due to the coalition government's inclusion of FPÖ, a radical right-wing party.

58 See *inter alia* L. Besselink, 'The Bite, the Bark and the Howl' in A. Jakab and D. Kochenov (eds), *The Enforcement of EU Law and Values: Ensuring Member States' Compliance* (OUP 2017) 131–133. See also <http://www.europarl.europa.eu/news/en/headlines/eu-affairs/20180222STO98434/rule-of-law-concerns-in-poland-how-the-article-7-procedure-would-work>.

59 The concerns arose as a result of collective deportations of persons of Roma origin by France; the Romanian government's disregard of its own constitutional courts' decision; and the effect on the make-up of Hungarian courts by a new system of early retirement of judges. See *inter alia* D. Kochenov and L. Pech, *Upholding the Rule of Law in the EU: On the Commission's 'Pre-Article 7 Procedure' as a Timid Step in the Right Direction*, EUI Working Papers RSCAS 24/2015, 2; and European Parliamentary Research Service (EPRS), *Understanding the EU Rule of Law Mechanisms* (2016) 2 <http://www.europarl.europa.eu/RegData/etudes/BRIE/2016/573922/EPRS_BRI(2016)573922_EN.pdf>.

60 Letter from the foreign ministers of Germany, Finland, Denmark and the Netherlands to the Commission President Barroso, 6 March 2013 <https://www.rijksoverheid.nl/binaries/rijksoverheid/documenten/brieven/2013/03/13/brief-aan-europese-commissie-over-opzetten-rechtsstatelijkheidsmechanisme/brief-aan-europese-commissie-over-opzetten-rechtsstatelijkheidsmechanisme.pdf>.

61 For the academic debate see *inter alia* C. Closa, D. Kochenov and J.H.H. Weiler, *Reinforcing Rule of Law Oversight in the European Union*, EUI Working Papers RSCAS 25/2015; A. von Bogdandy and M. Ioannis, 'Systematic Deficiency in the Rule of Law: What It Is, What Has Been Done, What Can Be Done', (2014) *CMLR* 59; J.-W. Müller, 'Should the EU Protect Democracy and the Rule of Law inside Member States', (2015) *Eur Law J* 141; C. Hillion, *Overseeing the rule of law in the European Union: Legal mandate and means* (SIEPS 2016) 1; D. Kochenov, *Busting the myths unclear: A commentary on Article 7 TEU*, EUI Working Papers LAW 10/2017; and the contributions in C. Closa and D. Kochenov (eds), *Reinforcing the Rule of Law Oversight in the European Union* (CUP 2016). See further L. Pech and K.L. Scheppele, 'Illiberlism Within: Rule of Law Backsliding in the EU', (2017) 19 *Cambridge YB of Eur Legal Studies* 3.

62 See <http://italia2014.eu/media/4288/conclusions_-ensuring-respect-for-the-rule-of-law.pdf>. For the report on the most recent dialogue in 2017 meeting see <http://data.consilium.europa.eu/doc/document/ST-13609-2017-INIT/en/pdf>.

the European Parliament issued a report on its own initiative, emphasising the importance of the rule of law in various ways, and also calling upon the other EU institutions to strengthen the mechanism, amongst other things.[63] Furthermore, in 2014 the Commission drew up a rule-of-law framework that creates a pre-Article 7 procedure, through which the Commission can assess risks of breaches of fundamental values, formalise these in an opinion and monitor the response to the opinion, all with the purpose of creating a dialogue with the Member State in question and instituting a softer initial tool.[64]

The purpose of both the Commission's framework and the Council's dialogue is thus to fill a gap and to have means to take action before Article 7 is activated.[65] In January 2016, the Commission used the framework for the first time and initiated a process against Poland. The process has continued in 2018 and relates *inter alia* to changes in the local law to limit the independence of the Polish Constitutional Court.[66] In December 2017, the Commission proposed to the Council that Article 7(1) be activated against Poland; in March 2018 the European Parliament also voted in favour of doing so.[67] However, the Council has not acted upon the proposal. The political rule-of-law mechanism in the TEU has been perceived as a measure of last resort, and also as insufficient to address such issues and to prevent them from arising.[68] Moreover, the additional

63 EPRS (n 59) 8–9; and Report with recommendation to the Commission on the establishment of an EU mechanism on democracy, the rule of law and fundamental rights, 2015/2254(INL), A8-0283/2016, 25 October 2016.

64 COM(2014) 158. For an analysis of the framework see Kochenov and Pech (n 59).

65 COM(2014) 158, 5–7. The framework is not intended to impact upon the authority of the Commission to bring infringement actions against Member States under Article 258 TFEU. The relationship between these mechanisms has been debated see K.L. Scheppele, *What Can the European Commission Do When Member State Violate Basic Principles of the European Union? The Case for Systematic Infringements* (2013) <http://ec.europa.eu/justice/events/assises-justice-2013/files/contributions/45.princetonuniversityscheppelesystemicinfringementactionbrussels version_en.pdf>. See also Closa, Kochenov and Weiler (n 61) 10–11 and 15–16; as well as Hillion (n 61) 4–9. The Commission also launched the first stages of an infringement procedure against Poland in relation to discrimination of judges <http://europa.eu/rapid/press-release_IP-17-2205_en.htm>.

66 See Pech and Scheppele (n 61) 14–21; and G. Halmai, *The possibility and desirability of economic sanction: Rule of law conditionality requirements against illiberal EU Member States*, EUI Working Papers LAW 6/2018, 6–12, for a detailed description of steps taken by the Commission, including four recommendations. For all the official documents of the Commission see <https://ec.europa.eu/info/strategy/justice-and-fundamental-rights/effective-justice/rule-law/rule-law-framework_en>. Ultimately the Commission seems to have resorted to proposing budgetary means to put pressure on Poland see <https://emerging-europe.com/in-brief/european-commission-formally-proposes-budget-ties-funds-rule-law/>; and COM(2018) 324 final. See further Halmai (this note) 15–20.

67 See COM(2017) 835 final; and <http://www.europarl.europa.eu/news/en/press-room/20180226IPR98615/rule-of-law-in-poland-parliament-supports-eu-action>.

68 Closa, Kochenov and Weiler (n 61) 2.

tools developed, the Council's annual dialogue and the Commission's framework have been heavily criticised as being inadequate or inadequately used, indicating the inherent limits of a political mechanism.[69]

The connection between the tools to support the rule of law and civil justice are demonstrated in some of the situations that have raised concern in the EU so far. A fair trial and effective judicial remedies can only be guaranteed if the judiciary is independent and impartial. The independence of the judiciary is considered to be an important component in the rule of law.[70] In the cases of Hungary and Poland, the actions of their respective governments have resulted in the concern that the local courts and court systems, including civil justice, may no longer be independent. This is of direct impact and importance in the EU because the trust that domestic authorities and citizens have in the legal systems of other Member States is central to the functioning on the EU's AFSJ. As mentioned in the preceding sections, due to legislative regulatory choices in the EU, Member State courts often have to directly recognise and enforce civil judgments from other Member States. Can such a system be legitimate if there is a risk that certain Member States are actively undermining or dismantling features of the rule of law?[71]

3.3. SOFT LAW

The 2004 Principles of Transnational Civil Procedure, which consist of 31 principles covering the key topics of civil procedure, were the result of a transnational project led by the American Law Institute (ALI) and UNIDROIT.[72] The project was primarily concerned with cross-border commercial disputes and has been widely hailed as a successful attempt to overcome the differences between the major legal families. However, the uptake or subsequent use of the model Principles seems to have been limited.[73] UNIDROIT has sought

69 See *inter alia* Pech and Scheppele (n 61) 26–34; and Besselink (n 58) 134–143, for critique and analysis of the limits to the actions and the different perspectives of the institutions.

70 COM(2014) 158, appendix 1, 1–3.

71 COM(2014) 158, 5. See also Case C-216/18 *Minister for Justice and Equality v LM (Défaillances du système judiciaire)*, pending before the CJEU, where questions on the rule of law in Poland have been raised by the Irish High Court in the similar, albeit criminal justice, context of an extradition requested under the European arrest warrant.

72 See <https://www.unidroit.org/civil-procedure#PrinciplesofTransnationalCivilProcedure>. The Principles are accompanied by a set of Rules of Transnational Civil Procedure, which were not formally adopted by UNIDROIT or the ALI, but constitute the reporters' model implementation of the Principles. See further *Principles of Transnational Civil Procedure* (CUP 2006).

73 X.E. Kramer, 'Strengthening Civil Justice Cooperation: The Quest for Model Rules and Common Minimum Standards in Europe' in M.A. Rodrigues and H. Zaneti Jr (eds), *Repercussões do CPC – Processo Internacional* (Juspodivm, 2018) (forthcoming).

to promote the Principles and other regional models. The ongoing research project by the ELI and UNIDROIT on European Rules of Civil Procedure[74] is an example of just such a regional project that takes the ALI-UNIDROIT Principles as its starting point. The project started in 2014 after an exploratory conference in 2013.[75] Since its start, when three Working Groups were set up as pilots, the project has grown to include nine Working Groups led by a Steering Committee and supported by an Advisory Board, as well as a Consultative Committee.[76] The various bodies consist of a mix of participants from different professional backgrounds and jurisdictions throughout Europe. The aim is to have a first consolidated set of works published in 2019.[77]

It is a soft law project that will hopefully provide a platform for debate among experts, practitioners and users across Europe to identify best practices in civil procedure. At present, the platform for a broader debate has been limited, as the work has been in progress and mostly not made public. However, there have been a few public events at which the ongoing project work has been presented to a wider audience. At such events there has already been interest in the project.[78] In addition, the project has a number of observer bodies that have had access to drafts and annual meetings. The observers include three EU institutions: the CJEU, the Commission and the European Parliament. Both the Commission and the Parliament have been active participants. In particular, the Parliament has shown an overt interest in the project by publishing its own report on it.[79]

As will be discussed further below, the European Parliament has also, in the wake of that report, passed a Resolution on Common Minimum Standards of Civil Procedure.[80] Annexed to the Resolution is a recommendation for a directive on common minimum standards of civil procedure in the EU. In other words, the Parliament has proposed a legislative initiative that would form the basis for

74 See project description and public reports <https://www.europeanlawinstitute.eu/projects-publications/current-projects-feasibility-studies-and-other-activities/current-projects/civil-procedure/>.

75 See contributions in the (2014) *Uniform Law Review* (issues 2 and 3) regarding the conference.

76 The author was one of the co-reporters for one of the first three Working Groups, the Working Group on Service and Due Notice of Proceedings, and is currently a co-reporter for the Working Group on Costs. See <https://www.europeanlawinstitute.eu/projects-publications/current-projects-feasibility-studies-and-other-activities/current-projects/civil-procedure/> for lists of all the members of each body.

77 See Kramer, 'Strengthening Civil Justice Cooperation' (n 73) for a more detailed description of the project work and analysis; see also the contribution of John Sorabji in this volume on the ELI/UNIDROIT project.

78 See ELI website (n 74); and the UNIDROIT website <https://www.unidroit.org/work-in-progress/transnational-civil-procedure> for public reports on the progress of the project.

79 U. Bux, *The European Law Institute /Unidroit Civil Procedure Projects as a Soft Law Tool to Resolve Conflicts of Law* (PE 556.972), Report upon the request of the Legal Affairs Committee, January 2017.

80 Resolution 4 July 2017 (2015/2084 INL) with underlying Report of its Committee on Legal Affairs, 6 June 2017 (PE 593.974).

some level of further harmonisation of civil procedure in the EU. Although there is no definite causal link between these developments, it seems clear that the soft law project has served as a trigger or tool for the European Parliament to further its agenda in civil justice matters. However, more than this, the soft law project can indicate best practices and provide a set of modern civil procedural rules that may highlight lacunae or deficiencies in current practice and legislation at both the domestic and supranational level. Thus, the soft law model rules may also potentially come to provide inspiration for future legislative reform at the domestic or supranational level.

4. RESHUFFLING THE CARDS

4.1. INSTITUTIONAL ROLES REVISITED

When it comes to the institutional actors in the EU, the pressures and triggers mentioned above have contributed to a slight reshuffling of their roles. Formally, the ordinary legislative procedure remains the relevant legislative procedure. There has been no formal change: the Commission remains the initiator of legislation and the European Parliament, together with the Member States in the Council, remain the legislators. However, the Parliament has always had the opportunity to make reports and legislative proposals on its own initiative. Since it does not have the formal power of initiative, it can under Article 225 TFEU propose that the Commission submits the same proposal. The Parliament did so in the case of its proposed directive on common minimum standards of civil procedure. However, the Commission is not obliged to support or act upon the Parliament's proposals – it has full discretion whether or not to initiate legislation – but it must respond to the Parliament. The Commission responded in October 2017 and declined to take the proposed directive on common minimum standards forward.[81]

In its response, the Commission stressed that a gradual harmonisation of procedural standards is already taking place in the context of the measures enacted so far, mainly regarding judicial co-operation in civil matters, i.e. the third strand mentioned above. Thus, the Commission argued that the way to promote further minimum standards is in the context of the implementation of the existing *acquis*.[82] The Commission further explained that it has ordered comprehensive studies on national procedural law and implementation of

81 SP(2017)539 of 16 October 2017 <http://www.europarl.europa.eu/oeil/popups/ficheprocedure.do?reference=2015/2084(INL)&l=en#tab-0>.

82 SP(2017)539 of 16 October 2017 (n 81) 1 and 5.

certain existing measures.[83] Reforms of specific existing measures, potentially initially including the Service and Evidence Regulations, are expected. The Commission, however, noted that it would take the Parliament's proposals into account in the context of further specific reforms. The Commission also noted that it is following the ELI/UNIDROIT project closely.[84]

Thus, in the short term, there appears to be no major regulatory shift. However, the Parliament's own initiative report and proposal demonstrates that it has a current political interest in taking an active role and putting pressure on the Commission to act.[85] In addition, it is notable that the Parliament's research assessment raises the issue of the relevant legal basis. There is an awareness of the cross-border limitation in Article 81 TFEU, but there seems to be an opening for a broader reading of the limitation than the Parliament has in practice taken before.[86] If the Parliament were in the future to support the Commission's broad interpretation of the legal basis, this could lead to a shift in the negotiations between the Parliament and the Council in the context of the ordinary legislative procedure.[87] How the Member States would react to such a development remains to be seen. As long as a qualified majority of Member States still want to protect national procedural autonomy, or consider that, for reasons of subsidiarity, civil procedure should mainly be left to be legislated at the national level, the limited and fragmented harmonisation, or rather approximation, approach will continue.

Notwithstanding this, the other pressures and triggers mentioned above have led to the advent of other types of measures that may also come to have a significant impact on civil justice. Both the problems encountered with mutual trust between the legal systems of the Member States and the risk of challenges to rule of law in the EU have demonstrated in a new way how dependent the EU is on the Member States to provide, at the domestic level, a functioning justice system to enforce EU law. These developments, which have been called

---

83 SP(2017)539 of 16 October 2017 (n 81) 6. See *inter alia An evaluation study of national procedural laws and practices in terms of their impact on the free circulation of judgments and on the equivalence and effectiveness of the procedural protection of consumers under EU consumer law* (Max Planck Institute, Luxembourg) <https://publications.europa.eu/en/publication-detail/-/publication/531ef49a-9768-11e7-b92d-01aa75ed71a1/language-en>.

84 SP(2017)539 of 16 October 2017 (n 81) 6. See subsequent proposal, COM(2018)378 final, to amend Regulation (EC) 1206/2001 on cooperation between the courts of the Member States in the taking of evidence in civil or commercial matters.

85 See further R. Bray, 'Common Rules and Best Practices From the Perspective of the European Parliament' in B. Hess and X.E. Kramer (eds), *From Common Rules to Best Practices in European Civil Procedure* (Nomos 2017) 35–42.

86 See M. Tulibacka, M. Sanz and R. Blomeyer, *Common minimum standards of civil procedure: European added value assessment (Annex 1)*, Study of the European Parliamentary Research service (PE 581.385), June 2016, 9–10 and 56–61. See further Bray (n 85) 41.

87 See above section 2.2.; and (n 24).

'constitutional capture'[88] and 'rule of law backsliding',[89] demonstrate a frailty that exists because of the procedural autonomy of the Member States. Even though there are several strands of development in the EU that have already created a limited harmonisation of procedural rules, as presented above, a justice system is not solely built on procedural rules themselves. It is also built on the actors and institutions, such as courts and judges that apply the procedural rules and oversee judicial proceedings, as well as on Member State governments and legislators.

Although it is uncertain whether the EU has legislative competence to harmonise the broader design of the Member States' legal systems, it may arguably have a political mandate to protect its values (rule of law) and support its policies (mutual recognition/mutual trust). It is this grey area that the Commission has in recent years stepped into. As noted above, the Commission did not follow the Parliament's call to back a more comprehensive procedural harmonisation act. However, it has launched other types of measures in recent years that may have a 'soft' impact on civil justice development. In this context, the Justice Scoreboards are one interesting development. Published since 2013 by the European Commission, the Scoreboards are a means for the Commission to annually collect information on the justice systems of the Member States and to evaluate certain indicators on key components (quality, independence and efficiency) that are considered important in achieving an efficient judicial system. The Scoreboards provide information on, *inter alia*, the length of proceedings and the number of pending cases. They also focus, among other things, on the training of judges, as well as on the efficiency, quality and independence of the justice systems.[90] The information is collected in the context of the EU's economic term (i.e. the EU budgetary process), and enables the Commission and ultimately the Council to make country-specific recommendations and have a dialogue with EU Member States on procedural reforms when allocating funds in the annual budget process via the EU Structural and Investment Funds.[91]

Considerable criticism can be levelled at how information is collected for the Scoreboards, at the opaque manner in which the data is presented, at the parameters chosen to indicate 'efficiency' of justice, and at the apparent lack of comparative procedural awareness.[92] In addition, it is regrettable that the

88 Pech and Scheppele (n 61) 21.

89 Pech and Scheppele (n 61) 8–9.

90 For the most recent Scoreboard see COM(2018) 364 final.

91 For older Scoreboards see COM(2014) 155 final, 6; and COM(2015) 116 final, 4. For the most recent Scoreboard see COM(2018) 364 final, 3 and 7. See further A. Dori, *The EU Justice Scoreboard – Judicial Evaluation as a New Governance Tool*, Max Planck Institute Luxemburg Working Paper (2015). See Halmai (n 66) 15–20 for a discussion on the usefulness of economic tools in the context.

92 Storskrubb, 'Några tankar' (n 5) 374–378.

Scoreboards have not yet resulted in a transparent dialogue with all Member States on how to address challenges in civil justice at the domestic level, and have thus not contributed to strategic learning cross-borders.[93] Nevertheless, they form a starting point that has the potential to support 'soft' impact and dialogue. There is also all the work that the Commission has stepped forward to do in the context of the political rule-of-law process mentioned above, as well as all the measures, including judicial networks, judicial training and e-justice, that the Commission co-ordinates and directs EU funds to – that is, all the measures included in the fifth strand of civil justice development mentioned above. There is thus considerable investment into structural matters that are central to the functioning of the domestic justice systems, and which is geared toward their development and modernisation. We should not ignore these actions in considering the role of the institutions and the context of the work being done that may have an impact on the domestic civil justice systems, and ultimately potentially contribute to the goal of a 'European judicial culture'.[94]

In contrast to the surge of activism on the part of the European Parliament or the development of potentially helpful new tools by the Commission, the role of the Member States in the Council appears to have remained mostly unchanged in relation to civil justice development. This is unsurprising, but also perhaps does not represent the full picture. Although the Council has played the role of the gatekeeper the most, it has nevertheless also allowed and enabled the constitutionally incoherent, gradual and fragmented approximation of procedural rules that we have today. In the future, the Council will be the key to unlocking potential legislative measures. In addition, the Member States in the Council arguably cannot remain unaffected by the pressures and triggers identified above. The Council is in the unique position to be able to conduct with authority a dialogue on the challenges and future of civil justice. It is the Council that can ultimately affect the choice of a regulatory strategy and heed the call for a more developed and coherent strategy. It is to be hoped that the pressures and triggers will inspire it to do so.

Finally, the institution that has historically been central to developing procedural principles in the context of the second strand presented above, namely the CJEU, remains important as regards impact on civil justice. The CJEU's case law on mutual recognition and mutual trust in the AFSJ context has been one of the central factors in creating the 'mutual trust trigger', as explained above. The Court's position has, as mentioned above, also been criticised. However, regardless, the Court has very clearly demonstrated through its case

---

93 Storskrubb, 'Några tankar' (n 5) 374–378.

94 See The Hague Programme: strengthening freedom, security and justice in the European Union [2005] OJ C53/1; and The Stockholm Programme – An open and secure Europe serving and protecting citizens [2010] OJ C115/1.

law, perhaps inadvertently, the challenges and limitations of mutual trust. In addition, in its more recent cases the CJEU has had – and in its upcoming cases will continue to have – the opportunity to further nuance and clarify the limits of mutual trust and mutual recognition. In this respect, the CJEU is engaged in a dialogue concerning the justice systems of the Member States. Furthermore, the CJEU has also recently had the occasion to address the importance of effective judicial protection in the domestic courts and the independence of the judiciary in the Member States, with a further case pending that raises issues related to the rule of law.[95]

4.2. TYPES OF FUTURE ACTION

Aside from the institutional perspective, the pressures and triggers identified may come to affect regulatory decisions. Even though the pressures and triggers ostensibly lead to further harmonisation, the present author has argued that to simply latch onto the promise of harmonisation may not lead to a functional regulatory strategy.[96] In addition, the European Parliament's proposal for a directive on common minimum standards of civil procedure brings to the fore the question of what kind of measures should be pursued. Some observations about the proposal will first be made from a regulatory perspective, after which other possible regulatory avenues and types of action will be discussed.

The European Parliament's proposal, though not covering close to all matters dealt with in any domestic set of procedural rules, nevertheless encompasses a wide range of procedural issues both general and specific.[97] What is concerning from a regulatory perspective is that the proposal suggests an added layer of rules between the current levels of civil justice measures. The report behind the Resolution acknowledges that there is a 'regulatory puzzle' of civil justice regulation in the EU, of which the Brussels I regime and other measures dealt with in this contribution are a part.[98] However, the proposal is not intended to supplant or improve them. Notably, the proposal includes rules on some procedural issues that are already covered by prior civil justice measures on the same issue. However, the proposed directive would add an extra layer of rules solely for cross-border cases. The scope of this layer is regrettably very unclear and is different from all other civil justice measures. Therefore, programmatically suggesting that the proposal will, if enacted, add 'systemisation' to EU civil justice appears to be optimistic. As such, the proposal has also been considered

95 See Case C-64/16 *Associação Sindical dos Juízes Portugueses v Tribunal de Contas* ECLI:EU:C:2018:117, paras 30–44; and pending Case C-216/18 (n 71).
96 Storskrubb, 'Mutual Trust and the Dark Horse' (n 40) 23.
97 Resolution (n 80) paras 14–20; Report (n 80) 34.
98 Report (n 80) 33.

by commentators as being 'unclear' as to regulatory method and in need of refinement.[99]

Furthermore, looking at the proposal from the perspective of the problems or challenges arising from the pressures and triggers identified above, it arguably cannot address all issues. What is required, rather, is improved co-ordination that would ensure mutual terminology and a common and overarching approach to procedural issues in the existing measures.[100] Further, it would be important to focus on specific procedural safeguards and work on specific remedies for human rights violations and other problems that might arise in cross-border litigation, including mutual recognition of judgments. Such an approach could arguably contribute more concretely to mutual trust and upholding the legitimacy of the EU civil justice measures. This could be compared to the field of criminal justice, where the very specific harmonising directives have all dealt with a particular issue of criminal procedure.[101] Thus, to continue a gradual legislative approximation process appears most concrete and useful, provided that it incorporates an overall understanding and co-ordination.

Furthermore, if the purpose of the European Parliament's proposal is to start a debate on civil procedural standards in Europe, it is concerning that its starting point is common minimum practices, rather than best practices.[102] It is true that assessing practices and identifying the best ones might be a sensitive issue. It is also true that practices often strike a balance between competing policy considerations and should not be taken out of that context. In addition, it is true that it may take a long time to promote, encourage and incentivise domestic actors to adopt best practices from other jurisdictions.[103] As a result, a level of comparative knowledge and openness will be needed to realise the goal of debating and identifying common best practices. However, such work is taking place under the auspices of the ELI/UNIDROIT project, and when the results of that project are more widely disseminated, discussed and debated among legal practitioners, there is a possibility that the best practices identified may be organically transferred to and implemented in the Member States' domestic justice systems. In addition, the European Judicial Network in Civil and Commercial Matters, which now has 505 members comprising public officials and professional associations of legal practitioners, hosts annual meetings to

99 See further B. Hess and X.E. Kramer, 'From Common Rules to Best Practices in European Civil Procedure: An Introduction' in B. Hess and X.E. Kramer (eds), *From Common Rules to Best Practices in European Civil Procedure* (Nomos 2017) 26–27.

100 Hess and Kramer (n 99), 26.

101 See *inter alia* Mitsilegas, 'Conceptualising Mutual Trust' (n 56).

102 Storskrubb, 'Mutual Trust and the Dark Horse' (n 40) 22; and Hess and Kramer (n 99) 29.

103 G. Cuniberti, 'The Promotion of Best Practices in European Civil Procedure' in B. Hess and X.E. Kramer (eds), *From Common Rules to Best Practices in European Civil Procedure* (Nomos 2017) 445–449.

discuss best practices in relation to EU civil justice regulations.[104] In addition, in the context of the work of the Council's Working Party on e-justice for example, recommendations have been issued on the use and sharing of best practices on cross-border videoconferencing at the EU level.[105] It is therefore apparent that cross-learning and discussion of best practices is already taking place in many relevant fora. While these influences may be slower to evolve and bear fruit than legislative harmonisation, they arguably contribute more to mutual trust and true approximation.

There are many difficult issues facing civil justice systems in Europe, including the opportunities provided by digitalisation and the challenges of public austerity. The soft regulatory techniques elaborated upon and proposed above that provide room for cross-learning and debate are thus ever more important. If they can complement gradual and targeted legislative initiatives, as well as case law that supports fundamental procedural rights, we may have the beginnings of a functioning and mixed regulatory strategy for civil justice in the EU. Finally, it is hoped that in the context of such a mix there will be room for a debate on civil justice values including the rule of law, and on how a modern civil justice system can meet its obligations and provide access to justice. It is only through such dialogue that a truly European area of justice can emerge.

---

104 See COM(2016) 129 final, Report on the activities of the European Judicial Network in civil and commercial matters ('EJTN'); and <https://e-justice.europa.eu/content_eventsnews-438-en.do> for the annual meeting agendas of the EJTN.

105 Council Recommendation [2015] OJ C250/1. See <https://e-justice.europa.eu/content_videoconferencing-69-en.do>.

THE ELI-UNIDROIT PROJECT

An Introduction and an English Perspective

John SORABJI

There is a long tradition of civil procedural reform in Europe. In England and Wales (England), for instance, a fetish is made of reform. It is embarked upon approximately every ten years.[1] Equally, there is a long tradition – although perhaps not one that has always been carried out consciously – which has seen national civil procedural systems across Europe converge. As Stürner noted in 2004,

> England is the motherland of the common law and common law procedure, but the [Woolf reforms of 1999] bring English civil procedure closer to the Continent and indicate a remarkable convergence between the different systems.[2]

---

1 J. SORABJI, *English Civil Justice after Woolf and Jackson – A Critical Analysis* (CUP 2014) 12–21.

2 R. STÜRNER, 'Anglo-American and Continental Civil Procedure' in M. ANDENÆS, N. ANDREWS and R. NAZZINI (eds), *The Future of Transnational Civil Litigation* (British Institute of International and Comparative Law 2004) 11.

To a common lawyer, the view from England would be much the same.[3] Convergence across systems has been a feature of the recent procedural past.[4] Notwithstanding such convergence as there has been, there have been few conscious attempts to produce common principles of European civil procedure, unlike, for instance, attempts to articulate common principles of European contract law.[5] There have been equally few attempts to produce a common code of civil procedure for Europe.[6] In this chapter, one such attempt, the most recent one, to develop a common code of civil procedure for Europe is examined. That attempt is the project, entitled 'From Transnational Principles to European Rules of Civil Procedure' (hereafter referred to as 'the project'), being carried out jointly by the European Law Institute (the ELI) and the International Institute for the Unification of Private Law (UNIDROIT). In particular, the project's background, methodology and early influence is examined. Finally, its potential future effect on both national and European Union civil procedure is considered.

1. BACKGROUND TO THE PROJECT

The project formally began in October 2013 via an initial exploratory workshop.[7] Three factors lay behind its inception. The first was the lack of any principled progress, noted above, in the development of a common European Code of Civil Procedure. There is a suggestion – and it can be put no higher than that – that Sir Jack Jacob, England's leading civil procedural scholar from the 1960s until the end of the 1990s, attempted to devise a 'uniform procedural code' for the then European Common Market in the 1970s. He is said to have given up 'because

---

3 On this see, for instance, C.H. van Rhee, 'Harmonisation of Civil Procedure' in X. Kramer and C.H. van Rhee (eds) *Civil Litigation in a Globalising World* (Asser 2012) 40 ff.

4 See, for instance, G. Canivet, 'The Interrelationship Between Common Law and Civil Law' (63 *Louisiana L Rev* 2003) 937; G. Seidman, 'The New Comparative Civil Procedure' in C. Picker and G. Seidman (eds), *The Dynamism of Civil Procedure – Global Trends and Developments* (Springer 2016) 23 ff.

5 See, for instance, O. Lando et al, *The Principles of European Contract Law*, vols 1–3, (Kluwer 1999, 2003).

6 An early attempt to articulate common principles can be found in Recommendation R (84) 5 of the Council of Ministers to Member States on the Principles of Civil Procedure designed to improve the functioning of justice, Council of Europe (1984) <https://rm.coe.int/CoERMPublicCommonSearchServices/DisplayDCTMContent?documentId=09000016804e19b1> accessed 22 June 2018.

7 ELI-UNIDROIT, *Initial Report on the ELI-UNIDROIT 1st Exploratory Workshop*, <http://www.europeanlawinstitute.eu/fileadmin/user_upload/p_eli/Projects/ELI-UNIDROIT_Workshop_initial_report.pdf> accessed 21 June 2018. The workshop was preceded by exploratory discussions by the ELI (Diana Wallis, Christiane Wendehorst, Matthias Storme, Remo Caponi and John Sorabji) and UNIDROIT (José Angelo Estrella Faria and Anna Veneziano).

of the difficulties inherent in integrating the different European traditions into a workable and acceptable home'.[8] If that is true, he was not deterred from making another attempt as a member of the Storme Commission, which examined the issue of European procedural harmonisation in the 1990s. It too concluded, albeit less pessimistically, when it reported in 1993 that the time was not ripe for a harmonised model code due to the level of procedural differentiation between the European Community Member States.[9]

Notwithstanding that general conclusion, it did set out 16 proposed Directives on areas where it concluded that progress could be made.[10] However, it did not yield a response from the European Commission, despite being the subject of detailed comment and scrutiny.[11] Its legacy in terms of the ELI-UNIDROIT project was twofold. First, that its recommendations ultimately did underpin the development of a number of discrete procedural instruments that now form part of the European Union *acquis communautaire*,[12] a point noted by Storme in 2005,[13] demonstrated that planned, principled harmonisation was possible at the European level. Convergence was not just a matter of separate systems growing together organically. As such, it was a clear inspiration for what could be achieved if an attempt was, once more, made to articulate a harmonised model code of European procedure. Secondly, that it had, despite its recommendations not being adopted directly, been influential in the development of the *acquis* demonstrated that a soft law instrument could produce concrete results in this area. It highlighted to ELI and UNIDROIT what was possible.

The second part of the background is directly linked to the Storme Commission's report: the growing procedural *acquis*. The European Union has

---

8 Reported in C. Glasser, 'A Transnational Civil Procedure Code' in M. Andenæs, N. Andrews and R. Nazzini (eds), *The Future of Transnational Civil Litigation* (British Institute of International and Comparative Law 2004) 14. It is doubtful, as Professor Glasser suggests, that Sir Jack Jacob was asked to carry out this project in the 1970s at the request of Sir Leon Brittan, the British European Commissioner. Sir Leon Brittan was not appointed as European Commissioner until 1989. It is possible therefore that Professor Glasser was misremembering Jacob's role in the Storme Commission.

9 M. Storme, 'General Introductory Report', 4 <https://www.law.kuleuven.be/personal/mstorme/Eu.Harmonis.Proced.intro.pdf> accessed 21 June 2018; M. Storme, *Approximation of Judiciary Law in the European Union* (Kluwer 1994) 61; also see R. Jacob, 'Towards a European Civil Procedural Code?' (1998) *The International Journal of Legal Education* 125 on the 'impossible subject' of devising a European civil procedural code.

10 Storme, *Approximation of Judiciary Law in the European Union* (n 9) 61.

11 As Storme noted in M. Storme, 'A Single Civil Procedure for Europe: A Cathedral Builders' Dream', (2005) *Ritsumeikan L Rev* 87, 88 it 'was commented upon, examined and criticised at a number of conferences and symposia.'

12 As acknowledged in 2002 by the European Commission, see Storme, 'A Single Civil Procedure for Europe' (n 11) 88.

13 And see B. Hess, 'Procedural Harmonisation in a European Context' in X. Kramer and C. H. van Rhee (eds), *Civil Litigation in a Globalising World* (Springer 2012) 164.

come a long way since the development of the Brussels Convention of 1968,[14] which even at that time was noted as forming a possible basis for the 'core of a unified European Civil procedure to come'.[15] A central part of that core, which drew together the European Community Member States and the EFTA Member States, was the Lugano Convention.[16] From that starting point, the *acquis* has grown significantly. Since the 1990s it has done so particularly significantly following the Storme Commission's work and, crucially, following the transfer of civil procedure from intergovernmental co-operation to an EU direct competence via the Treaty of Amsterdam in 1997. Harmonisation has advanced on a piecemeal basis then from the Brussels Convention to cover an increasingly wide field.[17] There are many examples,[18] from Brussels I[19] and Brussels I Recast,[20] to the Service Regulation,[21] the Evidence Regulation,[22] the European Enforcement Order,[23] the European Order for Payment,[24] and more recently the Mediation and ODR Directives.[25] What was in 1968 no more than a core from which procedural harmonisation could grow is now a considerable, albeit still far from complete, body of procedural law. Two points were again drawn

---

14 Convention of 27 September 1968 on jurisdiction and the enforcement of judgments in civil and commercial matters [1968] OJ L204/28.

15 P. Gottwald, 'The European Law of Civil Procedure' (2005) *Ritsumeikan L Rev* 37–38 cited in G. Seidman, 'The New Comparative Civil Procedure' in C. Picker and G. Seidman (eds), *The Dynamism of Civil Procedure – Global Trends and Developments* (Springer 2016) 41.

16 Ibid.

17 Seidman (n 15) 41–42.

18 For a concise summary see G. Wagner, 'Harmonization of European Civil Procedure – Policy Perspectives' in X. Kramer and C. H. van Rhee (eds), *Civil Litigation in a Globalising World* (Springer 2012) 95 ff; also see S. Prechal and K. Cath, 'The European acquis of civil procedure: constitutional aspects' (2014) *Uniform L Rev* 179; M. Tulibacka, M. Sanz and R. Blomeyer, 'Common Minimum Standards of Civil Procedure' (European Added Value Assessment, European Parliamentary Research Service, Study, PE 581.385, June 2016) <http://www.europarl.europa.eu/cmsdata/105660/EPRS_CIVIL_PROCEDURE.pdf> accessed 21 June 2018.

19 Regulation (EC) 44/2001 on jurisdiction and the recognition and enforcement of judgments in civil and commercial matters [2001] OJ L12/1.

20 Regulation (EC) 1215/2012 on jurisdiction and the recognition and enforcement in civil and commercial matters (Brussels I bis Regulation) [2012] OJ L351/1.

21 Regulation (EC) 1393/2007 on the service in the Member States of judicial and extrajudicial documents in civil or commercial matters (service of documents) [2007] OJ L324/79, and repealing Regulation (EC) 1348/2000 [2000] OJ L160/37.

22 Regulation (EC) 1206/2001 on cooperation between the courts of the Member States in the taking of evidence in civil or commercial matters [2001] OJ L174/1.

23 Regulation (EC) 805/2004 creating a European Enforcement Order for uncontested claims [2004] OJ L143/15.

24 Regulation (EC) 1896/2006 on a European order for payment procedure [2006] OJ L339/1.

25 Directive 2008/52/EC on certain aspects of mediation in civil and commercial matters [2008] OJ L136/3; Directive 2013/11/EU on alternative dispute resolution for consumer disputes and amending Regulation (EC) No 2006/2004 and Directive 2009/22/EC; Regulation (EU) 524/2013 on online dispute resolution for consumer disputes and amending Regulation (EC) No 2006/2004 and Directive 2009/22/EC (Directive on consumer ADR) [2013] OJ L165/63.

from these developments. First, the expanding yet piecemeal development was more than suggestive of a need for there to be a fully articulated, principled and holistic model code so that future developments were coherent and consistent. Secondly, the expansive nature of developments post-Storme demonstrated that the time was perhaps now ripe for a harmonised code; time and procedural harmonisation had developed to a degree since the 1990s that a fully harmonised code might no longer be beyond reach.

The third aspect of the ELI-UNIDROIT project's background goes beyond Europe. It was the ALI-UNIDROIT Principles of Transnational Civil Procedure of 2006.[26] They were the product of seven years' work, the aim of which was to produce what has been described as a 'balanced distillation of best practice (from common law and civil law learning), especially in the sphere of transnational commercial litigation'.[27] In what was then an increasingly interconnected commercial world, such a distillation was perceived to be an important means to reduce the cost, complexity and length of time to resolve transnational disputes:[28] reducing difference and promoting convergence was a way to reduce, even if not eliminate, what Bentham described as the 'vexation' caused by litigation.[29] In this regard, the ALI-UNIDROIT Principles sought to achieve transnationally what the Storme Commission sought to achieve for the European Communities' internal market.[30] We live in a far more connected world today than was the case in 1994 or 2006. The growth of the Internet, e-commerce and global markets has seen to that. And from the European perspective, the increasingly connected and regulated nature of the internal market since the start of the 1990s, as well as more recent developments in e-justice,[31] have added to that increase in connectivity, and mobility amongst potential litigants. The ALI-UNIDROIT Principles and their underpinning aim of enhancing convergence and reducing differences between systems in order to

---

26 American Law Institute and UNIDROIT, *Principles of Transnational Civil Procedure* (CUP 2006).

27 N. Andrews, 'Fundamental Principles of Civil Procedure' in X. Kramer and C. H. van Rhee (eds), *Civil Litigation in a Globalising World* (Springer 2012) 21.

28 See J. Sanchez-Cordero Davila, 'Preface' in American Law Institute and UNIDROIT, *Principles of Transnational Civil Procedure* (CUP 2006) xxxvii; and see S. McAuley, 'Achieving the Harmonization of Transnational Civil Procedure: Will the ALI/UNIDROIT Project Succeed?' (2004) 15 *Am Rev Int'l Arb* 231 on the importance of the 'divergent nature of procedural law in different judicial systems' increasing business costs and litigation risk and uncertainty when 'engaging in domestic litigation in a foreign jurisdiction'.

29 J. Bentham, 'Rationale of Judicial Evidence' in J. Bowring (ed), *The Works of Jeremy Bentham* (William Tait 1843) vol 6 at 212–213.

30 Storme, *General Introductory Report* (n 9) 8: 'It is common knowledge that the world of international business requires an effective and transparent system of procedural law. This is becoming all the more necessary with the multiplication of transnational contacts.'

31 For an interesting discussion see B. Hess and X.E. Kramer (eds), *From common rules to best practices in European Civil Procedure* (Nomos/Hart Publishing 2017).

improve efficiency and economy in securing civil justice was an ambition that was viewed as being all the more relevant today by both the ELI and UNDROIT. From the ELI's perspective it was a particularly pertinent issue. Two of its aims are to improve European law and law-making in ways that are beneficial to European citizens, first through stimulating the development of EU law, and second through facilitating pan-European (not just EU) research through drafting and improving principles common to European legal systems.[32] From UNIDROIT's perspective, it was equally pertinent given its aim of modernising and promoting the harmonisation of law; an aim which, by combining the ALI-UNDROIT approach and the Storme Commission's regional focus, could potentially be facilitated through the development of – in this case – a European harmonisation project.[33]

The ALI-UNIDROIT Principles thus provided the ELI and UNIDROIT with both a challenge and a template for what could be done. Equally, just as the incomplete albeit expanding *acquis communautaire* did, they drew attention to a continuing gap in European legal development. The template was both the Principles and the rules of transnational procedure that were produced by the ALI-UNIDROIT reporters: the production of a principle-based model code. The challenge was to see if, through the ALI-UNIDROIT Principles, the Storme Commission's aim could now be achieved. Could European rules of civil procedure, derived from the ALI-UNIDROIT Principles – and taking account of, but not being limited by, the *acquis communautaire* and other European legal developments – now be produced? Could rules be developed that would enhance the operation of the EU's internal market, of the operation of transnational litigation within Europe as a geographical whole? That was the nature of the challenge. From the ELI and UNIDROIT's perspective, the time was ripe, given the growth of the global market and the European Union, as well as its relations with non-EU European nations, to develop a draft set of European rules that would, as Professor Andrews is reported to have put it, 'piece together into one single "jigsaw" of soft law.'[34] In other words, to facilitate convergence through providing a coherent, consistent and 'commonly acceptable' single set of draft European rules that would be 'pitched at a level where they provide practical

32 ELI Statute, article 3.2 <http://www.europeanlawinstitute.eu/fileadmin/user_upload/p_eli/Statute/ELI_Statute_English_amended.pdf> accessed 21 June 2018.

33 As noted in EU Directorate General for Internal Policies, *The European Law Institute-UNIDROIT Civil Procedure Projects as a soft law tool to resolve conflicts of law* (PE 556.972) 11: 'From the point of view of UNIDROIT it may further represent a first attempt towards the development of other regional projects adapting the 2004 ALI / UNIDROIT Principles to the specificities of other regional legal cultures, leading the way to the drafting of further regional rules' <http://www.europarl.europa.eu/RegData/etudes/IDAN/2017/556972/IPOL_IDA(2017)556972_EN.pdf> accessed 21 June 2018.

34 Andrews, cited in EU Directorate General for Internal Policies (n 33) 11.

guidance, but avoiding the familiar tendency for procedural rules to contain over-detailed prescription of every imaginable eventuality.'[35]

It was against this tripartite background – the unfinished business of the Storme Commission, the growth of the procedural *acquis communautaire*, and the ALI-UNIDROIT Principles – that the ELI and UNIDROIT held the project's initial exploratory workshop, the immediate aim of which was to consider whether the project was viable, and if so, which aspects of civil procedure could properly be considered within it.[36] The view taken to the first question was positive but cautious. It was viable as a means to promote harmonisation, although as Professor Stürner noted, the 'idea of a common European civil procedure code may be realized by the European legislature in the coming decades, but it is quite certain it will not happen at the present time or in the near future.' Given this, as he put it, the project could facilitate the development of a 'common vision or idea of a European procedural model' and thereafter guide 'further harmonization for both European legislation and for Member States' legislation'.[37] Underpinning the latter point was recognition, and properly so, that any such development was not a matter solely for the European Union; it was a matter for it and for non-European Union European countries. Principled harmonisation via a model code was not a matter of political developments or entities, but rather of the convergence of procedural systems that predate such developments and go wider than them. The model code that the exploratory workshop understood to be viable was not a European Union model code, even if it could be used as such, but rather a European model code.

2. THE PROJECT'S SCOPE

The October 2013 workshop determined both the scope and methodology that the project was to adopt. Three issues were settled in terms of its scope.

First, it would not be limited to transnational, cross-border litigation. It would aim to provide as much of an inspiration for national procedural development as it would for the development of a pan-European code – European in the broad sense noted above. As such, it would seek to produce a model code that could, in principle, be adopted or adapted for use by a European state, the European Union and/or the European Free Trade Association or any

[35] N. Andrews, 'The European Law Institute/Unidroit Civil Procedure Projects: Reflections and Examples' (15 June 2016) 3 <http://www.europarl.europa.eu/cmsdata/105661/andrews.pdf> accessed 21 June 2018.

[36] A collection of papers derived from that initial exploratory workshop are published in (2014) 19(2/3) *Uniform L Rev*.

[37] R. Stürner, 'Principles of European civil procedure or a European model code? Some considerations on the joint ELI-UNIDROIT project' (2014) *Uniform L Rev* 322, 324.

combination of the three. As any such model code, if implemented or used as a source of inspiration for future development, would necessarily have to deal with cross-border questions, it was also to include provisions concerning cross-border disputes. The exact nature of this aspect of the project was not however finally determined until it had developed considerably, the final decision on this point being that cross-border rules should deal both with cross-border disputes concerning the European Union and those concerning non-European Union states.[38]

Secondly, the project's focus would be on civil, including commercial, litigation. As such, it would follow the approach taken by the Storme Commission and the ALI-UNIDROIT Transnational Principles. Consideration was, however, also given to the question whether it should encompass family disputes and/or employment disputes. While a complete civil – in the broadest sense – code of procedure could encompass such disputes, they do however demonstrate a degree of specialisation due to their substantive subject matter. Such specialisation has, by way of example, seen family disputes governed by their own procedural code in England.[39] It has equally seen employment disputes governed by their own procedural code in a specialist tribunal in England, albeit that employment disputes, such as those arising from a breach of the employment contract, can in certain circumstances also be prosecuted before the civil courts under the English Civil Procedure Rules. Although it would have been possible to develop the project such that it encompassed both family and employment disputes, it was considered that to do so would have introduced an element of complexity into it that would have rendered the model rules too unwieldy;[40] such rules might properly form the basis of future model rule projects, which could in turn build on and incorporate, as necessary, those produced by the immediate project. Here was the unstated, and perhaps largely unremarked, acceptance that the development of model harmonisation codes ought to develop in a deliberately cautious way, moving from one area of law to another. And implicit in this is the idea that it would, or should, be possible to build a fully trans-substantive code of procedure from the starting point of a model code the focus of which excluded specialist forms of civil, in a broad sense, proceedings.

Finally, the October 2013 workshop determined that the project would proceed in discrete phases. It would initially focus on developing model rules

---

38 ELI-UNIDROIT, 'Steering Committee – First Meeting Report' (12–13 May 2014) 8 <http://www.unidroit.org/english/documents/2014/study76a/s-76a-sc01-02-e.pdf> accessed 21 June 2018.

39 See the Family Procedure Rules (SI 2010/2955) <http://www.justice.gov.uk/courts/procedure-rules/family/rules_pd_menu> accessed 21 June 2018.

40 As noted by the Working Group on Access to Evidence, 'First Report' (27–28 November 2014) 3 <http://www.unidroit.org/english/documents/2014/study76a/s-76a-02corr-e.pdf> accessed 21 June 2018.

for three areas of procedure, which would form the basis of the project's first phase. Those areas were service and due notice of proceedings, provisional and protective measures, and access to information and evidence. Assuming work on these areas yielded positive results, the project would then move onto further phases, which would look at other discrete areas of procedure. Given the success of the initial phases, three further phases commenced. The second phase, which commenced in 2015, focused on *res judicata* and *lis pendens*, and obligations of parties and lawyers. In 2016, a third phase commenced, focusing on three further areas: parties and joinder, judgments, and litigation costs. Finally, in 2017 work began on a final area: appeals.[41] In addition to the work allocated to each of the discrete working groups, an overarching working group was identified as being necessary at the October 2013 workshop: a structure of the proceedings working group. It began its work in 2017.

The project is thus divided into ten work streams, each the responsibility of a specific working group. In terms of its scope, this was not the initial intent. The conclusion drawn at the October 2013 workshop was that three specific areas ought not to be pursued within the project: collective redress, appeals, and litigation costs. The reason for this was that each was taken to be too difficult an area to produce a harmonised approach, the continued and continuing failure of the European Commission to produce a coherent collective redress regime being an acute example of this.[42] While these three areas were initially viewed as posing intractable problems for harmonisation,[43] experience gained during work on the project led to this conclusion being revisited. Given the progress made on other areas, the conclusion was drawn that not only could the project properly leave these issues untouched, but that given the working groups' various experiences the apparently intractable often proves not to be so.

One area that was originally to be considered as part of the project,[44] but which is not however being pursued, is enforcement. The view initially taken was that enforcement was an essential feature of a civil procedural regime which aims to vindicate civil rights,[45] and ought therefore to be examined

---

41 Details of the work done is available at: < https://www.unidroit.org/work-in-progress/transnational-civil-procedure> and <https://www.europeanlawinstitute.eu/projects-publications/current-projects-feasibility-studies-and-other-activities/current-projects/civil-procedure/> both accessed 22 June 2018.

42 See, for instance, C. Hodges, 'Collective Redress: A Breakthrough or a Damp Squib?' (2014) 37 *Journal of Consumer Policy* 67; A. Stadler, 'The Commission's Recommendation on Common Principles of Collective Redress and Private International Law Issues' [2013] *Netherlands J of Priv Int'L* 483.

43 'Report of First Joint Meeting of the Steering Committee and Working Groups' (27–28 November 2014) 12 <http://www.unidroit.org/english/documents/2014/study76a/s-76a-05-e.pdf> accessed 21 June 2018.

44 Ibid, 11.

45 See, for instance, J. Bentham, 'The Constitutional Code' in J. Bowring (ed), *The Works of Jeremy Bentham* (William Tait 1843) vol 9 at 25–26.

and incorporated within a model code. However, it was later concluded that notwithstanding that fact, it was an area of such breadth that it ought properly to be considered as a separate, and future, project, one that would hopefully cohere with the present one. Having determined the scope of the project, the question was how it was to be carried out: what methodology was to be adopted.

3. THE PROJECT'S METHODOLOGY

3.1. EXPERTISE

The project could have been carried out in either of two ways. It could have been the singular product of a single mind, a latter-day Field Code,[46] or of a small group, such as the model rules of Transnational Civil Procedure produced by the ALI-UNIDROIT reporters, although they were not adopted by either the ALI or UNIDROIT.[47] Such an approach would have had much to commend it if the project's aim was to produce a model code or restatement of procedure for a single jurisdiction. It is an approach familiar to England and Wales, where individual judges are regularly asked to revise and restate its civil procedure code.[48]

The project's aim was not however to devise a model code for a single polity. It was to devise a model set of rules capable of inspiring procedural convergence and coherence both for the European Union and across Europe as a whole. As such, an aim would need to draw upon the experience of many systems, an alternative route was taken, that which was, again, evidenced by both the Storme Commission and the ALI-UNIDROIT Principles. It was to draw upon the experience of many minds, experts drawn from across Europe each of whom were, and are, well-versed in the common inheritance of ideas that underpin Europe's individual approaches to civil procedure. It would also draw upon the experience of individuals, such as Professors Hazard, Stürner, Andrews and Ferrand, all of whom had experience of the ALI-UNIDROIT project and would thus bring both their practical experience of taking part in such an endeavour, as well as their procedural expertise, to the project. Their experience has been of immense importance to the project's development. Additionally, the project

---

46 See the Code of Civil Procedure of the State of New York (Commissions on Practice and Pleading 1850); S. Subrin, 'David Dudley Field and the Field Code: A Historical Analysis of an Earlier Procedural Vision' (1988) 6 *L and History Rev* 311.

47 American Law Institute and UNIDROIT (n 26) 99 ff.

48 See, for instance, H. Woolf, *Access to Justice: Interim Report to the Lord Chancellor on the Civil Justice System in England and Wales* (HMSO 1995); H. Woolf, *Access to Justice: Final Report to the Lord Chancellor on the Civil Justice System in England and Wales* (HMSO 1996); H. Woolf, *Access to Justice – Draft Civil Proceedings Rules* (HMSO 1996).

would also draw upon the critical insight of an advisory body constituted of a number of experts from across the world nominated by both the ELI and UNIDROIT, as well the views of project observers, such as the European Commission and Parliament, the International Association of Procedural Law, Max-Planck Institute Luxembourg for International, European and Regulatory Procedural Law, and The Hague Conference on Private International Law.[49]

In order to draw properly upon European experience, it was decided at the outset that each of the project's areas of work would be carried out by a specific working group under the overall direction and co-ordination of a joint ELI-UNIDROIT Steering Committee.[50] Each working group was to have six to eight members,[51] although this was not prescriptive and some groups have more, others less, than that number. The essential feature of each of the groups was that they were to be drawn from each of Europe's legal traditions.[52] Consistently with the ELI's aims, each working group was also, in so far as possible, to have a blend of academics, practitioners and judges amongst its membership. The aim underpinning this requirement was that the project was not intended to

49 Full details can be found at: 'Report of First Joint Meeting of the Steering Committee and Working Groups' (n 43).

50 The Steering Committee's members are: Diana Wallis (ELI), Remo Caponi (ELI and Professor of Law, Dipartimento di scienze giuridiche, Università di Firenze), John Sorabji (ELI and Senior Fellow, Judicial Institute, Faculty of Law, UCL), José Angelo Estrella Faria (UNIDROIT Secretary-General until 2016), Anna Veneziano (UNIDROIT deputy Secretary-General), and Rolf Stürner (Professor of Law, Albert-Ludwigs-Universität Freiburg).

51 The working groups' membership is as follows: *Working Group on Service*: reporters: Astrid Stadler and Eva Storskrubb; members: Marco de Cristofaro, Emmanuel Jeuland, Wendy Kennett and Dimitrios Tsikrikas. *Working Group on Access to Information and Evidence*: reporters: Neil Andrews (until September 2016) and Fernando Gascón Inchausti; members: Frédérique Ferrand, Laura Ervo, Viktória Harsági and Michael Stürner. *Working Group on Provisional and Protective Measures*: reporters: Neil Andrews (until approximately September 2016), Gilles Cuniberti (until June 2016) and Xandra Kramer (from September 2016); members: Torbjörn Andersson, Fernando de la Mata, Alan Uzelac, Remo Caponi (from September 2016) and John Sorabji (from September 2016). *Working Group on Obligations of the Parties and Lawyers*: reporters: C.H. (Remco) van Rhee and Alan Uzelac; members: Emmanuel Jeuland, Magne Strandberg, Elisabetta Silvestri, Bartosz Karolczyk, John Sorabji and Walter Rechberger. *Working Group on Res Judicata and Lis Pendens*: reporters: Frédérique Ferrand and Burkhard Hess; members: Neil Andrews (until approximately September 2016), Alexander Arabadjiev, Remo Caponi, Marco de Cristofaro, Tanja Domej, Fernando Gascón Inchausti, Kalliopi Makridou, Jarkko Männistö and Karol Weitz. *Working Group on Judgments*: reporters: Chiara Besso and Christoph Kern; members: Lauro Ervo, Natalie Fricero, Andrew Higgins and Thomas Sutter-Somm. *Working Group on Costs*: reporters: Paul Oberhammer and Eva Storskrubb; members: Wendy Kennett. *Working Group on Parties (including collective redress)*: reporters: Astrid Stadler and Emmanuel Jeuland; members: Vincent Smith, Ianika Tzankova, Istvan Varga and Stefaan Voet. *Working Group on Appeals*: reporters: Frédérique Ferrand and Christoph Kern; members: Fernando Gascón Inchausti and Magne Strandberg. *Working Group on Structure of the Proceedings*: reporters: Loïc Cadiet and Xandra Kramer; members: John Sorabji and Rolf Stürner.

52 'Report of First Joint Meeting of the Steering Committee and Working Groups' (n 43) 20–21.

devise a perfect academic text, a work of crystalline but unworkable beauty akin to Wittgenstein's *Tractatus*.[53] On the contrary, it was to produce a workable, practical text, one informed as much by experience as it was by principle. Where practitioners and judges, or geographic diversity, could not be included within working groups, that deficiency was to be rectified within the membership of the project's advisory body. To ensure consistency of approach, each working group was to contain individual members drawn from other working groups.

A distinction does however need to be drawn between the Structure of the Proceedings Working Group (the Structure working group) and the other working groups. The Structure working groups is, unlike the other working parties, a horizontal one. Rather than focusing on a discrete aspect of procedure, such as service or evidence, its primary role is to draw together the final results produced by each of the other working groups and produce a single, coherent model code. As such, it will, for instance, need to determine the overall structure of the code and revise the working groups' work so that it is both linguistically and stylistically consistent. Moreover, it is also to fill in any procedural gaps, i.e. those areas not addressed by the other working groups but which are essential elements of a complete model code. It will, for instance, need to come to decisions concerning the approach to be taken to the pleading process and the relationship between the pre-trial and trial phases of proceedings. Difficult questions such as whether the trial process is to be concentrated or not will have to be answered. Unlike the other working parties, though, it has a small membership, with two members of the Steering Committee assisting Professors Cadiet and Kramer.[54] In order to ensure that it integrates effectively the discrete working groups' drafts into a final text, such that the whole is more than the sum of its parts, it will also, however, have to work closely with the reporters of those other working groups. This co-operation will, equally, be of importance if it becomes apparent that substantive changes to the working groups' drafts are required in order to produce a coherent, complete final draft.

3.2. DRAFTING THE RULES

The next question is how the working groups operate. Three general points can be made concerning the working method. The first concerns language. The project is being carried out in English, as a *lingua franca*. Working parties draft primarily in English. However, it is not the sole language.

53 L. Wittgenstein, *Philosophical Investigations* (Blackwell 1989) section 97.

54 Its membership is, as noted earlier: reporters: Loïc Cadiet and Xandra Kramer; members: John Sorabji and Rolf Stürner.

French-language versions of the draft rules have also been, and are being, prepared in order to ensure that the complete final draft is available in both languages. As importantly, bilingual drafting was taken to be an important aspect of the project for a further reason; it was adopted because of the benefits it brought from the perspective of clarity in drafting. It was noted at the project's outset – and this was particularly borne out in the Obligations of Parties and Lawyers Working Group – that comparative drafting between English and French highlighted ambiguities in the choice of drafting terms. Equally, it brought to light linguistic misunderstandings, highlighted superfluous wording, and drew attention to issues that had not otherwise been noted. For instance, it highlighted the differential scope of 'interested party' in English and in French, and differential meanings of 'order' and 'management' *qua* 'case management'. Ultimately it led, and is leading, to a clearer and better-drafted piece of work. It is hoped that – as is being done by the Working Group on *Res Judicata*, which is drafting its work in English, French and German, and intends to produce further drafts in, at least, Italian, Spanish and Polish[55] – ultimately the final draft rules will be translated into a number of different European languages.

The second general point concerns the nature of the rules to be drafted. Rules could have been drafted on the basis of compromise, i.e. what was broadly acceptable to most jurisdictions. Compromise was not however considered to be an effective way forward. The view was taken by the project's Steering Committee, following discussion with the working groups' reporters, that such an approach would lead to a sub-optimal result, or to no result at all. It would do no more than either set out a summary of what was acceptable to all jurisdictions. Such an approach would simply present a summary of uncontentious matters, or it would see a compromise struck on contentious matters. For example, it would leave undetermined whether a concentrated or an iterative or continuous[56] trial process should be adopted. This would thus result in no real decision being made within the model rules. The ultimate decision as to which to choose would then be left to be determined by national codes. If this approach were to have been adopted there would be little prospect of increasing procedural convergence; on the contrary, it would tend to reinforce difference. Another alternative approach was also rejected, that of drafting the model rules on a minimum standards basis. This was also rejected by the Steering Committee as being an approach that would tend to produce a sub-optimal approach. It would tend to produce, as the European Parliament's JURI Committee's Report

---

55 Working Group on *Res Judicata* and *Lis Pendens*, 'Third Report' (April 2016) 1 <http://www.unidroit.org/english/documents/2016/study76a/sc04/s-76a-sc04-03-e.pdf> accessed 21 June 2018.

56 P. Murray and R. Stürner, *German Civil Justice* (Carolina Academic Press 2004) 14.

on Minimum Common Procedural Standards shows,[57] a text more akin to a European Restatement of the ALI-UNIDROIT Principles than model rules of European civil procedure. A minimum standards approach would, given its very nature, accommodate the continuance of marked differences in approach across Europe, as the standards would be capable of being met by differential procedural approaches across – in the case of the European Parliament's draft – the European Union. It is an approach that does not promote harmonisation or convergence. Again, it is an approach that would tend to reinforce the continuance of difference.

The project took a third way. It adopted the position that, if real progress was to be made in terms of coherence and convergence, then a best practice approach to developing model rules was to be taken. As Stürner put it, this was an approach that would require clear decisions to be taken in favour of specific procedural approaches.[58] The working groups were thus to consider what was the best approach in formulating their rules. Inevitably this meant that some national system's approaches would not find their way into the final model rules. And inevitably this will mean that the final draft will be more controversial, in some parts, than an anodyne compromise or minimum standards approach. This was, however, a risk the Steering Committee concluded was more than worth taking. If progress towards harmonisation were to be made, it was not enough to accept – as the Storme Commission had had to do in the 1990s – that the time was still not ripe for a harmonised model to be developed. On the contrary, even if some of the proposed rules were still too outré for some systems to accept, if they were able to promote convergence amongst other systems, then an important step or steps towards a fully and properly harmonised, and best practice, approach could be taken. The approach taken was thus one that accepted that progress is and can be made by increments as much as by bold steps.

3.3. AN EXAMPLE OF THE WORKING PROCESS

Having set out these general points, the project's general working methodology can be further illustrated by the approach taken by the Working Group on Obligations of Lawyers and Parties.[59] As is to be expected, the starting point for each Working Group was to identify relevant principles from the ALI-UNIDROIT Principles and relevant European principles, whether contained, for instance, in the *acquis communautaire*, the European Convention

57 See, for instance, E. Radev, 'Report with recommendations to the Commission on common minimum standards of civil procedure in the EU' (RR\1127538EN.docx, 6 June 2017) <http://www.europarl.europa.eu/sides/getDoc.do?pubRef=-//EP//NONSGML+REPORT+A8-2017-0210+0+DOC+PDF+V0//EN> accessed 12 October 2018.

58 Stürner (n 37) 326.

59 Inevitably, different working groups took variants of the approach outlined here.

on Human Rights, the Storme Commission's report,[60] or the Council of Europe Recommendation (84) 5.[61] In this respect, the Obligations Working Group identified ALI-UNIDROIT Principles 11 and 14 – Obligations of the Parties and Lawyers, and Court Responsibility for Direction of Proceedings, i.e. active case management – as being of primary importance. Other principles were also identified, concerning procedural sanctions (Principle 17) and settlement in the context of encouragement of alternative dispute resolution (ADR) (Principle 24), as well as Principles 5 (due notice), 16 (access to evidence) and 19 (presentation of evidence).[62] The clear link to Article 6 of the European Convention on Human Rights is readily apparent.

Having identified relevant principles, comparative surveys of European jurisdictions' approaches were undertaken by the working group members. Each survey was to address a series of questions relating to case management.[63] This further preparatory work was either done by each working group member considering their own and related jurisdictions, or by members working together where there was a degree of commonality of approach as, for instance, was the case with the English and Welsh and Norwegian systems in respect of active case management.[64] Working group members were then given responsibility

---

60 Relevant rules from the Storme Commission were rules 2.1.1.1, 2.1.2 and 8.1–8.6: Storme, *Approximation of Judiciary Law in the European Union* (n 9).

61 For example, Principle 2.3. Consideration was also given to, for instance, Council of Europe, Recommendation (2000) 21 on the freedom of exercise of the profession of lawyer, and the Code of Conduct for European Lawyers of the Council of Bars and Law Societies of Europe.

62 For a comparable approach see Working Group on Access to Information and Evidence, 'First Report' (27–28 November 2014) <http://www.unidroit.org/english/documents/2014/study76a/s-76a-02corr-e.pdf> accessed 21 June 2018.

63 The questions were:

1. Does your system provide for a mechanism for the management of the pre-issue stage of a dispute? If so, what is that mechanism, how is it put into effect and what role, if any, does the court have in overseeing its operation?
2. Following issue of proceedings is there a clear distinction between the pre-trial and trial stage of proceedings? If so, how is the distinction drawn?
3. Does the pre-trial stage of proceedings have an explicit (or implicit) aim or aims? For instance, is pre-trial management intended and carried out in order to enable a claim to reach trial and judgment on the merits, is it intended to achieve this at reasonable cost and time, or is it intended to manage the claim to the most appropriate means of dispute resolution whether that is a merits-based judgment or consensual resolution?
4. Who is responsible for the management of the pre-trial stage of proceedings: the court, the party or both?
5. What duties and/or powers does the court have in respect of the management of the pre-trial stage of proceedings?
6. What duties and/or powers do parties have in respect of the pre-trial stage of proceedings?
7. What sanctions are available for party failure to comply with obligations that arise during the pre-trial stage of proceedings? What approach does the court take to granting relief from imposition of such sanctions, i.e. does it take a lenient or limited approach to granting relief?

64 Compare, for instance, Part 3 of the Civil Procedure Rules 1998 (England and Wales) and the Dispute Act 2005 (Norway), sections 94 to 9-11 and 11-5.

for considering the European approaches to a specific aspect of the area – such as potential pre-issue obligations, pre-trial case management, or the promotion (or otherwise) of ADR – and prepared comparative papers accordingly. From those papers, best practice proposals[65] were formulated, taking account of the approaches from each of the jurisdictions and traditions considered.[66] They were then discussed and revised at a number of meetings of, as well as via e-mail communication between, the whole group. Working drafts were then submitted to the project's Steering Committee and made subject to scrutiny and discussion by reporters and members of the other working groups and of the project's observers, at a number of project team meetings; in this way, different perspectives both from other jurists from the jurisdictions specifically considered by the working group and from those from other European jurisdictions could be brought to bear. The working group's drafts were also subject to discussion at a number of open meetings, i.e. at an open conference at the Academy of European Law in Trier in November 2016.

By adopting the above-illustrated approach, the working groups sought to ensure that their principle-based approach has produced rules that are both grounded in European procedural culture, but equally are not hidebound by it or by any particular approach. Final draft rules from the Working Groups on Service, Access to Information, Provisional Measures, and Obligations were produced by April 2017.[67] Final drafts from the remaining working groups are anticipated in 2018, with the final, consolidated draft to be produced by the end of 2019. No doubt, once finalised, it will be subject to detailed scrutiny and further discussion.

4. THE PROJECT'S INFLUENCE SO FAR

Having outlined the project and its working method, I turn now to the impact the project has had since its inception in 2013. The fear that must haunt any

65 Different groups will have adopted different criteria for determining best practice within their specific field of work. This will, for instance, have required consideration to be given to the growth in importance and use of digital and internet-based communication, for service of process and for case management. In respect of the Obligations Working Group, specific criteria applied to assess comparative approaches focused on, amongst other things, how well specific approaches promoted the aims of procedural efficiency, economy, and the court's ability to secure justice on the merits.

66 The specific jurisdictions considered were: Austria, Croatia, England and Wales, France, Germany, Italy, the Netherlands, Norway and Poland.

67 An examples of an early draft is Andrews (n 35) 7 ff. Also see the conference materials from the ELI-UNDROIT Project conference held in conjunction with the Academy of European Law in Trier in November 2016, where initial drafts of rules were presented by the first five working parties: Access to Information and Evidence; Provisional and Protective Measures; *Res Judicata* and *Lis Pendens*; Obligations of the Parties, Lawyers and Judges; and Service and Due Notice Proceedings.

project such as this is that, like David Hume's *Treatise on Human Understanding*, it falls 'dead-born from the press ... without reaching such distinction, as even to excite a murmur amongst the zealots'.[68] That is, it simply has no influence at all. That cannot be said for the ELI-UNIDROIT project. Its influence runs ahead of its completion.

First, and to a lesser extent, it has already started to influence national developments. Its timing has been serendipitous in respect of some European jurisdictions. Hungary, for instance, embarked upon a revision to its civil procedure in 2014. By 2016 a new draft code had been finalised and was subject to discussion and debate. As part of that discussion process, the ELI-UNIDROIT and a number of its working group members, most prominently Professor Andrews, outlined the nature and detail of the project in May 2016.[69] The project's work, and its insights, was brought to bear upon the developing Hungarian codification project.[70]

Influence at the European level has, however, been more significant, something which was anticipated by the European institutions at the very outset of the project.[71] First, it spurred the European Parliament in 2015, shortly after the project's first exploratory workshop, to consider whether the time was ripe for a European legislative proposal 'setting out common minimum standards of civil procedure law'.[72] The question was asked explicitly as a consequence of the project's then nascent work.[73] The answer reached, in stark contrast to the

---

68 David Hume quoted in T. Ritchie, *An Account of the Life and Writings of David Hume* (Cadell & Davies 1807) 9.

69 See the New Hungarian Civil Procedure Act and the Development of European Rules of Civil Procedure (May 2016) Programme <http://www.lb.hu/sites/default/files/sajto/new_hungarian_civil_procedure_act_programme_final_draft_30-31_may_2016.pdf> accessed 21 June 2019. And see *Acta Iuridica Hungarica*, vol 58, no 1, March 2017.

70 The new code is in force from 1 January 2018. See L. Pribula, *The New Civil Procedure Code in Hungary* (SUBB Iurisprudentia) 79.

71 Anticipated in the comments made by Michael Shotter at the Project's First Exploratory Workshop in 2014 <http://www.unidroit.org/english/documents/2014/study76a/201310-eli-news.pdf> accessed 21 June 2018.

72 European Parliament, Committee on Legal Affairs, 'Working document on establishing common minimum standards for civil procedure in the European Union – the legal basis' (DT\1079599EN.doc, 21 December 2015) 2 <http://www.europarl.europa.eu/sides/getDoc.do?type=COMPARL&reference=PE-572.853&format=PDF&language=EN&secondRef=01> accessed 21 June 2018. It had also, previously, resulted in an in-depth study on harmonisation and minimum standards by DG-Internal Policies, see B. Hess, 'Harmonized Rules and Minimum Standards in the European Law of Civil Procedure – In-Depth Analysis' (PE 556.971, 2016) <http://www.europarl.europa.eu/RegData/etudes/IDAN/2016/556971/IPOL_IDA(2016)556971_EN.pdf> accessed 21 June 2018. More recently, see U. Bux, 'The European Law Institute/UNIDROIT Civil Procedure Projects as a Soft Law Tool to Resolve Conflicts of Law' (PE 556.972, 2017) <http://www.europarl.europa.eu/RegData/etudes/IDAN/2017/556972/IPOL_IDA(2017)556972_EN.pdf> accessed 21 June 2018.

73 Ibid, 2: 'This document considers that – in line with the European Commission's past initiatives and the outcome of the joint projects of the European Law Institute and Unidroit – the time has come for a legislative proposal setting out common minimum standards of civil procedure law.'

position of the 1990s, was that the time was ripe. This decision yielded the first such minimum standards statement by the European Parliament.[74] The aim of that document is to foster a greater degree of convergence at the Member State level. It can however be questioned whether it is a step that takes convergence very far. It could be doubted (as noted above), for instance, whether any European state does not comply with such minimum standards, albeit that doubts may be raised in some respects at the present time.[75] Equally, and again as noted above, doubts arise whether a minimum standards approach can genuinely promote convergence, as such standards provide ample scope for differential implementation at the standard and above it. Notwithstanding these caveats, it is however a first concrete step – an important one, as any first step is important. And it is a step which, in July 2017, was referred by the European Parliament, via an own-initiative resolution, to the European Commission, calling upon it to take the proposal forward under Article 81(2) TFEU.[76]

The European Parliament's initiative does, however, in part, go beyond simply setting out common minimum standards as a way to foster greater convergence. In part, it also contains recommendations that suggest a clearer and more important influence by the project, one focused on what the project would understand to be rules of best practice. Amongst its proposals, the European Parliament's initiative contained a detailed proposal setting out what steps a court can take to engage in active case management. It is an idea familiar to English proceduralists, as such a power is detailed in rule 3.1 of the Civil Procedure Rules. It is an aspect of procedural best practice, drawn from both English and, it is right to say, Norwegian[77] procedure by the project's Obligations Working Group, and which forms an integral part of its draft rules. Here we can see the project's importance, through the access to its meetings and materials afforded to its institutional observers.[78] Best practice in that working group's draft rules

---

74 European Parliament, Committee on Legal Affairs, 'Draft Report with recommendations to the Commission on common minimum standards of civil procedure in the EU' (2015/2084(INL)) <http://www.europarl.europa.eu/sides/getDoc.do?pubRef=-//EP//NONSGML+COMPARL+PE-593.974+01+DOC+PDF+V0//EN&language=EN> accessed 21 June 2018.

75 For instance, concerns regarding the independence of the judiciary in Poland; see Commission Recommendation regarding the rule of law in Poland (C(2016) 5703 final, 27 June 2016) <http://ec.europa.eu/justice/effective-justice/files/recommendation-rule-of-law-poland-20160727_en.pdf> accessed 21 June 2018.

76 See further, P8_TA-PROV(2017)0282, 'Common minimum standards of civil procedure, European Parliament resolution of 4 July 2017 with recommendations to the Commission on common minimum standards of civil procedure in the European Union' (2015/2084(INL) <http://www.europarl.europa.eu/sides/getDoc.do?pubRef=-//EP//NONSGML+TA+P8-TA-2017-0282+0+DOC+PDF+V0//EN> accessed 21 June 2018.

77 Dispute Act 2005 (Norway), sections 9.4–9.11 and 11.5.

78 The project's institutional observers are: American Law Institute; Asociación Americana de Derecho Internacional Privado; Association for International Arbitration; Council of Bars and Law Societies of Europe; Council of the Notariats of the European Union; Court

has already become an accepted minimum standard through incorporation into the European Parliament's proposed legislative instrument. This can be seen most clearly through its adoption of the approach to case management. The Obligations Working Group's final draft text provided as follows:

Rule 8. Means of Case Management

(1) In order to further its general case management duty, the court may take any necessary step:
 (i) schedule case management conferences;
 (ii) set a timetable or procedural calendar;
 (iii) set deadlines for the parties to take procedural steps;
 (iv) determine the type and form of procedure;
 (v) limit the number and length of submissions;
 (vi) encourage the parties to take active steps to settle all or parts of their dispute including encouraging, and where appropriate taking part in, the use of alternative dispute resolution (ADR) processes or practices (Rules 24 and 25);
 (vii) determine the order in which issues should be tried, whether certain procedural or substantive issues should be decided jointly or separately, and whether the proceedings should be consolidated or split;
 (viii) determine changes related to the parties to the proceedings and on participation of other interested persons in the proceedings;
 (ix) consider whether a party is properly represented;
 (x) require party's appearance in person or require a party's representative to be present at a court hearing or meeting;
 (xi) ensure appropriate use of modern technology; or
 (xii) take any other necessary step.
(2) While exercising its general management duty, the court shall manage the proceedings so that that all relevant issues in the case are identified and may be decided in a complete and appropriate manner. The court may encourage the parties to identify the real issues in dispute, and discuss with them appropriate methods and steps for dealing with these issues.
(3) The court may vary any case management order, including abridging or extending the time to comply with them. Such orders are ordinarily not subject to appeal.[79]

---

of Justice of the European Union; European Commission; European Network of Councils for the Judiciary; European Parliament; Hague Conference on Private International Law; IBA Arbitration Committee; IBA Litigation Committee; International Association of Lawyers; International Association of Procedural Law; International Association of Young Lawyers; International Bar Association; International Union of Judicial Officers; Max Planck Institute Luxembourg.

[79] Itself inspired by the English civil procedural code, i.e. CPR r. 3.1.

By way of comparison, the European Parliament text adopts the approach, in simplified terms, as follows:

> To the extent reasonably practicable, the court shall manage the case in consultation with the parties. Specifically, active case management may include:
>
> (a) encouraging the parties to co-operate with each other during the proceedings;
> (b) identifying the issues at an early stage;
> (c) deciding promptly which issues need full investigation and disposing summarily of other issues;
> (d) deciding the order in which issues are to be resolved;
> (e) helping the parties to settle the whole or part of the action;
> (f) fixing timetables to control the progress of the action;
> (g) dealing with as many aspects of the action as possible for the court on the same occasion;
> (h) dealing with the action without the parties needing to attend in person;
> (i) making use of available technical means.[80]

While the European Parliament's draft does not go into as much detail as that set out in the Obligations Working Group's draft –for instance, it does not provide the necessary general case management power contained in rule 8(1)(xii) of the latter's draft – it includes the most significant powers contained in that draft. Soft law influence can already reasonably be seen to be having an effect before the project has been finalised.

The project's soft law influence goes further than the European Parliament. Unlike the Storme Commission, whose report was noted to bring no comment from the European Commission when it was finalised, the project has seen concerted engagement by the Commission from its inception. Project meetings and workshops have, for instance, seen the constructive engagement of Norel Rosner, acting as an observer on behalf of the Commission. The Commission's engagement has gone further than this; project members took part in a number of information sessions with the Commission in 2015 and in 2017. In the latter session, the view was expressed that the project's work was already being viewed as the most significant development since the Storme Commission.[81]

Given both the European Parliament and the Commission's ongoing interest in the project, it appears reasonable to conclude that when its work is finalised, it will not simply sit on shelf gathering dust. It is already influencing the development of minimum common standards. It might properly be expected that when its model rules are finalised, they too will influence future European

---

80 Article 9(2) of the European Parliament's proposal at <http://www.europarl.europa.eu/sides/getDoc.do?pubRef=-//EP//NONSGML+TA+P8-TA-2017-0282+0+DOC+PDF+V0//EN> accessed 21 June 2018.

81 Personal communication from D. Wallis.

Union developments, potentially laying the foundations for a common European Civil Procedural Code akin to the Federal Rules of Civil Procedure in the United States. With this in mind, I turn to consider, briefly, a number of issues that will arguably have an impact on the project's future influence both at the European level and in respect of national procedural codes.

5. THE PROJECT'S POTENTIAL: PROCEDURAL CULTURE AND DIGITISATION

An acceptable, practical model European code of civil procedure is a starting point. However, the successful implementation of any project requires more than that. It requires those who are interested in securing its influence to consider what happens after the model code is completed. Influence needs to be active if it is to succeed. This raises two particular issues: first, procedural culture, and second, digitisation.

The development of model European rules as a soft law instrument and any procedural convergence that that might, and hopefully will, promote at the national and European level cannot on its own secure effective convergence. Soft law's influence has its limits. Even if it is assumed that the model rules, when finalised and published, influence procedural design at national and European levels, that influence will be examined through the prism of prevailing litigation cultures. Different legal cultures can and almost inevitably will interpret and apply common rules consistently with local practice, a point recently emphasised by Professor Caponi.[82] National litigation culture will shape common rules and produce differential application. A common rule, or converging rules, on paper may thus produce, in reality, as many rules as there are states in which it is implemented, a point underscored by the European Union's approach, which posits autonomous interpretations of its legislative instruments.[83] For there to be genuine convergence, more will thus be needed than common rules inspiring convergence on paper. The first key issue will therefore be how to imbue the common or converging rules with a common or converging procedural culture. Experience in England and Wales, where attempts have been made on more than one occasion over the last two hundred years of procedural reform, demonstrate that not only is this easier said than done, but that, if it is to be

---

82 R. Caponi, 'The Performance of the Italian Civil Justice System: An Empirical Assessment' (2016) 2 *The Italian Law Journal* 15, 30–31.

83 The approach is not, of course, unique to the European Union; see M. Heidemann, 'The autonomous interpretation method in international law with particular reference to the proposed European Sales Law I' [2013] *Amicus Curiae* 91. The risk always remains that an autonomous interpretation will itself stand in need of application through an autonomous, common practice.

achieved, it requires concerted and consistent effort by judges and practitioners over at least a generation.[84]

A number of steps will arguably need to be taken to help foster a common procedural culture. First, and most obviously, a common culture will need to develop. This will only develop properly if, as Professor Caponi rightly notes, users of the common or converging code share a set of shared values. That may develop if a core number of judges and practitioners operate the common or converging code, and do so on the basis of a shared understanding and interpretation of those values; again, shared values can manifest themselves in differential practice through differential interpretation. For that to happen, consideration may have to be given to creating a common procedural framework, which would necessarily have to include: a common judiciary; common court structure; common court administration; and a common legal profession, with a common legal and vocational education and training.

This might seem to suggest the creation of a common, federal, court structure akin to that of the United States. There appears to be no reason, in principle, why this outcome might not be possible for European countries that wish to create a common European civil court, either with a general or a subject-specific civil jurisdiction, i.e. a functional equivalent of the Unified Patents Court, albeit one going wider than it in terms of judiciary, administration and lawyers. A confederal approach here is equally, in principle, a possibility, with – again – willing countries creating such a system. Either approach would, however, have to grapple with serious questions concerning sovereignty, the status of such a new court and judicial structure within their legal architecture, as well as questions such as the role and operation of precedent derived from the new court, whether federal or confederal. Equally, and this is the case irrespective of which of the two models is ultimately chosen (if either), there is no reason in principle that common judicial training (building on what already exists within the European Union)[85] and common legal training for practitioners separate from their national jurisdictions could start to develop, and in turn start to develop a common legal culture around the common rules.

This, of course, suggests a limit to the possible influence of the project's model rules – a limit arising from culture. Such potential limits ought, however, to be recognised. Recognition ought to provide a spur to further work, in order to build upon the project's rules. Rather than taking such limitations as undermining the project's utility, a better and more realistic approach is one that understands them to mark the outer limit of one phase of convergence and the beginning of its next phase. Common rules, as a soft law instrument, are a

---

84 J. Sorabji, *English Civil Justice after Woolf and Jackson – A Critical Analysis* (CUP 2014) 207 ff.

85 S. Benevenuti, 'The European Judicial Training Network and its role in the strategy for the Europeanization of National Judges' (2015) 7 *Int'l J for Court Administration* 59.

pre-condition to harmonisation. They provide the basis from which a common procedural court, and common court structure could, in time, develop. They are a necessary, but not sufficient, condition for harmonisation. That this is the case emphasises their importance rather than any weakness that might be thought to be inherent in the project.

Secondly, lessons could be learnt from history. Here two lessons are important. There is an English proverb that 'nothing succeeds like success'. If model European rules and a common court structure are to develop as well as they might, they will need to demonstrate to litigants that they are better able to secure the vindication and enforcement of rights, economically and expeditiously and with the least vexation. In the Middle Ages, following the Norman Conquest of England, the king's courts, through their new forms of procedure and remedies, were able to create a new, country-wide civil justice system because they demonstrated that they were better equipped to secure justice than the extant local courts. They succeeded in establishing a common court structure with common procedures across England and then Wales.[86] They did so because they were seen to be better than the alternative. If the model rules, and perhaps any future common court structure, are to ensure that convergence and harmonisation are to be maximised, they too must do the same. The rules must not only be best practice in name, but equally must be capable of convincing practitioners and policy-makers across Europe that they are in fact best practice, and provide better alternative means to secure effective civil justice than extant national rules and approaches.

The second lesson from history stems from the European Union's recent attempt to develop a Common European Sales Law (CESL). It was to form a second national sales contract code within each of the European Union Member States. It would sit alongside their national law and apply to cross-border sales contracts. Member States were to be given the option, however, to incorporate the CESL as their national law, thus creating the potential for harmonisation via common incorporation of a common European code into national law.[87] In the United States, the Federal Rules of Civil Procedure sit alongside each of the states' procedural codes and operate solely at the federal level. There has thus

---

86 R. van Caenegem, *The Birth of the English Common Law* (CUP 1988) 33; S. Milsom, *A Natural History of the Common Law* (Columbia 2003).

87 European Parliament and Council, Proposal for a Regulation of the European Parliament and of the Council on a Common European Sales Law [2014] OJ C285/638, 6: 'The Common European Sales Law will be a second contract law regime within the national law of each Member State. Where [contract] parties have agreed to use the Common European Sales Law, its rules will be the only national rules applicable for matters falling within its scope. Where a matter falls within the scope of the Common European Sales Law, there is thus no scope for the application of any other national rules. This agreement to use the Common European Sales Law is a choice between two different sets of sales laws within the same national law and does therefore not amount to, and must not be confused with, the previous choice of the applicable law within the meaning of private international law rules.'

been little incentive for state-wide procedure to converge, and where historically there has been such convergence, there has equally been a move towards an increase in local variations at state level of the federal rules.[88]

If European countries were to adopt the CESL approach rather than the US Federal Rules approach, the likelihood of convergence might potentially be greater than it would otherwise be. Even if there were no common court, the incorporation of a common procedure operative for cross-border matters and capable of incorporation as a new national code of procedure could properly promote greater harmonisation, through enabling litigants to opt to use the model European procedural rules rather than their national one. Such an approach would provide the means to demonstrate at the national level any benefits the model European rules had over those in place at the national level. It could thus help the model rules succeed at the national level through being a success at the cross-border, European level. In doing so it might, as was the hope with the CESL, over time result in those states that provide the option to use the model European rules incorporating it in substitution for, rather than as a mere optional complement to, their national code.

The final issue to consider is the effect that digitisation of process may have upon the project's influence. In this respect, England and Wales has currently embarked upon a radical set of court reforms, which will see the general digitisation of a significant proportion, and in all likelihood majority, of its civil procedure and civil litigation.[89] Electronic issue, filing and case management will become commonplace, and in some instances the norm. Digital hearings will also become commonplace. Procedure is adapting to the new online environment. England and Wales is not the only European jurisdiction, or country, to be developing such approaches.[90] Equally, the European Union's e-justice programme is developing in a similar vein.[91]

Digitisation of process presents an historic opportunity to develop a common European redesign, or at the least compatible redesign, of our civil processes. It provides the opportunity to move beyond doing what we have always done because that is the way we have always done it. Such a design process could start from common principles – minimum common standards. It could then be supplemented by draft model rules and processes – the project's model rules. They could then be adapted to fit the technology. Common rules and common technical design could produce comparable procedural design across the European countries and for the European Union.

---

88 M. La Belle, 'The Local Rules of Patent Procedure' (2015) 47 *Arizona State Law Journal* 63.

89 J. Sorabji, 'The Online Solutions Court – A multi-door courthouse for the 21st Century' (2017) 36 *CJQ* 86.

90 See for instance developments in France.

91 See the development of e-codex: <https://www.e-codex.eu> accessed 21 June 2018.

There seems to be no reason in principle why co-design across the European Member States and other European countries could not produce common, albeit jurisdiction-specific, online courts (an English online court, a French online court, a Norwegian online court), a common EU and/or EFTA online court or a common European online civil court, as referred to earlier, akin to the Unified Patents Court. Such a court or courts could share and operate a common trans-substantive procedure, processes and practices. Digitisation provides the basis for procedural convergence, just as Amazon provided the basis for a common online shopping experience across multiple jurisdictions.[92] It is to be hoped that the project and its model rules will provide the basis for such common co-design. As such, they would provide a soft law instrument to form the basis of a common market for civil justice.

6. CONCLUSION

Eighty years ago, Professor Clark, one of the two main drafters of the US Federal Rules of Procedure told a story about the annual migration of birds across the Mediterranean Sea.[93] It is a story recently retold by Lord Thomas CJ in a lecture on procedural reform. Professor Clark noted how the bird took the longest route across the sea. He asked the question why they did that. Why not take a shorter route?

> The answer he gave was simple: because when birds originally started flying from North Africa to Europe the present route was the shortest route. Time and geological had changed that, but the birds carried on each year just as they always had. For migrating birds so for lawyers 'habit has a tendency to become our master'.[94]

The project has provided those scholars, practitioners and judges who are taking part in it to consider and reconsider their procedural habits. When concluded, its draft model European rules ought properly to make us all consider and reconsider our national and European procedural habits. Given the ever-increasing growth in European markets and particularly the digital marketplace, there is no better time to do so if we are to ensure that our systems are able to properly secure civil justice for the Europe of tomorrow. We do not want to go the way of the birds.

---

92 For a more detailed consideration of these points, see J. Sorabji, 'Taking Justice Online: Developments in England and Wales and Their Potential Influence on European Procedural Harmonisation' in B. Hess and X.E. Kramer (eds), *From common rules to best practices in European Civil Procedure* (Nomos/Hart Publishing 2017).

93 C. Clark, 'The Challenge of a New Federal Civil Procedure' (1935) 20 *Cornell L Rev* 443, 443–444.

94 See J. Thomas, '*Cutting the cloth to fit the dispute: steps towards better procedures across the jurisdictions*' (2017) 29 *Singapore Academy of Law Journal* 1, 2.

EUROPEANISATION OF CIVIL PROCEDURE

Overcoming Follow-Up Fragmentation through Bottom-Up Harmonisation?

Wolfgang Hau

Starting from the well-known fact that the European law of civil procedure is fragmentary by nature, this chapter points to the unwanted phenomenon of follow-up fragmentation on the Member State level and considers whether and to what extent this could be overcome through bottom-up harmonisation, i.e. autonomous reception of European solutions into national law.

1. STARTING POINT: LIMITED EUROPEAN COMPETENCE

1.1. CROSS-BORDER CASES

According to Article 81 of the Treaty on the Functioning of the European Union (TFEU),[1] the European Union is competent to harmonise procedural rules for judicial co-operation in civil matters with cross-border implications. This explicitly includes the elimination of obstacles to the proper functioning of civil proceedings, if necessary by promoting the compatibility of the rules on civil procedure applicable in the Member States (Article 81(2)(f) TFEU). Over the years, an impressive number of legal instruments (regulations and directives alike) have been based on Article 81 TFEU,[2] providing the area of freedom, security and justice with a finely-meshed and mainly well-functioning legal framework for international civil litigation.[3]

Meanwhile, however, it seems as if the European legislative process is slowing down considerably, and the potential of Article 81 as a source for harmonisation in the field of civil procedure is almost exhausted. This is partly due to its express limitation to cross-border cases and partly due to the absence of political intent. But this is not a matter of course, as can be seen in the recent European Parliament resolution on common minimum standards of civil procedure in the EU.[4] Seizing upon an opinion that has been expressed on many occasions in the past, most notably by the European Commission, the Parliament contended that the current interpretation of 'cross-border implications' is too narrow and should therefore be construed in a broader manner.[5] As a consequence, the Parliament has made recommendations for a directive on common minimum standards of civil procedure that should be applicable even in cases in which both parties are domiciled in the same Member State as that of the court seized, provided either

1 Consolidated Version of the Treaty on the Functioning of the European Union [2012] OJ C 326/47.

2 And on its predecessor, Article 65 EC Treaty (Consolidated Version of the Treaty Establishing the European Community [2002] OJ C 325/33).

3 For a detailed account see the contributions in Paul Beaumont, Mihail Danov, Katarina Trimmings and Burcu Yüksel (eds.), *Cross-Border Litigation in Europe* (Hart 2017); for a brief overview see, for example, Wolfgang Hau, 'The European Union and Civil Procedure From a German Perspective' in Anna Nylund and Bart Krans (eds.), *The European Union and National Civil Procedure* (Intersentia 2016) 59, 62-64.

4 European Parliament Resolution of 4 July 2017 with recommendations to the Commission on common minimum standards of civil procedure in the European Union, 2015/2084 (INL), [2018] OJ C 334/39.

5 European Parliament (n 4) paras. 11-12.

that enforcement of the judgment takes place in another Member State or that the matter in dispute falls within the scope of EU law.[6]

Cross-border implications, like elephants, are easy to recognise but hard to describe.[7] It is, however, highly doubtful whether the very broad interpretation put forward by the Parliament stays in line with the intention of the TFEU and is likely to convince the Member States or eventually the European Court of Justice (ECJ).[8] As a consequence, the restrictive requirement of a cross-border implication would become close to meaningless, because today rights and freedoms guaranteed by the EU could be involved in some way in almost every civil dispute. By the same token, since each and every national court decision can at least potentially be recognised and enforced in another Member State (for example, in accordance with the provisions of the Brussels I *bis* Regulation),[9] this seems to be insufficient to constitute a significant international element of the proceedings leading to the decision when in every other respect the facts of the case are exclusively linked to the forum state. From this perspective, there

---

6 Article 3(1) of the proposed directive reads: 'For the purposes of this Directive, a dispute having cross-border implications is one in which: (a) at least one of the parties is domiciled or habitually resident in a Member State other than the Member State of the court or tribunal seized; or (b) both parties are domiciled in the same Member State as that of the court or tribunal seized, provided that the place of performance of the contract, the place where the harmful event takes place or the place of enforcement of the judgment is situated in another Member State; or (c) both parties are domiciled in the same Member State as that of the court or tribunal seized, provided that the disputed matter falls within the scope of Union law.' For what is meant by (c), see the proposed recital 6: 'The provisions of this Directive should apply to civil disputes having cross-border implications, including those arising from the violation of the rights and freedoms guaranteed by Union law.'

7 This requirement has been aptly labelled as 'the yeti of European law': André Lippert, 'Der grenzüberschreitende Sachverhalt – Der Yeti des Europarechts' [2014] *ZEuS* 273. For discussions of various approaches to construct the term 'cross-border implications' see Wolfgang Hau, 'Zivilsachen mit grenzüberschreitendem Bezug' in Stefan Arnold and Stephan Lorenz (eds.), *Gedächtnisschrift für Hannes Unberath* (C.H. Beck 2015) 139; Burkhard Hess, 'Binnenverhältnisse im Europäischen Zivilprozessrecht: Grenzüberschreitende v. nationale Sachverhalte' in Jan von Hein and Giesela Rühl (eds.), *Kohärenz im Internationalen Privat- und Verfahrensrecht der Europäischen Union* (Mohr Siebeck 2016) 67; Robert Magnus, 'Der grenzüberschreitende Bezug als Anwendungsvoraussetzung im europäischen Zuständigkeits- und Kollisionsrecht' [2018] *ZEuP* 507; Rolf Wagner, 'Grenzüberschreitender Bezug in der justiziellen Zusammenarbeit in Zivilsachen' 131 [2018] *ZZP* 183.

8 For a detailed and critical assessment of the preceding Report of the European Parliament's Committee on Legal Affairs see Astrid Stadler, 'Harmonisierung des Europäischen Zivilprozessrechts - Mindeststandards oder Modellregeln?' [2017] *JZ* 693 (on the lack of a legal basis, see 697).

9 Regulation 1215/2012 on jurisdiction and the recognition and enforcement of judgments in civil and commercial matters (recast) [2012] OJ L 351/1. This so-called Brussels I *bis* Regulation (or Brussels I Recast) succeeded the Brussels I Regulation 44/2001 ([2001] OJ L 12/1) that had already succeeded the Brussels Convention of 27 September 1968 ([1972] OJ L 299/32).

is no legislative competence for a directive (let alone a regulation) on common minimum standards of civil procedure in the EU reaching beyond international disputes. Therefore, the Commission would be well advised to settle for a mere recommendation (Article 292 TFEU).

1.2. DOMESTIC CASES

The legislative competence of the EU to harmonise or at least approximate civil procedure is even more limited as regards mere domestic disputes, because, in this respect, there is no general legal base equivalent to Article 81 TFEU. On the other side of that coin is what is often referred to as the 'procedural autonomy of the Member States': at least in principle, it is for each national legal system to designate which court has jurisdiction and to determine the procedural conditions governing actions at law to ensure the protection of rights of individuals.[10] Below the line, however, procedural autonomy is increasingly limited, if not eroding.[11] In addition to the self-evident relevance of European fundamental rights,[12] two important points must be kept in mind.

Firstly, several provisions of the TFEU (such as Articles 114, 115 and 169) allow for the adoption of measures for the approximation of the laws of the Member States. While such legal bases primarily aim at the harmonisation of substantive law in a number of areas of private law (for example, consumer protection, anti-discrimination, insurance law, labour law, company law and competition law), it is generally recognised that they may also cover the enactment of uniform procedural rules or standards even for purely domestic civil cases. Such procedural provisions can be included in instruments that otherwise only address issues of substantive law. Typical examples are Article 6 of the 2004 Directive on the enforcement of intellectual property rights[13] and, more recently, some provisions in the 2016 Directive on the protection of undisclosed know-how and business information (trade secrets) against their unlawful acquisition, use and disclosure.[14] In other contexts, the EU legislator chose to enact special instruments that predominantly deal with procedural questions. Examples of this are the 2014 Directive on certain rules

---

10 For recent accounts of this principle in the context of civil procedure, see Malte KRAMME, 'Verfahrensautonomie der Mitgliedstaaten im Zivilverfahrensrecht - Grundsatz des Unionsrechts oder Phantom?' in Caspar BEHME and Matthias FERVERS (eds.), *Perspektiven einer europäischen Privatrechtswissenschaft* (Nomos 2016) 407; Maciej SZPUNAR, 'Procedural Autonomy and Private Law' [2018] *ZEuP* 1.

11 This is criticised, for example, by STADLER (n 8) 693.

12 On this so-called 'first pillar' of European civil procedure see, for example, Bart KRANS, 'EU Law and National Civil Procedure Law: An Invisible Pillar' [2015] *ERevPrivL* 567, 568-569; Burkhard HESS, *Europäisches Zivilprozessrecht* (C.F. Müller 2009) 128-140.

13 Directive 2004/48/EC [2004] OJ L 195/16.

14 Directive 2016/943/EU [2016] OJ L 157/1.

governing actions for damages under national law for infringements of the competition law provisions of the Member States and EU[15] (which is mainly a procedural complement to and safeguard for the substantive rules provided for in Articles 101 and 102 TFEU) and, most recently, the 2018 Proposal for a Directive on representative actions for the protection of the collective interests of consumers.[16] Where applicable, the Member States' rules that are enacted to implement such European provisions override the ordinary rules of the national *lex fori processualis*.

Secondly, the increase in binding EU procedural law is flanked by the principles of effectiveness and equivalence. These principles were originally developed by the ECJ[17] but, meanwhile, have been taken up by the European legislator. This is again illustrated by the above-mentioned 2014 Directive, Article 4 of which reads:

> In accordance with the principle of effectiveness, Member States shall ensure that all national rules and procedures relating to the exercise of claims for damages are designed and applied in such a way that they do not render practically impossible or excessively difficult the exercise of the Union right to full compensation for harm caused by an infringement of competition law. In accordance with the principle of equivalence, national rules and procedures relating to actions for damages resulting from infringements of Article 101 or 102 TFEU shall not be less favourable to the alleged injured parties than those governing similar actions for damages resulting from infringements of national law.

As a consequence, these principles can give cause for sectorial modifications of the general rules of the national *lex fori processualis*.[18]

---

15 Directive 2014/104/EU [2014] OJ L 349/1.

16 COM (2018) 184 final.

17 See Case C-78/98 *Shirley Preston and others v Wolverhampton Healthcare NHS Trust and others and Dorothy Fletcher and Others v Midland Bank plc* ECLI:EU:C:2000:247, para. 31: 'First, it should be borne in mind that, according to settled case-law, in the absence of relevant Community rules, it is for the national legal order of each Member State to designate the competent courts and to lay down the procedural rules for proceedings designed to ensure the protection of the rights which individuals acquire through the direct effect of Community law, provided that such rules are not less favourable than those governing similar domestic actions (principle of equivalence) and are not framed in such a way as to render impossible in practice the exercise of rights conferred by Community law (principle of effectiveness)'.

18 As Szpunar (n 10) points out, even in some private law contexts the Member States are free to opt for a public law mechanism in order to comply with the principle of effectiveness, which makes modifications of the domestic rules of civil procedure unnecessary. This holds true, for example, for compensation under the Denied Boarding Regulation (Regulation 261/2004 of 11 February 2004 establishing common rules on compensation and assistance to passengers in the event of denied boarding and of cancellation or long delay of flights [2004] OJ L46/1), which in some Member States is safeguarded through private and, in others, through administrative law mechanisms. This dichotomy, however, goes beyond the scope of this chapter.

2. FOLLOW-UP FRAGMENTATION: TRANSFERRING FRAGMENTATION FROM THE EUROPEAN TO THE NATIONAL LEVEL

Notwithstanding the existence of such miscellaneous rudiments of harmonisation or at least approximation, the European law of civil procedure is fragmentary by nature, and this will continue to be the case for the foreseeable future. In particular, there is neither a legal basis nor a political majority for a comprehensive harmonisation of civil procedure within the EU, let alone for a general European Code of Civil Procedure.[19] Fragmentation as such should not be condemned wholesale; it is simply the flip side of the principle of conferral (Article 5(2) TEU)[20] and procedural autonomy of the Member States. Furthermore, while harmonisation of civil procedure within the EU is, for many reasons, an aim worth striving for,[21] fragmentation does not necessarily give rise to insuperable practical difficulties as long as the coexistence of European and national procedural rules is evident and their respective scopes of application are sufficiently co-ordinated. This holds true, at least for the most part, for the interaction between EU regulations and residual domestic rules in the context of international disputes.[22]

Much more scepticism, however, is warranted for procedural provisions (rules and standards) following from European directives or even unwritten from the principle of effectiveness. This phenomenon proves problematic especially because, in practical terms, it is sometimes rather difficult to identify such European provisions and draw a line between aspects that fall under EU law and those that are exclusively subject to domestic law. But even apart from such practical problems, European piecemeal harmonisation comes at a price: sectorial European procedural provisions are only meant to enhance the practical application of substantive rights as guaranteed by particular European

---

19 Cf. Burkhard Hess, 'Ein einheitliches Prozessrecht?' [2016] *IntJProcL* 55, 74.

20 Consolidated version of the Treaty on European Union [2012] OJ C 326/13.

21 For a recent discussion see, for example, C.H. van Rhee, 'Approximation of Civil Procedural Law in the European Union' in Burkhard Hess and Xandra E. Kramer, *From common rules to best practices in European Civil Procedure* (Nomos 2017) 63. For a global evaluation of cross-border convergence of procedure, see Oscar Chase and Helen Hershkoff, *Civil Litigation in Comparative Context* (2nd ed. West Academic 2017) ch. 12.

22 This assessment finds support in a report released in June 2017: MPI Luxembourg for Procedural Law, *An evaluation study of national procedural laws and practices in terms of their impact on the free circulation of judgments and on the equivalence and effectiveness of the procedural protection of consumers under EU consumer law* (JUST/2014/RCON/PR/CIVI/0082) - Strand 1: Mutual Trust and Free Circulation of Judgments. For a much more sceptical analysis, emphasising the in some respects still doubtful demarcation line between European and national rules, see Thalia Kruger, 'The Disorderly Infiltration of EU Law in Civil Procedure' 63 [2016] *Netherl. IntLR* 1.

instruments, but do not require the Member States to modify their national procedural regimes in general. As a result, fragmentary European law fragments national law, an effect that might be described as 'hook-up fragmentation' or 'follow-up fragmentation' on the Member States' level: due to the mere sectorial infiltration of EU law, every national procedural system becomes fragmented, with a (in many respects obscure) dividing line running between ordinary disputes on the one hand, and disputes with a relevant EU legal impact on the other hand.[23] It should be obvious, for various reasons, that an incoherent doctrinal system is not desirable, as over-complexity leads to uncertainty and thus makes the system more prone to errors. Even worse, a system with double procedural standards tends to yield unjust results; this is undesirable in and of itself, but may also raise concerns from a constitutional law perspective.[24]

3. BOTTOM-UP HARMONISATION: MODELLING NATIONAL PROCEDURAL LAW ON EUROPEAN SOLUTIONS

Since Member States cannot simply prefer doctrinal coherence to procedural rules and standards set by EU law, it makes sense to look for ways to overcome, or at least curb, the unwanted effects of follow-up fragmentation. This chapter discusses in particular one possible remedy, namely voluntary 'over-implementation' or 'bottom-up harmonisation'.[25] The idea behind this is rather simple: why not model national procedural rules on EU regulations or on the national rules that were made to implement directives or comply with the principle of effectiveness? Depending on the Member State's legal culture and the particular context, such autonomous reception and alignment could be effected through domestic legislation and/or case law, and it could happen either driven by European nudging or entirely spontaneously on the national level.

It goes without saying that this approach of taking European solutions as source of inspiration for national rule-making may not work in each and every

23 This is what KRANS (n 12) 582-585 labels as 'internal fragmentation' (as opposed to 'external fragmentation', which refers to differences between national procedural regimes notwithstanding the fact that all of them try to comply with the same European provisions).

24 KRANS (n 12) 586 illustrates this by referring to the Belgian discussion on the constitutionality of the national act to implement the (Recast) Directive 2011/7/EU of 16 February 2011 on combating late payment in commercial transactions [2011] OJ L 48/1.

25 Not surprisingly, there is no uniform nomenclature yet. Other authors propose terms such as 'legislative spill-over effect' (cf. Clement SALUNG PETERSEN, 'Danish Civil Procedure and the Internal Market' in Anna NYLUND and Bart KRANS (eds.), *The European Union and National Civil Procedure* (Intersentia 2016) 17, 26) or 'spontaneous harmonisation' (cf. Anna NYLUND and Bart KRANS (eds.), *The European Union and National Civil Procedure* (Intersentia 2016) 161, 163).

context. Moreover, it would be neither practical nor reasonable to model a national procedural system from scratch, only oriented towards the fragmentary European procedural law. But, as will be seen, there are at least some encouraging examples where fragmentation within national procedural systems was avoided by voluntarily extending the scope of application of suitable European solutions. And it seems that it is worth pointing out in passing that a similar manifestation of bottom-up harmonisation of civil procedure can also be found outside the EU. In the United States, the Federal Rules of Civil Procedure are only applied by the federal courts, and every state has to define rules for proceedings brought before their own courts. While some states (notably the most populous ones: California, Texas, Florida, New York and Illinois) take quite distinctive approaches, most states either have replicated the Federal Rules or vary the rules only slightly. Therefore, irrespective of some dissimilarities in detail, due to the role model function of the Federal Rules it is considered appropriate to speak of a general procedural system in the United States.[26]

4. LESSONS TO BE LEARNED FROM INTERNATIONAL CIVIL PROCEDURE

As already mentioned, the highest concentration of European procedural regulation today exists in the area of international civil litigation. It thus seems reasonable to expect that examples of bottom-up harmonisation will most easily be found exactly in this context. And indeed, as early as in 1986, the German legislator modified some of the rules on the recognition of third-country judgments (section 328 German Code of Civil Procedure) explicitly in accordance with rules that the then 1968 Brussels Convention provided for recognition within Europe.[27] Even more interesting, however, are instances in which national law-makers decide to adopt European solutions originally designed for international disputes to mere domestic cases. In the following, this will be illustrated mainly by taking examples from German law where such 'legislative copy and paste' has happened (or was at least discussed) on different levels and to various degrees.

---

26 Cf. Chase and Hershkoff (n 21) 33. For a more detailed (but rather sceptical) analysis, see Christopher A. Whytock, 'Harmonization of Civil Procedure: Is the United States a Model for the European Union?' in Burkhard Hess and Xandra E. Kramer, *From common rules to best practices in European Civil Procedure* (Nomos 2017) 133.

27 For details of this reform of 1986 cf. Jan von Hein, 'Comments on Christopher A. Whytock, Harmonization of Civil Procedure: Is the US a Positive or Negative Model?' in Burkhard Hess and Xandra E. Kramer, *From common rules to best practices in European Civil Procedure* (Nomos 2017) 159, 165-168.

4.1. ADOPTING ENTIRE LEGAL INSTRUMENTS

In Germany, as in other Member States, since the 1990s, there have been endless debates about whether and to what extent legislation should regulate alternative dispute resolution, but for many years this led to no result. Eventually, when the EU took the initiative, the scope of the Mediation Directive[28] was limited to cross-border disputes as defined in its Article 2. Recital 8, however, made it clear that 'nothing should prevent Member States from applying such provisions also to internal mediation processes'. Taking up this gentle hint, the German legislator opted for a voluntary over-implementation and enacted the Directive's provisions for international and purely national cases alike.[29] This was, however, not the route taken by all Member States. Austria, for example, already had a national law dealing with mediation and therefore implemented the Directive only in so far as was mandatory. Consequently, Austria now has two statutes on mediation (one with a European background, the other with a merely domestic one), and this reportedly tends to cause problems in practice.[30]

Another illustration of the adoption of entire European instruments is the Romanian approach to small claims. Romania has apparently replicated for domestic cases the Regulation establishing a European Small Claims Procedure,[31] which in itself only applies in cross-border cases, in Articles 1025–1032 of its new Code of Civil Procedure, which entered into force on 15 February 2013.

4.2. ADOPTING SPECIFIC PROCEDURAL PROVISIONS

The German Code of Civil Procedure dates back to 1877 and was originally characterised by nineteenth-century liberalism: while the judge is responsible for conducting proceedings in a manner that allows for a prompt, economic and just resolution of the case, his role is not understood as being paternalistic.[32] In particular, since legal representation is mandatory before the district courts and the higher courts, under the original German rules the court was in principle not required to warn the defendant of the legal consequences of

---

[28] Directive 2008/52/EC on certain aspects of mediation in civil and commercial matters [2008] OJ L 136/3.

[29] Mediationsgesetz (Mediation Act) [2012] BGBl. (Federal Law Gazette) I 1577. See Stefan Rützel, Gerhard Wegen and Stephan Wilkse, *Commercial Dispute Resolution in Germany* (2nd ed. C.H. Beck 2016) ch. 3.

[30] Cf. Peter G. Mayr, *Handbuch des europäischen Zivilverfahrensrechts* (Manz 2017) paras. 13.23–13.26.

[31] Regulation 861/2007 establishing a European Small Claims Procedure [2007] OJ L 199/1; meanwhile amended by Regulation 2015/2421 [2015] OJ L 341/1.

[32] See Peter L. Murray and Rolf Stürner, *German Civil Justice* (Carolina Academic Press 2004) 164 et seq.; Rützel et al. (n 29) 54.

his/her failure to notify the court of his/her intention to defend him/herself against the action.[33] Quite obviously, the European legislator does not subscribe to that point of view, which became apparent when the 2004 Regulation creating a European Enforcement Order[34] was enacted: according to its Article 6(1)(c), a judgment delivered in a Member State can only be certified as a European Enforcement Order if service of process and the summons met the minimum requirements set out in Chapter III. These requirements include, *inter alia*, that certain information was already clearly stated in the document instituting the proceedings. However, as recital 19 underlines, this does not mean that there is an obligation for the Member States to adapt their domestic laws of civil procedure to such European minimum standards. Rather, it 'provides an incentive to that end by making available a more efficient and rapid enforceability of judgments in other Member States only if those minimum standards are met'.[35] Interestingly enough, such nudging stimulates national legislation even for cases without any cross-border element. When one considers that in many cases enforcement in another Member State might be unlikely at the outset, but later on can turn out to be necessary, it makes sense for the Member States to modify their procedural regime accordingly even for merely domestic cases. And indeed, the German legislator reacted promptly by including new provisions into the Code of Civil Procedure, complying with the Regulation's requirements for cross-border and domestic proceedings alike.

A voluntary alignment between national and EU law can also take place for rather technical provisions. To give just one example, until recently, the German Code of Civil Procedure stipulated that a claimant's right to obtain or request certain information and data on the debtor's assets was subject to the condition that the value of the claim to be enforced amounts to at least €500. This minimum sum was abolished in 2017 on the occasion of the German implementation of the European Account Preservation Order Procedure,[36] which protects the claimant irrespective of the value of his/her claim. By doing so, the German legislator explicitly aimed at synchronising the rules on debt recovery, again regardless of whether the question arises in a cross-border or in a purely domestic setting.[37]

4.3. ADOPTING LEGAL CONCEPTS

Bottom-up harmonisation can concern not only legal instruments and rules, but also legal concepts and doctrine. In particular, a rich stock of concepts worth

33 Special rules apply in proceedings before the local courts.

34 Regulation 805/2004 creating a European Enforcement Order for uncontested claims [2004] OJ L 143/15.

35 Cf. Case C-300/14 *Imtech Marine Belgium v Radio Hellenic* ECLI:EU:C:2015:825.

36 Regulation 655/2014 establishing a European Account Preservation Order procedure to facilitate cross-border debt recovery in civil and commercial matters [2014] OJ L 189/59.

37 Cf. Bundestags-Drucksache (parliamentary documents) 18/9698, 23–24.

being considered for reception into national procedural law can be found in the Brussels I *bis* Regulation and its predecessors. For example, in Germany, there is much discussion about whether or not the very broad concept of congruence, as laid down for international *lis pendens* in Article 29 Brussels I *bis* Regulation, and in particular the equal treatment of actions for affirmative relief and actions for negative declarations, seems to be better suited to address the problem of parallel proceedings even in a merely domestic setting than the rather inefficient German approach. Furthermore, just to mention two more examples, it is debated whether the European *forum contractus* (Article 7(1) Brussels I *bis* Regulation) is to be preferred to the traditional understanding of the corresponding provision in section 29 Code of Civil Procedure and whether some narrowly defined provisions of the Code on jurisdiction and venue can be interpreted as coming close to a special forum for multiple defendants (which is provided for in Article 8(1) Brussels I *bis* Regulation but, as such, is unknown in German law). Without going into detail, it seems remarkable that such questions are not only academic topics but have been discussed by German courts when considering the interpretation of the corresponding German provisions.

It is noteworthy that European procedural law acts as a role model not only for Member States but sometimes even for third states. An example is Switzerland, which historically had no concept of an enforceable authentic instrument.[38] However, under the Lugano Conventions 1988/2007 (which essentially are replications of the Brussels Convention of 1968 and the Brussels I Regulation of 2000, respectively), Swiss courts are obliged to enforce authentic instruments formally drawn up in other Contracting States. Since it was felt inappropriate to deprive domestic creditors of an instrument that foreign creditors are allowed to make use of not only at home but also in Switzerland, the new Swiss Code of Civil Procedure of 2008 introduced this concept (*vollstreckbare öffentliche Urkunde*, as set out in Articles 347–352).

4.4. CONCLUSION

Against the backdrop of these examples, it stands to reason that Member States tend to prove rather open-minded when it comes to bottom-up harmonisation in the area of international civil procedure. This might be simply because some of them have rather limited legislative experience in this particular respect

[38] For a Norwegian perspective see Anna NYLUND, 'Norway: An insider outside – or an outsider inside – European Civil Justice' in Anna NYLUND and Bart KRANS (eds.), *The European Union and National Civil Procedure* (Intersentia 2016) 101. For further examples, see some of the contributions in Miklós KENGYEL and Viktória HARSÁGI, *Der Einfluss des Europäischen Zivilverfahrensrechts auf die nationalen Rechtsordnungen* (Nomos 2009).

and, therefore, are willing to fill the gaps that became manifest in the course of globalisation by adopting European rules. By the same token, it could be argued that the German legislator probably ordered the applicability of the provisions of the Mediation Directive in mere domestic cases not least to save the pain of negotiating a genuine German set of rules in the field of alternative dispute resolution. Such hypotheses, however, cannot explain all the examples presented above, which also illustrate a considerable degree of readiness to over-implement European procedural law, even in settings for which national rules already existed but were abolished in favour of supposedly more appropriate European solutions. Here, too, better is the enemy of good.

It seems remarkable that in some cases voluntary over-implementation is effected top-down by the national legislator, while, in other cases, the judiciary or legal doctrine takes the lead when the national codification allows room for a reorientation that is considered reasonable.[39] The impetus for such autonomous alignment between domestic and European law may come from the EU, in particular when a Member State is making arrangements to ensure compliance with a new directive or a ruling by the ECJ. In other contexts, it is instead the reaction to some sort of 'European nudging',[40] either through mere encouragement by the European legislator (as in recital 8 of the Mediation Directive) or through substantial incentives (as in the case of the Regulation creating a European Enforcement Order). This suggests that increased use of formal EU recommendations[41] as a means of voluntary approximation of procedural law is worth considering.[42]

But an external push is not always required. Reform of national justice systems is currently on the agenda of several Member States,[43] and in this context bottom-up harmonisation can happen entirely spontaneously, especially when litigation has revealed shortcomings of the domestic procedural regime and the legislator, courts or academics discuss alternative solutions.[44]

---

39 Cf. Krans (n 12) 585. For German examples in the context of international litigation, see von Hein (n 27) 169-176.

40 For a general introduction to this concept, see Cass R. Sunstein, *Why Nudge? The Politics of Libertarian Paternalism* (Yale UP 2014).

41 See Commission Recommendation of 11 June 2013 on common principles for injunctive and compensatory collective redress mechanisms in the Member States concerning violations of rights granted under Union Law [2013] OJ L 201/60; Council Recommendations 'Promoting the use of and sharing of best practices on cross-border videoconferencing in the area of justice in the Member States and at EU level' [2015] OJ C 250/1.

42 Rather sceptical in this respect: Stadler (n 8) 695.

43 This is one of the main findings of the 2017 EU Justice Scoreboard (COM (2017) 167 final) 4-6.

44 One could think that today such spontaneous law-making in the area of procedural law happens more often than it used to happen in the past (see Pamela K. Bookman and David L. Noll, 'Ad hoc procedure' 92 [2017] *NYULR* 767), but taking a closer look at the history of civil procedure reveals that it has always been a very busy legislative testing ground.

Apart from that, the autonomous enactment of national 'mirror proceedings' can be driven by concerns that unequal treatment of foreign and national creditors, or of cross-border and domestic cases, would be unconstitutional.[45]

5. BOTTOM-UP HARMONISATION BEYOND INTERNATIONAL CIVIL PROCEDURE

Assuming that in principle the voluntary transplant of European rules for international cases to merely domestic disputes seems feasible in many respects, it remains to be seen whether the concept of avoiding follow-up fragmentation by broadening the scope of European procedural solutions can gain momentum in other contexts too. Therefore, it may be advisable to take a closer look at European procedural rules that were designed for particular disputes (for example, over intellectual property rights, anti-trust or unlawful discrimination) and consider their transferability into the Member State's general law of civil procedure.[46] Other European rules worth scrutinising are those on the protection of particular groups of litigants (e.g. consumers or small and medium-sized enterprises). At this point, instead of going into detail, three reservations should be discussed.

Firstly, what has been set out here might fairly be derided as a 'trickle-down effect' from the European to the Member States' level and is obviously far less effective than a robust top-down harmonisation of procedural law.[47] Indeed, it is clear that this approach does not lead to Europe-wide harmonisation, if only because its application depends on every single Member State acting. They decide autonomously when and to what extent a European solution (instrument, provision or concept) is transplanted or, to continue the metaphor, allowed to trickle down into the national sphere. As a consequence, the harmonising and anti-fragmentary effect of voluntary over-implementation works directly only within a Member State, not horizontally between Member States. However, given the limited legislative EU competence in the field of civil procedure, trickle-down harmonisation accomplished in any event seems to be better than top-down harmonisation awaited: a bird in the hand is worth two in the bush. For another thing, there is also at least an indirect horizontal effect, in that the

---

45 Cf. Piet Taelman, 'Some European Challenges for Belgian Civil Procedure' in Anna Nylund and Bart Krans (eds.), *The European Union and National Civil Procedure* (Intersentia 2016) 5, 12.

46 Krans (n 12) 586 gets to the heart of the problem by asking why victims of a car accident or an environmental crime should have less procedural rights than holders of IP rights.

47 Cf. von Hein (n 27) 160 (see also 176: 'remains limited and insecure').

alignment with European solutions on the national level potentially strengthens mutual trust.[48]

Secondly, since the ECJ's role must be respected, over-implementation in practice does not completely eliminate the need to take into account whether or not a provision has a European law background. Therefore, for a court of last instance considering its obligation to bring a matter before the Court (Article 267(3) TFEU), it remains relevant whether the national rule in question was enacted in accordance with a European provision or rather in the spirit of voluntary bottom-up harmonisation. However, with regard to the right of a national court to require a preliminary ruling (Article 267(2) TFEU), it has to be kept in mind that the ECJ considers references to be admissible even when the situation in question is not directly governed by EU law, but where the national legislature, in transposing the provisions of a directive into domestic law, has chosen to apply the same treatment to purely internal situations, such that it has aligned its domestic legislation to EU law.[49] In doing so, the ECJ obviously honours and enhances the harmonising effect of voluntary over-implementation.

Last but not least, we should always bear in mind that bottom-up harmonisation is not about safeguarding minimum standards but about promoting best practice.[50] To give just one example, it has been said that the European Small Claims Procedure resembles a European code of civil procedure in a nutshell, and this might indeed have been at the back of the Commission's mind. Nevertheless, the Small Claims Regulation can hardly be recommended as a role model to national law-makers, given all its more or less obvious shortcomings and serious doubts whether some of its provisions are in line with Article 6 of the European Convention on Human Rights and Article 47 of the Charter of Fundamental Rights.[51] In other words, in so far as the EU lacks the authority to order reception, quality becomes crucial.[52] Although it seems reasonable to expect that the ongoing competition between civil justice systems (in particular in the wake of the British exit from the EU – Brexit)

---

48 By the same token, the aim of boosting mutual trust is at the heart of the Parliament's proposal for an instrument on common minimum standards of civil procedure (n 4).

49 Cf. Case C-28/95 *Leur-Bloem v Inspecteur der Belastingsdienst/Ondernemingen Amsterdam* ECLI:EU:C:1997:369; Case C-306/99 *Banque internationale pour l'Afrique occidentale SA v Finanzamt für Großunternehmen in Hamburg* ECLI:EU:C:2003:3.

50 With regard to the paradigm shift from approximation in itself (or minimum standards) to the promotion of best practice in European law of civil procedure see, for example, van Rhee (n 21) 67 et seq.

51 For a critical analysis see, for example, Hartmut Linke and Wolfgang Hau, *Internationales Zivilverfahrensrecht* (7th ed. Otto Schmidt 2018) para. 11.15 et seq; Johannes Wolber, 'Der Beitritt der Europäischen Union zur EMRK im Lichte des Europäischen Zivilprozessrechts' [2017] *ZEuP* 936, 939 et seq.

52 In this context, von Hein (n 27) 160 calls to mind that legal reception in general works through either power or prestige.

will in fact increase Member States' readiness for reception,[53] the concept of over-implementation stands or falls by the quality of each and every European procedural solution in question: Member States – legislators, courts and academics alike – will certainly not be prepared to cure one evil (i.e. follow-up fragmentation of their national procedural regimes) with an even worse one (i.e. voluntary alignment with suboptimal European rules).

---

53 Cf. Stadler (n 8) 695.

HARMONISATION OR FRAGMENTATION OF NATIONAL LAW?

An East Nordic Perspective

Laura Ervo

1. TREATY-BASED STARTING POINT

Judicial co-operation in civil matters simply means closer co-operation between Member States in order to minimise obstacles arising from the existence of varying legal systems.[1] The current definition and objectives of judicial co-operation in civil matters are, however, a result of historical development. Judicial co-operation was not one of the objectives of the European Community when the founding treaty was adopted. It was first officially included within the EU's sphere of activity by the Treaty of Maastricht.[2] Then, the Treaty of Amsterdam brought judicial co-operation in civil matters within the Community sphere, transferring it from the Treaty on European Union to the Treaty establishing the European Community.[3]

---

1 Judicial Cooperation in Civil Matters, Fact Sheets on the European Union <http://www.europarl.europa.eu/atyourservice/en/displayFtu.html?ftuId=FTU_4.2.5.html> accessed 29 January 2018.

2 Treaty on European Union [1992] OJ C191/1.

3 Treaty of Amsterdam amending the Treaty on European Union, the Treaties Establishing the European Communities and certain related acts [1997] OJ C340/1, and Judicial Cooperation in Civil Matters (n 1).

Initially, governed by international conventions, judicial co-operation in civil matters was included in the Maastricht Treaty as a *'matter of common interest'*, and subsequently in the Treaty of Amsterdam, which places judicial co-operation in civil matters on the Community level by associating it with the *free movement* of persons, which is a milestone in this development. In theory and in practice, this constitutes a great leap from the common interest to free movement. As a matter of fact, free movement requires far greater harmonisation and co-ordination than that dictated by a common interest. Therefore, the change between the Maastricht Treaty and the Treaty of Amsterdam was a very significant one in terms of harmonisation, and meant that even procedural law has come to be covered by common EU law. The free movement of persons is a core principle of EU law, and is also the one with which the general public is most familiar. To introduce co-operation in civil matters into the principle of free movement is not only radical, but revolutionary. Let's see how successful this introduction has been, especially in the East Nordic countries, namely Finland and Sweden.

East Nordic countries are comparable because of their common history and similar codes for judicial procedure. Finland was a part of the Kingdom of Sweden from the thirteenth century until 1809, when the vast majority of the Finnish-speaking areas of Sweden were ceded to the Russian Empire (excluding the areas of modern-day northern Sweden), making this area autonomous. Despite the fact that Finland was from 1809 onwards an autonomous part of Russia, Swedish laws were still valid in Finland – and remained valid through the entire Russian period. In 1917, Finland became an independent country, but the originally Swedish laws remained in force. Today, for instance, the Finnish Code for Judicial Procedure dates from 1734, when the Swedish Empire enacted its important new – and still well-known – Civil Code. Finnish legislation continues to be similar in many ways to modern Swedish laws because of the active legislative co-operation between the Nordic countries, which was particularly marked before the EU era. Moreover, Finland has adopted many reforms that were first carried out in Sweden, especially if the Swedish experience was positive. A particularly notable example would be the comprehensive reform of Finnish district court proceedings at the beginning of the 1990s, which followed the Swedish example in many respects.[4]

Swedish and Finnish courts are broadly divided into administrative courts and general courts. The administrative courts deal with cases related to public administration. The general courts deal with civil and criminal cases.

---

4 Laura Ervo and Amie Dahlqvist, 'Delays in Civil Proceedings: Comparative Studies Between Finland and Sweden' in Laura Ervo and Anna Nylund (eds.), *The Future of Civil Litigation. Access to Courts and Court-annexed Mediation in the East-Nordic Countries* (Springer 2014) 250.

In addition, there are several specialised courts or court divisions in both countries. In Sweden, it is possible to use the small claims procedure or the payment order procedure by turning to the Swedish Enforcement Agency, which handles economic claims. The authority not only handles the recovery of claims, but also takes decisions on applications for injunctions to pay. If the claim is not contested, the Enforcement Agency has the right to make an enforceable decision. The creditor can choose between starting proceedings before the district court or with the Enforcement Agency, but the latter is faster and cheaper. In Finland, only the general courts handle applications for injunctions to pay.[5]

2. MUTUAL RECOGNITION AS A TOOL

The main tools for facilitating access to cross-border justice are the principles of mutual recognition based on mutual trust between Member States and direct judicial co-operation between national courts.[6] Mutual recognition could be replaced with substantive harmonisation of national laws, which is always an alternative if mutual recognition is not working in the case of judicial co-operation. However, a system based on mutual recognition is friendlier to the unique features of national law than substantive harmonisation while allowing for national variety. Therefore, national variety is not endangered; rather, it is specifically protected by using mutual recognition instead of harmonisation. However, Niemi is of the opinion that, for instance, the abolition of *exequatur* in the enforcement of judgments is a small step towards harmonisation. She seems partly to equate real harmonisation – like that of European procedures – with mutual recognition.[7]

Still, harmonisation is often understood as softer than unification.[8] However, Delmas-Marty has said that harmonisation and unification are complementary rather than antagonistic processes.[9] In terms of judicial co-operation, harmonisation must mean unification, as otherwise it is difficult to see systems – courts and authorities – working. But if the same can be achieved through mutual

5 Ervo and Dahlqvist (n 4) 252, 253 and 266.

6 See <http://www.europarl.europa.eu/atyourservice/en/displayFtu.html?ftuId=FTU_4.2.5.html> accessed 22 June 2018.

7 Johanna Niemi, 'Prosessioikeus ja eurooppalaistumisen haaste' (2014) *Lakimies* 1058, 1061. On the history and current situation in the harmonisation of procedural law, see also Eva Storskrubb, 'Några tankar om hur EU-rättens tentakler genomtränger processrätten' (2017) *JFT* 360.

8 See Martin Boodman, 'The Myth of Harmonisation of Laws' (1991) *AJCL* 700–702 and Melander Sakari, 'Rikosoikeuden harmonisointi Euroopan unionissa – harmonisointiteoreettisia näkökulmia' (2005) *Lakimies* 218.

9 Mireille Delmas-Marty, 'The European Union and Penal Law' (1998) *EurLJ* 106.

recognition, there is no need to harmonise or unify. Mutual recognition also, at the same time, protects national diversity in the decision-making processes. However, Storskrubb has stressed the problems and doubts that still exist even at the European level as what mutual recognition actually involves.[10]

Zimmerman argues for finding the European core – in other words, the 'grammar' in common, or the bridge that links different and varying national jurisdictions across Europe. He thinks that this should be the main aim of the harmonisation process, rather than simply harmonising the minor details of individual issues.[11] Still, even this problem of the harmonisation of details can be avoided through mutual recognition in judicial co-operation. National diversity can be fully protected if decisions and judgments have the status of free movement through mutual recognition. Therefore, real harmonisation or unification in the field of substantive procedural law is not especially necessary, so long as it is sufficient to make the system well-functioning through the free movement of decisions and judgments.

In the field of criminal law, this more procedural track of 'harmonising' the law has been used more extensively than substantive unification. It means that European co-operation in criminal proceedings is replacing the need to harmonise or unify the substance of criminal law.[12]

Mutual recognition is, therefore, an easier route towards integration. In particular, it seems easier at the national level to accept mutual recognition than harmonisation or unification, because mutual recognition does not directly affect national law by changing it. Mentally, it is a much simpler way to do integration and get even such legal cultures to come along, which otherwise are quite hesitant to do so. In Finland, at least, Sormunen has underlined the good odds that mutual recognition has of success, and he considers the principle to be a dynamic, multi-level one. According to him, the principle of mutual recognition can even be used when the substantive field has already been harmonised or unified to make this process more effective and comprehensive. In his opinion, this kind of double check by using harmonisation as well as mutual recognition in the same field would intensify both the rule of law and the single European market. Sormunen was mainly approaching the issue from the single-market perspective, but the same views are also applicable even when mutual recognition is considered from a wider perspective, including legal co-operation. Sormunen also described the

---

10 Storskrubb (n 7) 383.

11 Reinhard Zimmerman, 'L'Héritage de Savigny. Histoire du droit. Droit compare, et émergence d'une science juridique Européenne. De Boeck Supérieur' (2013) *Revue internationale de droit économique* 107–111.

12 Kimmo Nuotio, 'Euroopan unioni kriminaalipolitiikan tekijänä – järkevän kriminaalipolitiikan päätepiste?' (2003) *Lakimies* 1228.

principle of mutual recognition as infectious, by which he meant that the principle has been transferred from the single market to other fields too.[13]

In Sweden, the reception of mutual recognition has been mainly positive, although it has been recognised that the concept of mutual recognition also casts a shadow of mutual suspicion. Namely, according to Nilsson, the concept of mutual recognition should first be developed using minimum standards and the rule of law. In addition, it has been argued that harmonisation should be used for some national details as a way to guarantee that mutual recognition can be used in an effective and fair way in all Member States. Still, it has been stressed that it is time to adopt and follow the principle of mutual recognition because cross-border situations are a daily feature of life in the EU.[14] This idea of using harmonisation as a tool to guarantee the functioning of mutual recognition ultimately shows us that the principle of mutual recognition is in fact not an especially simple way forward, as mutual suspicion can be deep and some jurisdictions seem to require harmonisation of national laws in order to be able to accept mutual recognition.

3. EAST NORDIC CLASSIFICATIONS

To understand whether the situation in the East Nordic countries is one of harmonisation or fragmentation, we need to look at the characteristics of the European tools of harmonisation first. Two groups of these are generally mentioned, namely, the European procedures (European small claims procedure and European payment order) and co-operation in civil matters. At first sight, these group classifications are very clear. However, many instruments relating to co-operation in civil matters also have, to a significant extent, the goal of harmonisation and, even though they are not European procedures, they have similar characteristics and come close to European procedures. Therefore, the distinction between procedures and other tools is perhaps not that significant; rather, it is possible to view all tools from the functional perspective. That is why the first category in my classification consists of European instruments, which are as follows: fundamental rights, payment orders, the small claims procedure, insolvency proceedings, mediation, enforcement of judgments, protection measures in civil matters, and interim and precautionary measures.

The second category in the classification of co-operation in civil matters is pure co-operation, without the aim of harmonising but simply of making European life easier in cross-border situations. This category comprises European co-operation in the taking evidence, service of documents, legal

13 Ari Sormunen, 'Vastavuoroisen tunnustamisen periaate muutoksessa' (2008) *Defensor Legis* 121 and 126.

14 Hans G. Nilsson, 'Ömsesidigt erkännande' (2005) *Svensk Juristtidning* 895–898.

aid in cross-border cases, the European judicial network, and automatic processing (for instance, taking evidence by video-conferencing and the use of dynamic forms).

The harmonisation of conflict-of-law rules falls somewhere between the categories of instruments and pure co-operation. It has harmonisation as its aim, and thus, from this perspective, belongs into the first category. However, it is not an instrument as such, but rather a way to make European life easier in cross-border situations. Therefore, I would nevertheless classify conflict-of-laws harmonisation as belonging in the second category, pure co-operation.

From the perspective of harmonisation, or having the question of fragmentation in mind, the classification of European procedures and co-operation in civil matters becomes difficult as soon as one starts to describe the procedural content of these different instruments. Both European procedures and some examples of European co-operation in civil matters strongly harmonise the national procedural systems. Therefore, it is not possible to finish the classification with this distinction; rather, it is necessary to consider which European procedural instruments need to be harmonised and whether there are also other types of non-instrumental co-operation in civil matters. This distinction between European instruments and other types of co-operation in civil matters leads to a more fruitful result. The first group (instruments) includes such procedural tools that aim at harmonisation and 'pure' co-operation, which means co-operation without any aims to harmonise national jurisdictions but rather to make cross-border situations easier to handle in Europe.

Niemi has classified the effects of the Europeanisation of procedural law into three categories. First of all, the EU has placed procedural demands on the Member States when they apply EU law. Secondly, Europeanisation means procedural tools to make cross-border situations effective, as I described earlier. This level was reached following the Amsterdam Treaty. Thirdly, following the Lisbon Treaty, the EU has also set out substantive requirements for criminal proceedings. Niemi also mentions European fundamental rights in the context of substantive requirements.[15]

Storskrubb has five categories in her classification of the effects of Europeanisation in national procedural law. In the first category, she places effective legal protection based mainly on Article 47 of the EU Charter of Fundamental Rights. The second category consists of two principles created by case law, namely the principles of equality and effectiveness. National procedural laws in the Member States need to follow these principles even if national procedural laws cannot otherwise be harmonised directly.[16]

15 Niemi (n 7) 1058.
16 Storskrubb (n 7) 363–367.

Co-operation in civil matters is Storskrubb's third category. She has also paid attention to the diversity of constituents of this category; she even says that the name 'co-operation in civil matters' is misleading.[17]

Storskrubb's fourth category is the invisible harmonisation of national procedural law in the context of substantive harmonisation in various specialist fields. This harmonisation often includes procedural rules too. As an example, Storskrubb mentions the Mediation Directive. These special procedures do not need to have a cross-border aspect to be harmonised by the EU, but they can be harmonised even at the national level if this is carried out in conjunction with the harmonisation of substantive law.[18] In my opinion, this category is the most important one and is rather problematic, as it is an invisible but effective tool to harmonise national procedural law.

The last category according to Storskrubb is the EU's soft law tools – like the judicial networks or e-justice – which can be used to strengthen the other categories of harmonisation. Even though these tools do not count as hard law, their effects in practice can be very significant. Therefore, this category can in fact play an important role in harmonisation.[19]

The European Parliament mentions all of the above in its factsheet,[20] except for fundamental rights, as the achievements in co-operation in civil matters worthy of inclusion. The Parliament does not set out its own classification, but rather mentions all the types of tools as achievements without making any distinction between them. For my part, I would place the Charter of Fundamental Rights above all other tools in the context of co-operation in civil matters. The Charter provides a common foundation of rights that are naturally fundamental to this harmonisation and co-operation process.[21] Secondly, I think that some kind of classification of these achievements is needed to avoid drifting without a common aim in relation to harmonisation and co-operation. Namely, some of them are more comprehensive and, therefore, more harmonising, like the European procedures; others are softer and less harmonising.

4. EUROPEAN INSTRUMENTS

As mentioned before, there are a number of European instruments available to achieve harmonisation. Some of them are European procedures such as

17 Storskrubb (n 7) 364–365.

18 Storskrubb (n 7) 365. Normally EU law does not cover national procedural law except in cross-border situations. See, for instance, Storskrubb (n 7) 360.

19 Storskrubb (n 7) 366.

20 Judicial Cooperation in Civil Matters (n 1).

21 In addition, Niemi has paid attention to the significance of European fundamental rights in the process of harmonising European procedural law. Niemi (n 7) 1063.

the European Payment Order Procedure and the European Small Claims Procedure. Others are procedural tools that do not aim at harmonising as such, but rather at promoting or strengthening integration in practice, for example in relation to the enforcement of judgments or protection measures in civil matters. These types of instruments are not entire procedures, but they are based either on mutual recognition (like measures relating to the enforcement of judgments), or they are linked to national procedures or procedural instruments and strengthen them in cross-border situations (like protection measures in civil matters or interim and precautionary measures).

Because of these differences in their characteristics and function, not all European instruments change national law; sometimes they just strengthen it and make it effective in cross-border situations. Therefore, the Europeanisation of procedural law is not only about harmonisation or unification, but is also more often about strengthening and extending national procedural instruments so that they also cover cross-border situations.

As Niemi has written in relation to Finland, despite the fact that harmonisation has not affected procedural law as such very much, there are many situations where the Europeanisation of procedural law has had direct or indirect effects on national procedural law.[22] Moreover, as early as 1996, Lindblom underlined that the free movement of persons would have a huge effect in terms of the Europeanisation of civil procedural law, because the majority of civil proceedings are in some way linked with this key EU principle.[23]

Still, there can be some fragmenting effects too, especially when the European tool does not already exist in the national toolbox in advance and is therefore unfamiliar to the local legal culture. In such situations, the new European tool does not fit well into the national system; moreover, the national legal culture is opposed to adopting it, this type of tool often remains outside the national toolbox, as a legal fragment, as happened in Sweden with the adoption of the Mediation Directive.[24]

---

22 Niemi (n 7) 1058.

23 Per Henrik Lindblom, 'Integrera mera? Regeringsförhandlingar om (bl.a.) civilprocessrätten i EU!' (1997) *Svensk Juristtidning* 316.

24 See Amie Dahlqvist, 'Mediation in the Swedish Courts: Change by EU Directive?' in Laura Ervo and Anna Nylund (eds.), *The Future of Civil Litigation. Access to Courts and Court-annexed Mediation in the East-Nordic Countries* (Springer 2014) 137. Directive 2008/52/EC of the European Parliament and of the Council of 21 May 2008 on certain aspects of mediation in civil and commercial matters has, of course, been formally implemented in Sweden, but its effects are yet to be seen in practice. Since 2011, the Mediation Act (2011:860) and some changes in other acts have been in place, but the situation in practice is still more or less the same as before the Directive. In the other words, mediation does not play a significant role in Swedish legal culture and Swedish adjudication, and the implementation of the Directive did not change the fact that mediation is not an important tool in Swedish dispute resolution. Swedes trust in courts, and there is also a long and successful tradition of arbitration in Sweden. In Finland, on the other hand, the academic discussion on mediation was

This type of partial harmonisation received criticism early on. In Sweden, Lindblom was worried about this in 1996 and wrote that partial harmonisation would lead to duplicate instruments and increase complexity. At the same time, he was sceptical about whether full harmonisation of civil proceedings would be possible, for example because of a lack of resources, which would make creating a well-functioning and living European civil procedure challenging.[25]

In the Netherlands, Krans has also paid attention to the invisible latent effects that European law exerts on national procedural law. By this he refers to the directives that include a large number of procedural rules without being instruments intended to harmonise national procedural law as such.[26] He finds that this kind of 'harmonisation' gives rise to problematic fragmentation both internally and externally. By internal fragmentation he means that EU law itself is inconsistent and patchy. External fragmentation refers to similar results in national procedural laws, which can also be fragmented by EU instruments of this type.[27]

Where the East Nordic perspective is concerned, sometimes EU tools can be transposed onto the national system quite technically without actually changing the actual content of the national procedural law. One Swedish example is the Mediation Directive already mentioned above. In Finland, there is the unusual situation that national law includes only the European Payment Order Procedure, but no national payment order procedure. It is fairly strange to have a particular tool that only applies to cross-border disputes when the same instrument does not exist at the national level. However, Finland is not the only Member State with this problem. This shows that there is a certain amount of fragmentation in East Nordic procedural law. Sweden has been obliged to adopt mediation even though it does not fit well into the national

---

already lively even before the EU Directive, and therefore the Directive fell on fertile soil. Finnish court proceedings are considered too inflexible, lengthy and costly, and therefore parties are keen to avoid them. Arbitration is also not that popular, as it is believed to preserve of rich businesspeople, in the main. That is why there was a place for a new conflict-resolution tool in Finland. However, both examples show us that a society's habits and legal culture are the most important factors in determining whether new legislation will be successful or merely a dead letter. See also Anna-Liisa Autio, *Lainkäyttö yritysten riidanratkaisussa* (Lakimiesliiton Kustannus 2014) 16; Anna Liisa Autio, 'The Main Problems in Access to Court Regarding the Dispute Resolution of Finnish Companies' in Laura Ervo and Anna Nylund (eds.), *The Future of Civil Litigation. Access to Courts and Court-annexed Mediation in the East-Nordic Countries* (Springer 2014) 213–229; and Laura Ervo, 'Välimiesmenettely vaihtoehtoisena riidanratkaisumenettelynä Suomessa ja Ruotsissa' (2017) *Defensor Legis* 661–679.

25 Per Henrik Lindblom, 'Rättssfärernas harmoni. Om arbetet på en enhetlig europeisk processrätt' (1996) *Svensk Juristtidning* 831–834.

26 Bart Krans, 'EU Law and National Civil Procedure Law: An Invisible Pillar' (2015) *EurRevPL* 567–568 and 571–573.

27 Krans (n 26) 582–585.

legal culture, where there is a preference for court proceedings instead of court-connected mediation.[28] Finland, on the other hand, has implemented the European Payment Order and Small Claims Procedure despite the fact that they do not exist at the national level and there does not seem to be any particular practical need to include them in the national procedural tools. Therefore, the European and East Nordic national tools are not the same, and this leads to a degree of fragmentation. However, this kind of fragmentation is only marginal and does not have significant effects. As far as I can see, the national procedural law is still a unified whole both in Sweden and Finland. The fragmentation is not a substantial problem as described above. There is not even formal fragmentation due to the fact that in both countries European legislation has been incorporated into national law – not by incorporating it into the national codes of procedure, but rather by enacting as special acts like the Swedish Act on the European Small Claims Procedure (2008:1038).

5. EUROPEAN PAYMENT ORDER PROCEDURE AND EUROPEAN SMALL CLAIMS PROCEDURE

The European Payment Order Procedure and the European Small Claims Procedure are the only real European procedures we have. They are based on harmonised European regulation where procedural rules are concerned, which is novel at the international and even at the European level. Previously, according to the *lex fori* principle, the national court had always followed the national procedural rules, even if the case had international connections.[29] However, the European procedures cover only cross-border situations and are alternatives to the national procedures. They have not abolished any national procedural tools but are instead parallel instruments. That is why national procedural law has not been harmonised at all with these European procedures.[30] As a result, they are not tools that give rise to in-depth harmonisation, but rather provide a different way to react compared to national tools and get access to court in Europe. Still, they do differ from the Brussels I Regulation in as much as they are independent procedural instruments that are not linked to the national procedures.[31] This was a radical step taken at the European level when these purely European procedures were introduced.

---

28 Dahlqvist (n 24) 137–155.

29 Heidi Lindfors, 'Eurooppalainen maksamismääräysmenettely ja eurooppalainen vähäisten vaatimusten menettely – jäsenvaltioittain eroavat yhtenäistetyt menettelyt?' (2012) *Defensor Legis* 499.

30 Lindfors (n 29) 500.

31 Lindfors (n 29) 502.

The European Payment Order Procedure and the European Small Claims Procedure are usually conducted in writing, using standard claim forms, which makes it simple to use these tools in cross-border situations.[32]

However, the European procedures leave a lot of procedural issues, many of them significant, to the national level. Only the main points are governed by the European-level provisions, and everything else about the procedures is left to be governed by domestic principles and systems. Therefore, the implementation of the procedures in practice varies depending on the local procedural laws. This interplay with national law is one of the weaknesses of these European procedures. For instance, the provisions of the European Small Claims Procedure do not establish a fully-fledged process, but rather only a partial process that must be inserted into the domestic procedural system, including the judicial structure and organisation, of the Member State. This makes the system a complex one that comes at a price.[33] Lindfors considers it paradoxical that European procedures, which are meant to be harmonised procedures for all EU Member States, still use national, varying proceedings.[34] For instance, the appeals process comes entirely from national law.[35]

In relation to these procedures, the East-Nordic situation on a national level varies quite dramatically. In Finland, there is no national small claims procedure or payment order system, whereas both exist in Sweden. Naturally, the European Payment Order Procedure and the European Small Claims Procedure have been implemented in both Member States. For some reason, these European procedures have ceased to cause much discussion in the East Nordic countries. When they were new, there were some doubts raised, especially in Finland, about these totally new systems and how they would function, but that debate has since fallen silent.[36] The reasons for this might be that the European procedures are not actually used that much, and that in those cases where they have been used, they have likely worked as they should without

32 European Order for Payment Procedure, European Consumer Centre Finland <https://www.ecc.fi/en/about-us/court-proceedings-in-cross-border-trade-consumer-disputes/european-order-for-payment-procedure/>; and European Small Claims Procedure, European Consumer Centre Finland <https://www.ecc.fi/en/about-us/court-proceedings-in-cross-border-trade-consumer-disputes/european-small-claims-procedure> accessed 27 February 2018. Lindfors (n 29) 498; and Eva Storskrubb, *Civil Procedure and EU Law. A Policy Area Uncovered* (OUP 2008) 203–219 and 220–232.

33 Cristian Oro Martinez, 'The Small Claims Regulation: On the Way to an Improved European Procedure?' in Burkhard Hess, Maria Bergström and Eva Storskrubb (eds.), *EU Civil Justice. Current Issues and Future Outlook* (Bloomsbury 2016) 134.

34 Lindfors (n 29) 500.

35 Lindfors (n 29) 502. Nylund has also paid attention in the co-ordination problems; she covers them in detail from the Finnish perspective in Anna Nylund, 'Europeiskt betalningsförläggande och småmålsförfarande' (2008) *JFT* 256–258.

36 Nylund (n 35) 241–259; and Lindfors (n 29) 498–508.

major problems. In Sweden, the recent amendments to the European small claims procedure to improve access to court have been seen as useful.[37]

There are no official statistics on the use of these European procedures, but it has been possible to obtain a certain set of statistics by contacting the Helsinki District Court, which is the correct forum in Finland, and the Swedish Enforcement Authority in Sweden. In the early stages, there were only a handful of cases, but the amount has been steadily increasing since then, especially in Finland. The reason for the very high figures in Finland in 2016 and 2017 is that one Estonian firm has been very active and has been making extensive use of the European Payment Order Procedure in Finland.[38] In Sweden, the use of this tool has been more stable.

Year	**Finland**	**Sweden**
2008	1	0
2009	16	45
2010	71	34
2011	142	39
2012	259	59
2013	633	91
2014	990	71
2015	861	73
2016	2,547	125
2017	1,704	126
Total	**7,224**	**663**

The harmonisation effect of the European Payment Order Procedure seems to be based significantly on the actors who use this tool. Even one active firm using the procedure can make a major difference. Therefore, the active promotion and marketing of the European tools seems to be necessary to make them effective in practice. For instance, in the case of the United Kingdom, the reason for the low usage rates of these European procedures is said to be potential litigants' lack of awareness and knowledge of them.[39] The fragmentation or harmonisation effect of the European Payment Order Procedure is linked with the active actors. As such, the effect of the European Payment Order Procedure in an individual Member State seems to depend on how widely the tool is used, which in turn

37 *Nya regler för europeiska småmål – lättare att pröva tvister inom EU.* Departementsserien 2016:10 (2016).

38 Based on information received via email from the Helsinki District Court.

39 Carla Crifò, 'Trusted with a Muzzle and Enfranchised with a Clog: The British Approach to European Civil Procedure' in Burkhard Hess, Maria Bergström and Eva Storskrubb (eds.), *EU Civil Justice. Current Issues and Future Outlook* (Bloomsbury 2016) 89.

seems to vary dramatically between Member States and to hinge on individual actors and their activity in the field, which is somewhat confusing.

As far as the Small Claims Procedure is concerned, the statistics from Finland show that it has not been as popular a tool as the European Payment Order Procedure, and has been used only in a small number of cases. At least in Finland, it seems to be mainly a dead letter.[40] One reason for this could be the fact that there is no domestic small claims procedure in Finland. On the one hand, it might be that the lack of procedural experience with small claims and/or the lack of procedural systems to fix the problems mean that the European procedure is not functioning well in Finland – however, this is just speculation. On the other hand, that very same reason, i.e. the failings of the national system, could in another context be a reason to in fact use the European procedure in cross-border cases to get its benefits, because the alternative of using the domestic small claims procedure does not exist. However, the result seems to be that domestic procedures are chosen in cross-border cases instead of these European alternatives. Perhaps this is because there is trust in the well-functioning in domestic procedures, which are otherwise frequently used. In Finland, the domestic alternative is the summary proceedings for uncontested debt cases. The procedure is simple and quick even though it happens before the district court.[41] If the case is contested, it is automatically transferred to full civil proceedings, which can also be seen as one benefit. Simply, and surprisingly enough, there seems to be no need to use the European procedures in Finland.

Year	Finland
2008	0
2009	12
2010	7
2011	9
2012	46
2013	21
2014	12
2015	11
2016	42
2017	26

40 The Finnish statistics received by email from the Helsinki District Court, which is a competent forum in Finland. In Sweden, all district courts are competent forums (Act on the European Small Claims Procedure (2008:1038), section 2) and therefore the statistics are not available. The national court authority was approached for statistics but European small claims are not recorded separately in Sweden.

41 Finnish Code of Judicial Procedure, Chapter 5, section 3.

As for Sweden, statistics are not available for before 1 November 2016, but in 2017 a total of eight European Small Claims Procedures were started and three cases decided.[42] This low figure is a bit surprising because a domestic small claims procedure also exists in Sweden. Therefore, whereas we might have expected that the European Small Claims Procedure would be more extensively used in Sweden than in Finland, perhaps the existing domestic systems (both the small claims procedure and the payment order procedure) are also widely used in cross-border cases and so there seems to be no need to use the European procedures. If not, the other alternative is that claimants are not familiar enough with the European procedures. Still, the recent Finnish statistics mentioned above show us that as soon as just one foreign debt collection agency starts to use the European procedure, the amount of cases increases rapidly.

Compared with the United Kingdom, the East Nordic results are not that surprising. The number of the applications to issue a European payment order in the UK was 85 in 2009, 62 in 2010, 242 in 2011, and 250 in 2012. The number of the applications to issue a European small claims decision was 138 in 2009, 202 in 2010, 183 in 2011, and 164 in 2012.[43] In the Netherlands, the numbers for the use of the European Payment Order Procedure were 295 cases in 2009, 343 cases in 2010, 372 cases in 2011, 334 cases in 2012 and 282 cases in 2013.[44] The two European procedures are not used much in the Netherlands either. One reason for that might be that there is no similar domestic procedure and therefore litigants are probably not used to using this type of instrument as a way of collecting debts. Still, the lack of a domestic equivalent does not explain why foreign creditors are not using the European procedure to collect debts from Dutch debtors.[45]

Therefore, the result seems to be that this tool has not been very successful at harmonisation and not changed the national procedural tools very much.[46] On the other hand, this also means that the European Small Claims Procedure has not given right to much fragmentation either. Still, if considered systematically, some fragmentation does nonetheless exist because of the fact that it is in principle possible to use the European Small Claims Procedure instead of the national procedure. However, the variety of options available in terms of access to court cannot be seen as negative, and these types of European procedures

---

42 Based on information received by email from the Swedish national court authority.

43 Crifo (n 39) 88.

44 Xandra Kramer, 'European Procedures on Debt Collection: Nothing or Noting? Experiences and Future Prospects' in Burkhard Hess, Maria Bergström and Eva Storskrubb (eds.), *EU Civil Justice. Current Issues and Future Outlook* (Bloomsbury 2016) 107.

45 Kramer (n 44) 116.

46 In advance, the expectations or fears were bigger than the result today seems to be. See, for instance, Nylund (n 35) 241 and 258.

only make life easier when the claim has cross-border elements. Therefore, I hesitate to call this 'fragmentation', which has certain negative implications. The European procedures are more about development.

The European Small Claims Procedure has been added to national proceedings but has not abolished anything. Even from that perspective, its effects are not that crucial where the parallel national procedures are also concerned.[47] As Nylund has put it, these European procedures were about minimum harmonisation because only the main questions have been regulated at the EU level and many details about how to implement the European systems at the national level have been left open, in line with the subsidiarity principle.[48]

Earlier, it was also considered whether the European procedures could act as a stimulus and change national procedural law – for example, whether those Member States that do not have a payment order system could adopt one based on the European example. This was even recommended as a way to make the harmonisation process easier and less fragmented.[49] However, Finland, for instance, which does not have a payment order system, has not adopted it at the national level – there was not even any discussion of this possibility – despite implementing the European Payment Order Procedure to govern for cross-border situations. Nevertheless, even without a corresponding tool at the national level, the European procedure seems to be working well without any major problems. Indeed, the number of the cases has even recently been increasing, as the statistics above show. As a result, this procedural law fragmentation, where there are different tools for domestic and cross-border debt cases, has probably not been seen as a problem in Finland, and the legislative branch has therefore presumably not felt the need to re-establish the domestic payment order system (the original system was abolished in 1993).[50] The other example is the Netherlands, where there is also no payment order system at the national level. The domestic procedure for judgment in default works well and therefore the Dutch legislative branch ultimately recommended that the payment order should not be adopted at the national level.[51]

Another problem is that the European procedures are not that well designed as compared to other European instruments. For instance, the relationship

---

47 There seem to be more effects of Europeanisation in the area of enforcement law, where at least some scholars already speak about European enforcement law. See LINDFORS (n 29) 49–54.

48 LINDFORS (n 29) 502–504; and NYLUND (n 35) 257.

49 NYLUND (n 35) 248 and 258. Lindfors has also considered the fact that in those Member States where the national procedural system is similar to the European tools – for example, where it is flexible and simple, rather than a formal or complicated system – the implementation of new European procedures is likely to be easier. LINDFORS (n 29) 505.

50 *Laki maksamismääräyslain ja -asetuksen kumoamisesta* 593/1993.

51 KRAMER (n 44) 116.

between the European Small Claims Procedure Regulation and the Brussels I Regulation is not successful. This is because the interplay with other EU instruments is not working well enough.[52] This could be one reason why the European procedures have not been complete successes so far.

Nylund wrote in 2008 that the European Payment Order Procedure belongs on the periphery of civil procedure. Therefore, according to her, the harmonisation effect of this European tool is not that profound. Still, she found the harmonisation effect of the Small Claims Procedure to be much more significant and also riskier because of its lack of respect for the main EU procedural principles, such as the right to be heard in a fair trial. The European Small Claims Procedure had been created to be quick and cheap and, as a result, the principles on which it is built differ from those on which traditional court proceedings are built at the national level in most Member States.[53] Nylund was worried about the lack of oral communication, an important component in a fair trial, in the written Small Claims Procedure and her doubts from the perspective of the fair trial are justified.[54] Nylund also predicted that these two original European procedures would be just the start of the harmonisation of civil procedural law.[55] However, the next level is still failing and the harmonisation of civil procedural law has not been as quick as was expected when European Payment Order Procedure and the European Small Claims Procedures were introduced. Lindfors was more sceptical as to what harmonisation of procedural law is concerned with and wrote in 2012 that it is not that easy to cut loose the strong national tradition in procedural law even in cross-border cases. Therefore, she was a bit more cautious when predicting the future of the harmonisation of European procedural law. According to Lindfors, the indirect effects of Europeanisation would be more likely in the field of procedural law. As an example, she mentioned the possibility of adopting national payment orders as a result of the European Payment Order Procedures.[56] When the European procedures were being drafted, as with Finland, there were also some critical views in Sweden. For instance, the Small Claims Procedure was not considered to be effective enough and there were concerns about whether the planning at the EU level had been comprehensive enough.[57]

---

52 Oro Martinez (n 33) 136–137.
53 Nylund (n 35) 258.
54 Nylund (n 35) 258; and Laura Ervo, *Oikeudenmukainen oikeudenkäynti* (WSOY 2005) 113.
55 Nylund (n 35) 258.
56 Lindfors (n 29) 507–508.
57 Johan Lindholm, 'Det europeiska småmålsförfarandet – en liten början på något stort?' (2008) *Svensk Juristtidning* 863–866.

6. OTHER TYPES OF CO-OPERATION

There are still three examples of the other type of EU co-operation in the field of civil and commercial matters. These tools are mainly instrumental, and therefore I call this type of co-operation 'pure co-operation', which means co-operation without any significant harmonisation aims.

The three examples of pure co-operation are the regulations on the taking of evidence, the service of documents and automatic processing. These are technical instruments to make the handling of cross-border situations easier. Due to the free movement of persons and capital, many claims in Europe have cross-border effects; the current way of life in Europe is a very mobile one. In addition, technical development is rapid and there are increasingly easy and safe ways to improve and assist cross-border proceedings. Therefore, these instrumental forms of EU co-operation in civil and commercial matters are necessary and viable tools that mostly have practical effects and benefits. They are not particularly intended as harmonising instruments, but rather as practical tools to make the common way of life in Europe easier.

The Regulation on the taking of evidence[58] seeks to improve, simplify and accelerate co-operation between courts in this area. The Regulation provides for two methods for the taking of evidence between Member States: taking of evidence through the requested court and the direct taking of evidence by the requesting court. The requesting court is the court before which the proceedings are commenced or contemplated. The requested court is the competent court of another Member State that is asked to perform the taking of evidence. Each Member State needs to designate a central authority that is responsible for supplying information and seeking solutions to any difficulties that may arise in relation to a request.[59] This tool helps in the cross-border situations because the taking of evidence in civil proceedings is not restricted to the boundaries of a Member State. It may be necessary to hear witnesses or experts in other Member States, or the court may have to visit a scene of occurrence situated in another Member State.[60]

The Regulation 1393/2007 on the service of documents[61] aims to put in place a fast, secure and standardised transmission procedure for judicial

---

58 Regulation (EC) 1206/2001 of 28 May 2001 on co-operation between the courts of the Member States in the taking of evidence in civil or commercial matters.

59 See <http://eur-lex.europa.eu/legal-content/EN/TXT/?uri=LEGISSUM:l33130> accessed 2 March 2018.

60 See <https://e-justice.europa.eu/content_taking_of_evidence-76-en.do> accessed 2 March 2018; and Storskrubb (n 32) 114.

61 Regulation (EC) 1393/2007 of 13 November 2007 on the service in EU countries of judicial and extrajudicial documents in civil or commercial matters.

and extrajudicial documents in civil or commercial matters between parties located in different EU countries. Documents must be transmitted directly and as soon as possible by any appropriate means of transmission, as long as they are legible and faithful to the original. The documents are exempt from legalisation or any equivalent formality.[62]

Both Regulations are directly applicable in Sweden (and completed by the Acts 2003:493, 2003:483 and 2008:808 respectively). The Act on the taking of evidence takes precedence in Sweden over provisions in earlier international agreements, such as the 1970 Hague Convention.[63] Neither Regulation has given rise to any specific debate in Sweden.[64] Both Regulations are directly applicable in Finland. In addition, there is a secondary Act (426/2015) on international legal aid[65] in Finland, which, however, is secondary to the European regulations. The named European regulations have not caused any specific debate there either. Therefore, European co-operation in the fields of service and taking evidence seem to be working from the East Nordic perspective. These instruments to strengthen European co-operation are accepted in the East Nordic countries.

In recent years, more and more Member States have introduced changes to their laws that allow for the use of modern information and communication technologies in civil judicial proceedings. This automatic processing covers, for instance, the taking of evidence via video-conferencing and the use of dynamic forms. These changes allow communication between the judicial authorities and the parties via new channels, such as the internet. The national legislation should ensure that communication via the internet does not threaten the appropriate protection of sensitive data used in the course of the proceedings. Other human rights principles should, of course, also still be protected.[66]

Especially in Sweden, the use of modern technology in court is comprehensive and used intensively to make proceedings more effective – in other words, to make them quick, easy and cheap. There has been an extensive debate in Sweden as to whether the recent developments and amendments are too radical, for instance because they remove the positive psychological effect

---

62 'Transmission of judicial and extrajudicial documents between EU countries' <http://eur-lex.europa.eu/legal-content/EN/TXT/?uri=LEGISSUM:l16031> accessed 3 March 2018; and Storskrubb (n 32) 92.

63 Rättslig hjälp i civila mål och ärenden, Regeringskansliet <http://www.regeringen.se/sveriges-regering/justitiedepartementet/internationellt-rattsligt-samarbete/rattslig-hjalp-i-civila-mal-och-arenden/> accessed 29 March 2018.

64 *Domstolarnas handläggning av ärenden. Statens offentliga utredningar* (SOU) 2007:065.

65 Laki kansainvälisestä oikeusavusta sekä tuomioiden tunnustamisesta ja täytäntöönpanosta siviili- ja kauppaoikeuden alalla.

66 See <https://e-justice.europa.eu/content_automatic_processing-280-en.do> accessed 2 March 2018.

of a face-to-face session. Therefore, the development in Finland has been more cautious, although modern technology is still also used widely in Finnish courts.[67]

As stated at the beginning of this chapter, these instruments are mainly European 'tools'. They are technical instruments in the field of procedural law that do not have a significant harmonising effect. Still, it could be argued that, for instance, the taking evidence framework goes against state sovereignty,[68] according to which the state has jurisdiction only over its own geographical space. However, the world and society are changing. Therefore, state sovereignty is in many ways old-fashioned and no longer a very serviceable concept. In modern societies, it is difficult to argue that the way to handle cross-border situations is through state sovereignty, especially now that technical developments facilitate the conduct of hearings that go over borders and jurisdictions. The law, especially procedural law, is an instrument too: it is a way to make life easier. The law should not be seen as an isolated island; rather, there is always a bridge to current society, and this connection should be alive. That is why it is difficult to see the named three EU instruments as harmonising tools in the substantive sense; instead, they are mostly just technical instruments to handle cross-border situations, which are needed now more than ever because cross-border situations have become part of daily life in today's society and especially in Europe.

7. EAST NORDIC PROCEEDINGS TODAY: IS THERE ANY NATIONAL VARIETY LEFT?

The legal culture particularly affects law and its development. According to Tuori, law does not consist only of a legal order; rather, a legal order is only the visible and discursively formulated surface of law. I would argue that it is the most trivial level of law. Below a legal order there are still two more stable levels, namely the legal culture and the underlying structure of the law.[69]

The differences in legal culture in many cases explain the differences in interpretation and adoption of international norms at the national level. The common international norms are – of course – common to all states that have

---

67 Laura Ervo, 'Swedish-Finnish Preparatory Proceedings: Filtering and Process Techniques' in Laura Ervo and Anna Nylund (eds.), *Current Trends in Preparatory Proceedings. A Comparative Study of East-Nordic and Former Communist Countries* (Springer 2016).

68 The Helsinki Term Bank for the Arts and Sciences, *Oikeustiede: sisäinen valtiosuvereniteetti.* <http://www.tieteentermipankki.fi/wiki/Oikeustiede:sisäinen valtiosuvereniteetti> accessed 2 March 2018; and Storskrubb (n 32).

69 Richard Mohr (review), '*Critical Legal Positivism* by Kaarlo Tuori' (2003) *Adelaide L Rev* 24; and Kaarlo Tuori, *Critical Legal Positivism* (Routledge 2002) 147.

ratified or implemented them. Still, the factual situation may vary from state to state; in the other words, the implementation and interpretation are not identical but culturally based.

This is true even in similar legal cultures where the underlying structure of the law is more or less identical and where the visible law in the case of common international conventions is identical too. Due to the varying legal culture and the second level of the law, the real, current situation in applying the common international instrument can, however, be rather different.

The legal culture differs between East Nordic countries, in spite of common EU law. As Tuori has said, legal culture is not that easy to change. It stays below the level of legislative norms and the change of a single norm does not directly change the legal culture on which the application of norms is based.[70] Storskrubb has questioned whether we were in fact ready to accept the common European legal culture in the context of European civil procedural law. She seems to have some doubts, but emphasises that mutual understanding and discourse is also necessary to achieve a common European legal culture and this first step is just now taken.[71]

Too often it has been taken for granted that Finland and Sweden have similar societies, similar cultures and even a similar legal mentality. It is true that the two countries very often have shared or similar jurisprudence – sometimes even identical individual legal rules – due to their shared history, the deep co-operation of East Nordic legislators (especially before either country joined the EU), and because Finland has often copied Swedish legislation where something has been working well in Sweden. Still, the way of thinking about the law, and therefore also the interpretation of the law, may differ between the two countries, owing to the differences that exist at the micro level between the two cultures' ways of thinking.

East Nordic legal culture has been said to be democratic, transparent, human, flexible, pragmatic and reformistic.[72] Still, there are some key differences between Finnish and Swedish legal culture. Swedish legislative culture is much more dialogic compared with that in Finland: the Finnish approach lacks the elements of discussion and reflection that are so visible in Swedish culture. Finnish legal culture can be characterised by quick solutions and rapid reforms, which can be realised whenever needed through new interpretations of the case law if the legislator has not reacted to relevant new needs in society. This makes for flexibility. Creative solutions and common

---

70 Mohr (n 69) 141–142 and Tuori (n 69) 147.

71 Storskrubb (n 7) 384.

72 Johan Hirschfeldt, 'Domstolarna som statsmakt – några utvecklingslinjer' (2011–2012) *Juridisk Tidskrift* 5–6; and Thomas Wilhelmsson, 'Suomen kansanomaisen oikeuskulttuurin uhat' (2003) *Lakimies* 85.

sense are trademarks of the Finnish legal culture.[73] This type of legal culture creates a lot of space and fertile ground for adapting foreign models and international instruments to the national context. There are no major cultural obstacles to adopting new approaches. Swedes, however, being used to the discursive legislative procedure for changing how the law is interpreted, are less comfortable with European instruments to make changes without extensive, and sometimes time-consuming, public discussions first. This difference can be seen, for instance, in the fact that Finnish courts will develop the law through case law when needed, such as when the European instruments require new ways to go. Swedish courts, by contrast, wait for the legislator to respond and new national statutes to be enacted for advice on the next step.[74]

Other differences between the East Nordic countries relate to their mentalities.[75] Swedes seem to be pleased and satisfied with their legal system for the most part.[76] By contrast, in Finland it is typical to underrate local solutions and focus on what could be imported to make the country's legal system better. The domestic climate, or in other words this type of general systemic mentality, evidently has an effect on legal decision-making - and especially on interpretation and application. Mentality is one crucial factor in the opposite of judicial activism, i.e. judicial self-restraint, and is at the same time connected to the sources of law. According to one study of 11 countries' attitudes to this, Sweden was shown to be one of the most restrained countries, together with the Soviet Union, whereas the United States was the most active. Finland was unfortunately not among the countries included in the research.[77] This empirical study is unfortunately very old, but because legal culture changes slowly, there might still be something relevant in it today. Taking an autoethnographical method,[78] my own observations suggest a similar result.[79] In Sweden, harmonisation has been carried out more formally, compared with

---

73 See also Jussi Sallila, 'Eurooppalainen oikeuskulttuuri, pohjoismainen perinne ja juristi-identiteetti. Oikeushistoria Suomen oikeustieteellisissä aikakauslehdissä n. 1945–1970' [2011] *Oikeus* 466.

74 Laura Ervo, 'Comparative Analysis Between East-Nordic Countries' (2015) *Scandinavian Studies in Law* 144–145.

75 Ewoud Hondius, 'Pro-active Comparative Law' (2007) *Scandinavian Studies in Law* 147.

76 Hondius (n 75) 147.

77 Kenneth M. Holland, 'Introduction' in Kenneth M. Holland (ed.), *Judicial Activism in Comparative Perspective* (Macmillan Houndmills 1991) 2.

78 Autoethnography is a form of qualitative research in which the authors uses self-reflection to explore their personal experience and connects this autobiographical story to wider cultural, political and social meanings and understandings. 'Autoethnography' in Albert J. Mills, Gabrielle Durepos and Eliden Wiebe (eds.), *Encyclopedia of case study research* (Sage Publications 2010) 43–45.

79 I took my exams in Finland and have worked for about 20 years at Finnish universities. Since 2010, I have been working in Sweden at Örebro University.

the more substantial change in Finnish court culture. For instance, where human rights and, for example, fair trial are concerned, the Finnish Supreme Court has taken the European case law into consideration more often when applying European fundamental rights in the national context, in order to fill gaps in the national legislation and find a solution by interpreting the European Convention on Human Rights or EU fundamental rights directly. The Swedish Supreme Court follows the letter of the national law and expects that the legislator to respond by making a change where there is a need for one, whereas the Finnish Supreme Court finds the solution itself with the help of direct interpretation of European norms.[80] Another example of this can be seen in the differences described above in implementing the European Mediation Directive. In Sweden, the changes made were mostly formal ones, and were carried out only because of the duty to implement; there was no effort made to 'implement' the Mediation Directive in practice by changing procedures and practices substantively too. In Finland, by contrast, a great deal of effort has been put into developing mediation as a substantive tool in dispute resolution.[81]

The differences in legal culture lead to national variations, which still exist in spite of harmonisation. The implementation of EU law can be substantive and deep, and affect into the whole legal culture – or it can be more or less superficial and done mainly formally, with the real substance of law still continuing to be based on the national way of thinking. Which approach is used depends on the national legal culture and mentality. I used the term 'used' on purpose, instead of using 'chosen', because of the fact that legal culture is a long-lasting tradition and habit instead of a pure choice.

[80] Laura Ervo, 'The status of the case-law from the European court of human rights in the national legal practice – A question of the local legal culture? East-Nordic comparisons' (2018) *Law Review* 15–16; and Laura Ervo, 'Ne bis in idem-problematiken i Norden: varför är det så svårt att acceptera Europadomstolens rättspraxis?' in Andreas Anderberg (ed.), *Festkrift till Josef Zila* (Iustius förlag 2013) 39–52.

[81] Ervo (n 24) 661–679.

AN EXAMINATION OF THE INFLUENCE OF EUROPEAN UNION LAW ON ENGLISH CIVIL PROCEDURE

John SORABJI

1. INTRODUCTION

Since the United Kingdom joined the European Economic Community in the early 1970s, English and Welsh (English) civil procedure has been subject to significant reform. It underwent radical change, which was described at the time as the most important set of reforms since the 1870s,[1] in the early 1990s as a result of the Civil Justice Review.[2] They were however as nothing compared to reforms implemented less than a decade later. In 1999, as a direct consequence of the Woolf Reforms,[3] English civil procedure saw its two codes of civil procedure replaced by a new, unitary code – the Civil Procedure Rules[4] (the CPR) – applicable to all civil proceedings in all civil courts. While the CPR was understood to be drafted so as to be consistent with the provisions of the European Convention on Human Rights,[5] specifically its Article 6, the influence

1 J. JACOB (ed), *Supreme Court Practice* (Sweet & Maxwell 1993) vol 1 at vii.

2 Report of the Review Body on Civil Justice (Command Paper 394 of 1988).

3 H. WOOLF, *Access to Justice: Interim Report to the Lord Chancellor on the Civil Justice System in England and Wales* (HMSO 1995); H. WOOLF, *Access to Justice: Final Report to the Lord Chancellor on the Civil Justice System in England and Wales* (HMSO 1996).

4 SI 1998/3121.

5 See, for instance, J. JACOB, *Civil Justice in the Age of Human Rights* (Ashgate 2007). It is arguable that its influence on the exact nature of English procedure has in fact been rather muted given that it is shaped by the common law right to fair trial, the elements of which mirror those within the Convention; see further J. SORABJI, 'Article 6: A Triumph of Style over Substance?' in D. HOFFMAN (ed), *The Impact of the UK Human Rights Act on Private Law* (CUP 2011).

of European Union law on both it and its predecessors, and on English procedure in general, has been limited.

Two areas of development are examined here and are illustrative of the absence of significant influence: first, the impact of the European Small Claims Procedure on the comparable English procedure; and secondly, the impact of the European Order for Payment on the manner in which debt claims are dealt with in England. In both cases, the European developments significantly post-date comparable ones in England. And both cases, those European developments have had no real, if any, influence on the English mechanisms. On the contrary, in both cases English and European procedures run parallel within England and no more than that: EU legislation has had no real positive influence in the sense of promoting new developments or revisions to the procedural code.[6] I look at each in turn.

2. SMALL CLAIMS PROCEDURES

In this section the impact of European Union developments in the areas of small claims, payment orders and mediation is examined. In each case it will be seen that this influence has been, at best, minimal. The reason for this is that these developments arise in areas where English procedure already has a longstanding and well-developed regime, the consequence of which is a blunting of the possibility of influence. That there was such a well-developed regime in place meant that what European Union developments there have been have simply been adopted alongside but separate from the established English procedure. There was simply no real scope for those developments to have any real influence.

The English civil justice system has had a uniform small claims process since the creation of the county courts in 1846, now the single County Court for England and Wales.[7] At that time their jurisdiction encompassed claims up to a value of £20.[8] By 1903, their jurisdiction had been increased to £100,[9] while by 1955 their jurisdiction was £400.[10] The county courts' jurisdiction was not only

---

6 One further area of EU developments is not dealt with here: the effect of the Brussels Regulation and its successor on the use of anti-suit injunctions is not considered (Regulation (EC) 44/2001 on jurisdiction and the recognition and enforcement of judgments in civil and commercial matters (Brussels I Regulation) [2001] OJ L12/1; Regulation (EC) 1215/2012 on jurisdiction and the recognition and enforcement in civil and commercial matters (Brussels I *bis* Regulation) [2012] OJ L351/1). It is not because it has not influenced the development of anti-suit injunctions, but has rather simply prohibited their use where the Regulation applies: see *Turner v Grovit* [2005] 1 AC 101.

7 County Courts (England) Act 1846; Crime and Courts Act 2013, s 17.

8 County Courts (England) Act 1846, s 57.

9 County Courts Act 1903, s 3.

10 County Courts Act 1955, s 1.

limited to low value claims, it also provided a simple form of procedure through which they could be pursued.[11] By the early 1970s, the provision of a simplified form of procedure for low-value claims was not considered to be suitable for all such claims, and for the lowest-value claims a simpler form of process was introduced.

This new procedure for the lowest-value claims was originally built on a statutory power that enabled a County Court judge, with the consent of the parties, to direct their dispute to be dealt with informally through arbitral proceedings, known as a 'small claims arbitration'.[12] In 1973, this power was extended. The informal, consent-based, arbitral procedure became a small claims process carried out by a County Court Registrar,[13] the most junior judicial office-holder at the time. It remained informal, but was no longer based on consent as it formed part of the normal adjudicative process, i.e. it concluded with a trial and judgment. It was applicable to all claims with a value below £100.[14] That limit stood until 1991, when it was raised to £1,000. It was then raised again in 1996 to £3,000. In 1999, when following the Woolf Reforms, the small claims procedure was further formalised as one of the procedural case tracks of the Civil Procedure Rules (CPR), it became known as the small claims track. Its limit was then set at £5,000.[15] It remained at that limit until 2013, when it was raised to £10,000.[16] The majority of all civil claims are dealt with on the small claims track.[17] As Cortes has rightly noted, such claims tend to be 'related to debts, compensation for faulty services or goods and disputes between landlords and tenants',[18] as well as road traffic accidents and low-value personal injury claims. Litigants may be individuals or businesses; there is no restriction on who may bring or defend a claim.

---

11 See, for instance, County Court Rules 1981 (1687/1981) Ord. 19; for an outline of the history and development, see N. Madge, *Small claims in the county court* (2004) 23 *CJQ* 201.

12 Madge (n 11) 202.

13 The office of County Court Registrar is now that of District Judge.

14 Woolf, *Access to Justice: Interim Report* (n 3) 102: 'The small claims procedure has been progressively refined over the 20 years since it was first introduced in 1973 ... The first scheme built on an existing statutory procedure which allowed a county court judge to refer cases to arbitration with the consent of the parties.'

15 CPR Pt 27; R. Scott (ed), *Civil Procedure* (Sweet & Maxwell 1999) 260.

16 Civil Procedure (Amendment) Rules 2013 (SI 2013/262) Art 9. The limit for personal injury claims remained, however, at its historic limit of £1,000. The small claims procedure was also available for claims above the financial threshold with the consent of the parties. Consent is no longer necessary for the court to allocate a high value claim to the small claims track: Civil Procedure (Amendment) Rules 2013, Art 8 as explained in R. Jackson (ed), *Civil Procedure: The White Book 2015* (Sweet & Maxwell 2015) 26.7.1.

17 R. Jackson, *Review of Civil Litigation Costs: Preliminary Report* (Judicial Office 2009) vol 1 at 47 and 108.

18 P. Cortes, 'Does the proposed European procedure enhance the resolution of small claims?' (2008) 27 *CJQ* 83, 86.

This small claims procedure was, when introduced, intended to be 'an accessible, quick, cheap and informal means of deciding disputed civil claims which involve comparatively small sums of money.'[19] While what is understood to be such an amount of money has, as noted above, changed since 1973, the intention remains the same. It remains a straightforward, accessible, inexpensive and – importantly – proportionate means for determining low-value disputes. The procedure itself differs in three fundamental ways from English civil procedure generally, each way being an aspect of its simplicity and proportionality.

First, there is an expectation that a significant number of litigants whose claims are allocated to this track will not be legally represented: their claim will neither be formulated and drafted by a lawyer, nor will they have an advocate representing them in court. To facilitate this, the normal restriction on rights of audience, which ordinarily only permits barristers or solicitors to represent litigants before a court, are relaxed.[20] Litigants will either represent themselves or they may be represented by non-lawyers. In this way, the expectation that the cost of litigating for claims allocated to this track is intended to be achieved. It should, however, be noted that, notwithstanding this approach, small claims proceedings are not typically lawyer-less proceedings. While no figures are available concerning the percentage of small claims where the parties are represented, it is commonplace for such proceedings to be the effective starting point for the careers of junior barristers, who will typically be instructed to represent parties in road traffic accident claims.

This leads to the second feature of the small claims track: the role of the judge. The traditional and general approach in English procedure is that, as an aspect of its adversarial process, the parties are in control of presenting their respective cases during a trial hearing. Parties present and challenge evidence. They examine and cross-examine witnesses. And they present legal argument. While the judge may, and often does, ask clarificatory questions of parties, witnesses and the parties' legal representatives, the judicial role remains one of ensuring that the parties abide by applicable rules of procedure in presenting their cases. The approach in small claims proceedings is markedly different. From the early 1990s, the judicial role in such proceedings (at the time still small claims arbitrations) has been markedly inquisitorial or interventionist.[21]

---

19 Report of the Review Body on Civil Justice (Command Paper 394 of 1988) cited in WOOLF, *Access to Justice: Interim Report* (n 3) 104.

20 Legal Services Act 2007, Part 3; The Lay Representatives (Rights of Audience) Order 1999; CPR PD27 para 3.1.

21 J. BALDWIN, 'Small claims hearings: the "interventionist" role played by district judges' (1998) 17 *CJQ* 20.

Appleby described the change in approach from that adopted previously in small claims and that adopted generally in English civil procedure, at the time:

> The Civil Justice Review recommended a more interventionist role for judges, dispensing with the formal rules of evidence and assuming control of the questioning of the parties and witnesses by the arbitrators.[22]

That change in approach was introduced in 1992. It was confirmed in the transformation of small claims arbitration into the CPR's small claims track in 1999, when the nature of the judicial role was explained by Lord Woolf in the following terms:

> The role of the judge in small claims is not only that of an adjudicator. It is a key safeguard of the rights of both parties. In most cases, the judge is effectively a substitute for a legal representative. His duty is to ascertain the main matters at issue, to elicit the evidence, to reach a view on the facts of the matter and to give a decision. In some cases he may encourage the parties to settle. In doing so he should ensure that both parties have presented the evidence and called the witnesses germane to their case and that he has identified and considered any issue of law which is pertinent to the case in hand. He must also hold the ring and ensure that each party has a fair chance to present his own case and to challenge that of his opponent.[23]

This approach is now set out in CPR r.27.8(1), which provides that: 'The court may adopt any method of proceeding at a hearing that it considers to be fair.' This is non-exhaustively elaborated in CPR PD28 paragraph 4.3, which clarifies the nature of the interventionist role concerning evidence-taking at trial:

> Rule 27.8 allows the court to adopt any method of proceeding that it considers to be fair and to limit cross-examination. The judge may in particular:
>
> (1) ask questions of any witness himself before allowing any other person to do so,
> (2) ask questions of all or any of the witnesses himself before allowing any other person to ask questions of any witnesses …

This stands in marked contrast to the general restriction on judges questioning witnesses, where robust judicial intervention is generally discouraged and can, if it is seen to be too interventionist, result in judgments being set aside on appeal.[24]

22 G. Appleby, 'Legislative Comment – New county court rules for small claims' (1993) 12 *CJQ* 20, 21.

23 Woolf, *Access to Justice: Interim Report* (n 3) 108.

24 *Jones v National Coal Board* [1957] 2 QB 55; *Southwark LBC v Kofi-Adu* [2006] EWCA Civ 281; [2006] HLR 33; *Shaw v Grouby* [2017] EWCA Civ 233.

The interventionist approach on the small claims track will, even where parties are legally represented, typically see the District Judge explain the purpose of the trial hearing at its outset. They will then go on to explain their role, before moving to ask the parties to explain what the dispute concerns. They tell which party to speak and in which order, and will question them and their witnesses. Parties' legal representatives are also able to question and cross-examine, but their scope for doing so can and may well be circumscribed depending on how interventionist an approach the District Judge adopts.

In order to facilitate the interventionist approach, procedure – the third distinct feature of the small claims track – differs fundamentally from the general approach in English civil procedure.[25] In the first instance, pre-trial case management is kept to a minimum. Statements of case are generally straightforward; as Baldwin put it in 1998, and the position remains true today, 'For the most part the papers are very straightforward, consisting of a summons and a defence, and they usually require no more than a few minutes to read in their entirety'.[26] Standard case management directions apply, with a pre-trial case management conference being very much the exception rather than the rule. Evidential disclosure is kept to a minimum. Parties are only required disclose to their opponent evidence on which they intend to rely. It is often the case that disclosure does not occur until the hearing, particularly where the parties act in-person. Expert evidence is generally not permissible. The court may also recommend that parties take part in a small claims mediation scheme while they await their claim coming to trial.[27] The trial itself takes place in the judge's chambers rather than in a formal courtroom. It generally takes place with the parties sitting round the judge's table. Evidence is not given on oath, although parties are informed at the start of the hearing that they are expected to tell the truth. The formal rules of evidence do not apply. The trial length is generally limited to an hour, although some hearings may last up to three hours. The general costs rules do not apply. While the 'loser pays' rule applies, recoverable costs are limited to a fixed amount covering the fee to issue the claim or defence and, if legally represented, a very low fixed legal fee.[28] Witnesses for the successful party may recover reasonable expenses. The parties may also agree to have the claim determined entirely on the papers, i.e. they may agree to waive the right to a trial hearing.[29] Additionally, at a small claims trial hearing, the District Judge may encourage parties to try to reach a settlement. Judgments tend to be delivered

---

25 See CPR Pt 27 and PD27.

26 Baldwin (n 21) 23. The 'summons' is under the CPR equivalent to the claim form and particulars of claim.

27 See J. Sorabji, 'Austerity's effect on English Civil Justice' (2015) *Erasmus L Rev* 159.

28 CPR r.27.14(2)(g).

29 CPR r.2.7.10.

orally at the end of the hearing. Appeals are possible; however, as is the case generally, they may only be brought with the court's permission.[30]

By the time the European Small Claims Procedure (ESCP) was proposed in 2005 and came into force in 2009, England had had a fully developed small claims procedure since the 1970s.[31] It was well-established and had been reinvigorated through its incorporation as a fundamental aspect of the Woolf Reforms' procedural case track approach introduced in 1999 via the CPR. The ESCP introduced a cross-border small claims procedure that in many ways was analogous to that provided for by the English small claims track. It applied to low-value civil and commercial claims (initially below €2,000 and then post-2017 below €5,000). It provided a streamlined procedure designed to be used by litigants-in-person. It was primarily paper-based, albeit with an option for an oral hearing. It was introduced into English civil procedure not through any amendment to CPR Pt 27, i.e. the domestic rules governing small claims, but via a new and separate part of the CPR, Pt 78.[32] More significantly, in terms of its treatment within the overall architecture of English civil procedure, claims brought under the ESCP are 'treated as if they were allocated to the small claims track' except in respect of costs, matters such as the written nature of the procedure, time limits and, since the increase in the small claims track's financial threshold to £10,000, the financial threshold.[33] Since its introduction it has, as noted in the leading English procedural commentary, 'not been widely or frequently used'.[34] It was, for instance, only used 526 times in 2012–2013. This compares with 54,575 small claims trials (which necessarily form a small percentage of the total usage of the small claims track procedure itself) in the same period.[35]

Setting aside questions as to its lack of use,[36] its impact, in terms of the development of English procedure, has amounted to no more than a dead letter. It can fairly be said to have had no influence on English procedure. No changes

30 CPR Pt 52.

31 See Cortes (n 18) 88, for an outline; Regulation (EC) 861/2007 establishing a European Small Claims Procedure [2007] OJ L199/1.

32 Civil Procedure (Amendment) Rules 2008 (SI 2008/2178).

33 CPR r.78.14 on allocation, and see CPR rr.78.13–78.19 for specific differences in approach.

34 G. Vos (ed), *Civil Procedure* (Thomson Reuters 2018) ch 3L-16.

35 ECC-Net, *European Small Claims Procedure Report* (ECC-Net 2012) 23; The Law Society, *Response to consultation on European Small Claims Procedure* (The Law Society 2013) 3; The Law Society of England and Wales, *Review of the Balance of Competences between the United Kingdom and the European Union – Civil Judicial Co-operation* (The Law Society 2013) 38 ff; Court Statistics, Main Tables <https://www.gov.uk/government/statistics/court-statistics-quarterly-april-to-june-2014> accessed 21 June 2018.

36 Briefly put, its lack of utility appears to stem from its low financial threshold and the unwieldy nature of its language translation requirements. Questions might also be raised concerning litigant confidence in using a system which is entirely paper-based and in which they have little to no practical participation.

were effected to the small claims track procedure in the light of its introduction. No consideration was, for instance, apparently taken to alter the default position under the small claims track that the trial would be an oral one to that provided by the ESCP. In other words, the civil approach to adjudication via a paper-based determination[37] was not considered for adoption via amendment to CPR Pt 27. On the contrary, the ESCP was not integrated into CPR Pt 27; it was compartmentalised within 'European Procedures' in the CPR in Pt 78, and the small claims track procedure was applied to it. Rather than influencing English procedure, it was simply treated as an extension of English procedure. Two reasons can explain this.

First, the ESCP incorporated no real developments of or improvements upon the small claims track procedure in terms of domestic procedure. Apart from its approach to paper-based determinations, which are antithetical to the common law approach to the trial process, it did not differ in any substantive way from the streamlined process available via the small claims track. If it were to have had any impact, it would have had to have not only differed substantively but in such differences it would have had to provide a better, more efficient and more effective mechanism than that already provided for in English procedure. It did neither of these things. If the depth of impact is a function of the nature of a novel processes improvement over existing procedure, then, conversely, a lack of novelty and improvement cannot but point towards a shallow impact, if any at all.

Secondly, and this follows from the previous point, the success of the small claims track and the fact that it is long-established, provides a structural disincentive to consider procedural revision in the light of the ESCP. If England had only recently introduced its own small claims procedure, or if its own procedure were seen to suffer from structural or procedural weaknesses, an alternative mechanism such as the ESCP might have provided the basis for a principled reconsideration of the domestic approach. If this had been the case, the ESCP might have been able to exert a significant and positive influence on domestic developments. Neither of these points held true, however. As such, the potential for influence did not arise in fertile ground. Exactly the same considerations arose in respect of European Union developments concerning the European Order for Payment.

3. PAYMENT ORDERS

The European Order for Payment (EOP) introduced a cross-border mechanisms for low-value uncontested debt claims.[38] As with the ESCP, it provides a

37 Cortes (n 18) 92.

38 Regulation (EC) 1896/2006 on a European order for payment procedure [2006] OJ L339/1.

simplified form of procedure with short procedural time limits. The procedure is written. Where a defendant opposes the application, it is transferred to the applicable national process for contested claims. It was introduced into English civil procedure in the same way as the ESCP was introduced, i.e. they were both introduced via CPR Pt 78. As with the ESCP, it was not incorporated into the existing English mechanisms, but was treated as a discrete measure; it too was compartmentalised. Its influence has consequently been equally muted. The underlying explanation for this is the same as that which underpins the negligible impact of the ESCP on procedural reform. Both the EOP and the ESCP deal with matters where there were well-established domestic mechanisms and approaches.

As noted above, the EOP's focus is uncontested debt claims, although it necessarily provides a means to exit the process where the debt claimed under it is, in fact, disputed. It is thus, in essence, a means of facilitating debt enforcement through a simple and cost-effective court procedure. English procedure has had such a process since 1855, when the statutory Summary Procedure on Bills of Exchange Act was introduced.[39] It was introduced in order to provide, as with the EOP, a means to secure, via a truncated process, the means by which a creditor could demand payment from a debtor where they believed there was no defence to the debt claim, which, unless the debtor then contested the claim, would result in judgment being entered for the creditor. As Clark and Samenow described it, under the 1855 procedure,

> judgment may be entered summarily for the plaintiff in the more usual types of civil actions, on motion setting forth his demand and his belief that there is no defense to it, unless the defendant, by counter-affidavit, shows that the facts are in dispute.[40]

That statutory procedure was formally incorporated into English civil procedure via the Rules of the Supreme Court (RSC) when it was introduced in 1875: the specific rule on summary judgment being set out in RSC Ord. 14. The lineal successor to that rule is now contained in the procedure for judgment in default of either an acknowledgment of service or a defence in CPR Pt 12.[41] This provision enables the court to award judgment as an administrative act

---

39 J. Bauman, 'The Evolution of the Summary Judgment Procedure: An Essay Commemorating the Centennial Anniversary of Keating' (1956) 31(3) *Indiana LJ* 329.

40 C. Clark and C. Samenow, 'The Summary Judgment' (1929) 38 *Yale LJ* 423.

41 This is to be contrasted with the present summary judgment process contained in CPR Pt 24, which is the means by which a claimant or a defendant in a contested claim can seek an early final judgment on the merits where the claim or defence is not sufficiently robust as to justify the application of the full pre-trial and trial process. It enables a claim or defence to be determined on its merits on the basis that the case taken at its highest has no real prospect of success at a full trial or, where that is the case, there is no other good reason why it should be permitted to continue to trial: CPR r.24.2.

where a defendant chooses not to contest the claimant's claim by either failing to acknowledgment receipt of the claim form or, having acknowledged receipt, failing to submit a defence to the claim. Judgment can be obtained in this way 28 days after service of the claim form and particulars of claim on a defendant.[42]

In addition to the default judgment process, English procedure also provides a means to seek the payment of debt claims for a specified amount up to £100,000 through a streamlined online process: Money Claims Online (MCOL).[43] Again, this simple process enables a claimant to obtain a judgment in default to secure payment of the debt where a defendant chooses to, or fails to, submit an acknowledgement of service or defence to the claim. By way of illustration, from October to December 2017, 225,000 out of 265,000 judgments were determined by way of default judgment, i.e. 85% of all civil judgments.[44] Additionally, in respect of claims pursued through MCOL, this was noted in the Civil Courts Structure Review (admittedly in 2015) to process approximately 750,000 claims per annum, of which 95% were undefended and hence resulted in a default judgment.[45]

Both the English default judgment procedure and MCOL and the EOP provide truncated processes through which creditors can achieve an enforceable judgment on a claimed debt. They each provide the possibility for a debtor to challenge the claim. English procedure achieves this straightforwardly: all a defendant need do is submit a defence, and the claim, whether online or otherwise, then proceeds normally through the pre-trial case management process. The default judgment and MCOL processes are just a specific application of general civil procedure process. The EOP achieves the same, as it provides for a contested claim to be transferred to the relevant EU Member State's domestic civil procedure.[46] It may not be a specific instance of the generally applicable process, but it is incorporated into it via the transfer process. In England this is achieved through CPR r.78.5, which deems a contested EOP to be a claim commenced under its regular civil process, i.e. as where a defendant defends a domestic civil claim it proceeds through the normal CPR pre-trial case management process. In this

---

42 CPR r.12.3, r.15.4.

43 See Money Claim Online (MCOL) – User Guide for Claimants <https://assets.publishing.service.gov.uk/government/uploads/system/uploads/attachment_data/file/684567/MCOL_Userguide_for_Claimants_August_2017.pdf> accessed 21 June 2018. For an interesting discussion of MCOL, see G. Lupo, 'Building Interoperability in European Civil Procedures Online – England and Wales Case: The Case of Money Claim Online and Possession Claim Online in England and Wales' (2012) <http://www.irsig.cnr.it/BIEPCO/documents/case_studies/MCOL_Lupo_FINAL%20REVISION.pdf> accessed 21 June 2018.

44 HMCTS, 'Quarterly Statistics October to December 2017' 6 <https://assets.publishing.service.gov.uk/government/uploads/system/uploads/attachment_data/file/684410/civil-justice-statistics-quarterly-oct-dec-2017.pdf> accessed 21 June 2018.

45 M. Briggs, *Civil Court Structure Review – Interim Report* (Judicial Office 2015) 16.

46 Regulation (EC) 1896/2006 on a European order for payment procedure [2006] OJ L339/1, Art 17(1).

way it mirrors the relationship that the ESCP has with the English small claims process: the EOP provides a cross-border mechanism which to all practical purposes replicates a well-established domestic procedure.

Here lies the reason why the EOP has had no real impact on English civil procedure. As with the ESCP, there was a well-established, effective domestic procedure. And again, as with the ESCP, the EOP provided no real and specific procedural improvement over and above that which was already available through the domestic civil procedure. For instance, it provided a process that offered the prospect of a payment order being made in a comparable timeframe to that available under the CPR default judgment process: 30 days in comparison to 28 days under the CPR's default judgment process.[47] It equally provided a simplified form through which an EOP could be sent.[48] Again, this mirrors the simplified process under MCOL[49] and that which is available under the CPR;[50] the latter permitted claims to be drafted in very simple terms. Apart from its ease of enforceability across the European Union, the EOP provided no procedural advantage or innovation that could have been drawn upon to reshape English procedure. Again, the depth of influence in domestic procedure by hard law is a function of innovation and advantage over domestic procedure. In the absence of perceived defects in the domestic procedure and perceived advantage or innovation in the EOP, both the impetus for and means to influence procedural development in the field of default judgment was lacking.

4. CONCLUSION

The English civil justice system is, historically, a product of many sources. Its process for issuing claims can be traced back to the Anglo-Norman formulary system introduced after the Norman conquest of 1066. Its disclosure process, unique to the common law, is a direct inheritance from Canon law procedure.[51] It might have been expected that, as has been the case in respect of substantive EU law and jurisprudence arising from the UK's accession to the European Convention on Human Rights, these historic influences would have been reinvigorated as a result of EU procedural law developments. In the main, that has not been the case. What has, however, been seen is minimal influence. EU developments have not brought about reform in England. On the contrary, they have been absorbed into English procedure through their transformation

[47] Ibid, Art 12(1).

[48] Ibid, Form A.

[49] CPR PD7E paras 5.1 and 5.2.

[50] CPR r.16.4.

[51] R. van Caenegem, *European law in the past and the future* (CUP 2002) 2; H. Coing, 'English Equity and the Denunciatio Evangelica of the Canon Law' (1955) 71 *LQR* 223.

into discrete, and self-contained, aspects of it, having effected no change to extant English process.

With Brexit on the near horizon in March 2019, European influence on English procedure ought not therefore be substantively affected. This ought to be the case for two reasons. First, direct EU influence through hard law, as illustrated by the impact or lack of it which the ESCP and EOP have had on the structure and process within England's CPR, has been minimal. What may then be lost post-Brexit would appear to be the possibility of comparably minimal influence in the future. Secondly, as noted by Stürner, English procedure has been moving towards the approach taken by continental European civil procedure for some time now.[52] The common and civil law traditions are moving closer together. That they have been doing has not been a consequence of European Union law, but rather due to a wider exchange of ideas between academics, policy-makers and judiciaries. There the European Union has perhaps had real influence: through facilitating and encouraging intra-European dialogue, it has helped promote greater understanding, commonality and exposure to different and sometimes better ways of approaching questions of civil process. This influence may be unacknowledged and unconscious; it is, for instance, arguable that the CPR's approach to case management owed as much to the unconscious influence of Franz Klein through a greater understanding of German civil procedure in the 1990s in England as it did to developments in case management in the United States of America. Equally, this influence may also flow from a greater understanding of EU Member States' domestic developments, which will itself continue unabated post-Brexit. The influence, for instance, that developments in online justice via the Rechtwijzer in the Netherlands had on reforms to the English civil justice system is a case in point. Those developments underpinned the arguments for developing an online court process in England in 2015, developments which, at the time of writing in 2018, are being implemented.[53] Via such soft forms of influence, EU hard law developments may well, through reforming Member States' procedural systems, indirectly influence future English developments. Perhaps the lesson to take is that where procedural convergence is concerned, at least in England's case, soft law influences will prove in future to be more effective as means to shape procedural reform than hard law ones have in the past. Influence comes in many forms. At least in English terms, perhaps the most effective form of influence is one that flows from soft rather than hard sources.

---

52 R. Stürner, 'Anglo-American and Continental Civil Procedure' in M. Andenæs, N. Andrews and R. Nazzini (eds), *The Future of Transnational Civil Litigation* (British Institute of International and Comparative Law 2004) 11.

53 See, for instance, M. Briggs, *Civil Courts Structure Review – Interim Report* (Judiciary of England and Wales 2015) 51; M. Briggs, *Civil Courts Structure Review – Final Report* (Judiciary of England and Wales 2016); Civil Justice Council, *Online Dispute Resolution for Low Value Claims* (2015); for a discussion see J. Sorabji, 'The Online Solutions Court – A multi-door courthouse for the 21st Century' (2017) 36 *CJQ* 86.

THE EU'S INFLUENCE ON NORWEGIAN CIVIL PROCEDURE THROUGH NATIONAL SUBSTANTIVE LAW

Maria Astrup Hjort

1. INTRODUCTION

European Union Member States are said to have procedural autonomy as long as national civil procedure rules comply with the principles of equivalent and efficient enforcement of EU law.[1] However, over the years, the EU has increased its influence over national civil procedure on the pretext of adopting measures to establish and improve the functioning of the internal market.[2]

Not being part of the EU, it might seem like Norway has been largely a spectator to this development. However, Norway is a party to the Agreement on the European Economic Area (EEA), which extends the single market and free movement of goods, persons, services and capital between EU Member

1 Anna Nylund and Bart Krans, 'The European Union and National Civil Procedure – a Rocky Road or a Smooth Process?' in Anna Nylund and Bart Krans (eds), *The European Union and National Civil Procedure* (Intersentia 2016) 1.

2 Cf. Treaty of the Functioning of the European Union (TFEU), Arts. 81 and 114.

States and non-EU EEA Member States.[3] The Agreement, which is between the EU and European Free Trade Association (EFTA), came into force in 1994. National courts interpret the EEA Agreement in national proceedings. When interpretation of EEA law is unclear, the national court may request an advisory opinion from the EFTA Court.[4]

The EEA Agreement does not include any procedural regulation, but according to Article 3 of the agreement, '[t]he Contracting Parties shall take all appropriate measures ... to ensure fulfilment of the obligations arising out of this Agreement'. To reach the goal of the EEA Agreement – legal homogeneity and effectiveness in the EEA region – effective application of substantive law often requires changes to the national civil justice system.[5]

The EU/EEA principles of homogeneity and effectiveness were recognised in the preparatory works to the Norwegian Dispute Act, which was drafted in 2001, but the EU influence on Norwegian civil procedure was presented as being only modest.[6] The law commission that drafted the Dispute Act highlighted Article 3 of the EEA agreement, mentioned above, which is almost identical to Article 4(3) of the Treaty on European Union (TEU). It stated that being an EEA Member State had not led to a similar development to the one found in the EU, in terms of harmonisation or specific procedural rules. On the other hand, the law commission underlined that ongoing reforms in the EU could mean a greater impact on the national civil procedure rules of EEA Member States. The conclusion was, therefore, that the impact of the EU and of EEA membership on Norwegian civil procedure rules was 'uncertain'.[7]

The law commission also highlighted the principle of non-discrimination, as set out in Article 4 of the EEA Agreement, which is almost identical to Article 18 of the Treaty on the Functioning of the European Union (TFEU). Two of the provisions in the Dispute Act were designed to meet these conditions, as will be explained in more detail in sections 2 and 3 of this chapter. Finally, the law commission acknowledged that the EU and the EEA had resulted in the need for civil procedure rules in the two regions to be coordinated, but they argued that this had been attempted through separate treaties, particularly the Lugano Convention of 1988, the Brussels Convention of 1968 and the European Convention on Human Rights of 1950.[8]

---

3 See more about this relationship in Anna Nylund, 'Norway: An Insider Outside – or an Outsider Inside – European Civil Justice' in Anna Nylund and Bart Krans (eds), *The European Union and National Civil Procedure* (Intersentia 2016) 101.

4 EEA Agreement, Arts. 106–111; and Agreement between the EFTA States on the Establishment of a Surveillance Authority and a Court of Justice, Arts. 31–37.

5 Nylund (n 3) 101.

6 NOU 2001: 32 *Rett på sak* 154. See also the presentation of the Law commission's point of view in Halvard Haukeland Fredriksen, 'Tvisteloven og EØS-avtalen' (2008) *TfR* 289, 290–292.

7 NOU 2001: 32, 154.

8 NOU 2001: 32, 151–154.

In 2001, when the Norwegian Dispute Act was drafted, the EU's influence on Norwegian substantive law seemed quite limited. Article 81 TFEU on judicial co-operation in civil matters with cross-border implications and Article 114 TFEU on approximation of laws to ensure the functioning of the internal market were not considered to apply in Norway if the content was primarily procedural,[9] since this was beyond the scope of the EEA Agreement. The fact that secondary legislation from the EU does not have direct effect in the EEA reinforces this impression.[10] Norwegian case law points in the same direction.[11]

Despite this stance, EU directives have resulted in changes to the Dispute Act since its entry into force in 2008. This chapter will deal with how Norwegian civil procedural provisions are adapted to align with EU law through the EEA Agreement, what changes have been made to such provisions to accommodate EU law, why these changes have been made, and how the changes fit into the framework of national substantive law.

In addition to the Dispute Act,[12] the Courts Act[13] and the Enforcement Act,[14] civil procedural rules can be found in assorted provisions in other Norwegian acts. This chapter is limited to addressing changes to general procedural legislation.

2. EEA LAWYERS' ACCESS TO NORWAY IN ORDER TO PROVIDE LEGAL ASSISTANCE AND ACT AS COUNSEL

As described above, there are two provisions in the Dispute Act that already showed the influence of the EEA Agreement when the act was drafted. One of these is section 3-3(6), which contains the obligation to give lawyers from other EEA states access to Norway to provide legal assistance and act as counsel, with reference to the rule of free movement of services and the principle of non-discrimination. In the preparatory works for section 3-3(6) of the Dispute Act, the law commission referred to the Norwegian Regulation of Advocates[15] and stressed that EEA lawyers are not dependent on any discretionary approval from the court. In Norwegian case law, only two cases from Norwegian courts have

9 Nylund (n 3) 102.

10 EEA Agreement, Art. 7(a).

11 Rt. 2000, 1811 and Rt. 2005, 1365.

12 Act 17 June 2005 no. 90.

13 Act 13 August 1915 no. 5.

14 Act 26 June 1992 no. 86.

15 Pursuant to chapter 11 of the Courts Act, this is further regulated in the Regulation of Advocates of 1996, chapters 9 and 10.

considered the question of approval of lawyers from other EEA states,[16] and in neither case was the EEA Agreement at the forefront. In other words, the question of allowing lawyers from other EEA states to provide legal assistance and act as counsel in Norway has minimal significance as a form of EU influence on substantive Norwegian civil procedure law.

3. SECURITY FOR LIABILITY FOR COSTS

The second provision from the Dispute Act that already showed the influence of the EEA Agreement when the act was drafted, is section 20-11. The provision applies to claimants who live abroad and requires them to provide security for liability for the litigation costs they may have to pay the other party as compensation. Such a rule conflicts with Article 4 of the EEA Agreement, which prohibits discrimination based on nationality within the scope of the Agreement, and EFTA Surveillance Authority pointed this out already in 1999.[17] An amendment was passed in 2001 in the previous Dispute Resolution Act where the following was added to the provision: 'Security cannot be required if the dispute falls within the scope of the EEA Agreement.'[18] In drafting the Dispute Act, the law commission stated that the 2001 amendment included cases covered by the EEA Agreement.[19] In order to cover bilateral agreements on not requiring security from claimants from the country concerned, the chosen wording was not directly linked to the EEA Agreement:

> Security cannot be required if it would be contrary to an international obligation to treat parties resident abroad and parties resident in Norway equally, or if it would seem disproportionate to the nature of the matter, the relationship of the party and the circumstances in general.

However, court practice has shown that there may be cases where this wording is still not sufficient. In the Supreme Court's decision of 16 February 2016, the Supreme Court's appeal committee stated that it was not only the direct discrimination that was contrary to Article 4 of the EEA Agreement, but also *indirect* discrimination.[20] The case concerned compensation for breach of a

16 A search on 1 November 2018 in the databases on <www.lovdata.no> for decisions in civil cases from all national instances about 'LOV-2005-06-17-90-§3-3' (Dispute Act section 3-3) and the keyword 'EØS' (EEA) returned seven results. Of those, only two decisions, LB-2013-186586 and LB-2010-112288, concerned access for lawyers from other EEA countries to provide legal assistance and act as counsel.

17 Ot.prp. no. 63 (2000–2001) *Om lov om endring i tvistemålslova (trygd for sakskostnader)* 1.

18 Act 13 August 1915 no. 6 on Dispute Resolution, section 182.

19 NOU 2001: 32, 938.

20 HR-2016-407-U.

contract for the purchase of a house in Norway, and the defendant demanded security for liability for the costs incurred because the claimant lived intermittently in Greece. The claimant alleged that this was contrary to Article 4 of the EEA Agreement on discrimination based on nationality. The appeal committee referred to the *Dr Kottke* case from the EFTA Court, stating that Article 4 also covers discrimination that is not directly related to nationality, but where the result is better treatment for the country's own citizens.[21] A claim that a claimant resident abroad should provide security would typically affect foreigners and could therefore lead to indirect discrimination and violation of Article 4 of the EEA Agreement.

The Supreme Court's appeal committee considered that real estate investment, which was at issue in this case, was to be considered as capital movement in the sense of EU law. The defendant's claim that the dispute fell outside the scope of the EEA Agreement was not upheld. With reference to the *Dr Kottke* case, the appeal committee stated that a claim for liability for costs appears to fall within the scope of the EEA Agreement, regardless of the underlying transaction.[22] The Court of First Instance's ruling was, therefore, overturned.

By letter of 13 July 2016, the EFTA Surveillance Authority concluded that the Dispute Act section 20-11 violated Article 4 of the EEA Agreement, as well as the rules on free movement of goods, persons, services and capital (Articles 28, 31, 36 and 40 of the EEA Agreement). On this basis, the wording of section 20-11(1) was changed:

> Security cannot be required *if the claimant is domiciled in an EEA State*, if it would be contrary to an international obligation to treat parties resident abroad and parties resident in Norway equally, or if it would seem disproportionate to the nature of the matter, the relationship of the party and the circumstances in general. (emphasis added)

The appeal committee referred to the *Dr Kottke* case, where a claim for liability for costs appeared to fall within the scope of the EEA Agreement regardless of the underlying transaction. Despite this, the Ministry of Justice and Public Security stressed in the preparatory works for the amendment that a claim for security for costs would depend on whether the object of the dispute fell within the scope of the EEA Agreement or not.[23] The claim for liability for costs would in the ministry's view only violate Article 4 of the EEA Agreement if the object of the dispute fell within the scope of the EEA Agreement. However, it acknowledged that a general prohibition on claiming collateral for costs for claimants living

---

21 Case E-5/10 *Dr Joachim Kottke v Präsidial Anstalt and Sweetyle Stiftung*, EFTA Ct. Rep. 320, paras. 29 and 30. See the Supreme Court appeal committee's summary of the case in HR-2016-407-U, para. 13.

22 HR-2016-407-U, para. 16.

23 Prop. 42 L (2016–2017), *Endringer i tvisteloven (sikkerhet for sakskostnader)* 7.

in an EEA state would create predictability, would be practicable and might seem less process-driven than the existing legal situation.[24] The new wording, therefore, applies regardless of the object of the dispute.

The Ministry's emphasis on the fact that some cases might fall outside the scope of the EEA Agreement appears hollow, all the time the amendment in the end included all types of cases, irrespective of the object of the dispute. It may seem as if the ministry finds a point in itself to emphasise that Norway's obligations are limited and that the legislation is made on a voluntary basis.

4. INFORMATION ORDERS

Chapters 26, 27 and 28 of the Dispute Act contain different procedures for gaining access to evidence. The procedures are applicable in all sorts of civil cases. In 2013, a new chapter, chapter 28 A, was added to the Dispute Act. This chapter only applies to intellectual property disputes. Through so-called 'information orders', the provisions seek to ensure the ability to identify both the manufacturer and the distribution networks of goods or services which infringe an intellectual property right. Before chapter 28 A came into force, there were no rules expressly giving the intellectual property rights holder this ability. Admittedly, the more general rules in chapter 28 on the securing of evidence do provide for the securing of evidence if 'there is a clear risk of the evidence being lost or considerably impaired, or if there are other reasons why it is of particular importance to obtain access to such evidence prior to the lawsuit being initiated'. However, it was emphasised in the preparatory works that 'this is an exception rule with a relatively narrow scope'.[25] Furthermore, the rules on information orders give the rights holder both a greater possibility of accessing information than the other evidence rules in the Dispute Act and the ability to access information in much greater detail. Information that is not necessarily important as evidence in the case but is important as a tool to track down the manufacturer and distribution team could typically be given to the rights holder according to the rules on information orders, but not according to the other evidence rules. The rules on information orders actually provide the ability to carry out something resembling an investigation, in order to find the person who has infringed the rights holder's rights.

Chapter 28 A of the Dispute Act is based on Article 8 in Directive 2004/48/EC on the enforcement of intellectual property rights. The Directive contains procedural rules, but since such rules fall outside the scope of the EEA Agreement, Norway is therefore not obliged to implement the Directive. In the

---

24 Prop. 42 L (2016–2017) 7–8.

25 NOU 2001: 32, 988.

preparatory works to chapter 28 A, the Ministry of Justice and Public Security emphasised that the current Norwegian law was 'as favourable to the rights holder as the minimum requirements of the Directive with regards to the means of enforcement available at the time of intervention'.[26] However, the ministry acknowledged that the Directive's rules on the right to information on the origin and distribution networks gave rights holders a stronger position than under Norwegian law. Referring to the Directive and amendments made in Denmark and Sweden as a result of the Directive, the Norwegian government found that Norway also should have rules that satisfied the requirements of the Directive.[27] It was a guiding principle for the drafting of the provisions that the rules should be at least as favourable to rights holders in Norway as in the EU.[28] The Directive was implemented on a voluntary basis. The chapter is a lightly adapted version of Article 8 of the Directive on 'right of information'.

So far, the rules on information orders seem to have had limited impact. A search for cases in the Lovdata database for all civil cases at all instances mentioning provisions from chapter 28 A of the Dispute Act returned just two results.[29] It is, of course, possible that there exist some cases that were heard in the lower courts but not registered in the database; however, the search still paints a picture of a set of rules that are seldom used.

5. THE LUGANO CONVENTION

The Convention on jurisdiction and the recognition and enforcement of judgments in civil and commercial matters was settled in Lugano on 16 September 1988, long before the work on the EEA Agreement was commenced and before the discussion on the EU's impact on Norwegian litigation had started. The Convention was incorporated into Norwegian law in 1993 through a separate act.[30] For EU Member States, the Convention on the jurisdiction and enforcement of judgments in civil and commercial matters of 27 September 1968 (the Brussels Convention) is a parallel instrument to the 1988 Lugano

26 Prop. 81 L (2012–2013), *Endringer i lovgivningen om industrielt rettsvern m.m. (styrking av håndhevingsreglene)* 9.

27 Prop. 81 L (2012–2013) 68.

28 Prop. 81 L (2012–2013) 13.

29 Lovdata is a Norwegian database containing all judgments from the Supreme Court, all judgments from the six Courts of Appeal, and selected judgments from the District Courts. Search in Lovdata 1 November 2018 with the search term 'LOV-2005-06-17-90-§28A-*', i.e. provisions from the Dispute Act chapter 28 A. The search resulted in two decisions: The Supreme Court's decision from 17 January 2018 (HR-2018-110-A) and Frostating Court of Appeal's decision from 26 May 2015 (LF-2015-27853).

30 Act 8 January 1993 no. 21 on implementation of the Convention on jurisdiction and the recognition and enforcement of judgments in civil and commercial matters.

Convention. These two regulations exist side by side, but have only to a small extent been influenced by each other.

In drafting the Dispute Act, the law commission emphasised that the rules on jurisdiction in the Dispute Act should be harmonised as far as possible with the rules in the Norwegian Lugano Act of 1993, incorporating the Lugano Convention from 1988 into Norwegian law.[31]

However, after the Dispute Act has been enacted, a new Lugano Convention was negotiated in 2007. This came into force in 2010 and replaced the former Lugano Convention from 1988. The material content is essentially the same as the former Convention, but the relationship to the EU is different. Firstly, the 2007 Lugano Convention was conceived as a parallel to Regulation (EC) 44/2001. Admittedly, the two are no longer completely parallel because a revised version of the Regulation has since come into force, but the similarity is still striking.[32]

Secondly, the EU itself is a party to the Convention, rather than each individual Member State.[33] Thus, the Convention's geographic scope has extended to include states that were not parties to the 1988 Convention. This was also important in the negotiation process because the EU negotiated the Convention on behalf of all Member States. The EU, Norway, Denmark, Iceland and Switzerland have today ratified the Convention.[34]

Thirdly, the European Court of Justice (ECJ) is given the status of a supreme court to interpret both Brussels I and the Lugano Convention. Protocol 2 to the Lugano Convention states in Article 1 that any court 'shall take due account of the principles arising from any relevant decision taken by the courts of the Constitutional States and the Court of Justice of the European Union'. In theory, the ECJ should have studied how the Convention is interpreted in Norway, Switzerland, Iceland and Denmark. All Member States are equal to the Lugano convention, so decisions on interpretation of the Convention in other Member States are legal sources regardless of Member State. However, in practice, everyone looks to decisions from the ECJ.[35]

The Lugano Convention of 2007 entered into force on 1 January 2010 and was, at the same time, integrated into Norwegian legislation by incorporation

---

31 NOU 2001: 32, 676.

32 Regulation (EC) 1215/2012 on jurisdiction and the recognition and enforcement in civil and commercial matters (Brussels I *bis* Regulation) [2012] OJ L351/1. See also Nylund (n 3) 104.

33 Convention of 13 October 2007 on jurisdiction and the recognition and enforcement of judgments in civil and commercial matters (Lugano Convention) [2007] OJ L339/3, Art. 69.

34 Denmark is an independent party to the Convention because it does not participate in internal justice co-operation in the EU, which provides the basis for the EU to act as a party in cases on behalf of the Member States. See Ot.prp. no. 89 (2008–2009), *Om lov om endringer i tvisteloven m.m. og om samtykke til ratifikasjon av Luganokonvensjonen 2007 om domsmyndighet og om anerkjennelse og fullbyrdelse av dommer i sivile og kommersielle saker*, 6.

35 Nylund (n 3) 104 with further references.

into the Dispute Act. As the Convention is not part of the EEA Agreement and is a convention to which the EU itself is one of the parties, it is not entirely unreasonable to say that incorporation of the Convention into the Dispute Act is a direct legal impact of the EU on Norwegian law. However, the ECJ in fact has the last word in interpretation of the Convention. The Convention is one of the legislative amendments that has the greatest EU legal impact on Norwegian legislation on civil procedure.[36] While the other adjustments to EU law described above have given rise to very few decisions reported in the Lovdata databases, hundreds of cases related to the Lugano Convention have been dealt with in Norwegian courts.[37]

6. ADAPTATION OF NORWEGIAN LEGISLATION

The changes made to Norwegian civil procedural legislation as a result of the influence of the EU and EEA have differed. The rules on both the right of lawyers from other EEA states to provide legal assistance and act as counsel in Norway and on security for liability for costs are minor adjustments to existing rules. The provisions are formed by the Norwegian legislative technic with a limited level of detail and leaving room for interpretation.

For information orders, it is different. In terms of content, chapter 28 A adds something new to the Dispute Act. Including a right to information into intellectual property rights gives rights holder far greater opportunities to track down the manufacturer and distribution networks of goods or services which infringe an intellectual property rights that constitute a breach of intellectual property rights beyond what was possible before. However, what really distinguishes chapter 28 A on information orders from the two adjustments described above are the legislative techniques used.

First of all, the provisions on information orders are not an addition to, or an adjustment of, an existing provision. The legislator has inserted a whole chapter into the act that is designed with little substantive anchoring to other provisions of the act. This implies that it is difficult to make the provisions of the Directive merge with existing Norwegian rules.

Secondly, the chapter is characterised by its use of the wording of the Directive. EU law is far more detailed than Norwegian law. Instead of discretionary formulations about what information rights holders can get, the Directive lists exactly what may be required and from whom. As an example, section 28 A-1 (2)

---

36 Cf. for example Rt. 2004, 981 para. 22; Rt. 2006, 391 para. 21; Rt. 2007, 1759 para. 42; Rt. 2011, 1532 para. 21; and HR-2017-1297-A para. 37.

37 A search in Lovdata on 1 November 2018 for all civil decisions containing 'Lugano*' returned 424 results.

of the Dispute Act states that 'origin and distribution information includes a) the name and address of manufacturers, distributors, suppliers and others who have had the goods in their possession, or delivered or received the services, b) name and address of intended wholesalers and retailers, and c) information about the amount of goods that has been manufactured, delivered, received or ordered and what price has been paid and achieved for the goods or services'.

Thirdly, the chapter breathes new life into a debate that arose in the drafting of the Dispute Act, namely the assessment of whether the Dispute Act should contain provisions on specific types of cases or whether such provisions should appear in separate, specific legislation. Chapter 28 A of the Dispute Act on information orders is a special chapter that goes against the general conception of the Dispute Act as a general procedural act. In the preparatory works to the Dispute Act, the issue of whether specific procedural rules should be included was discussed separately, and the law commission stated:

> The Law commission thus considers that, to the extent that there is a need for specific sets of procedural rules, these should be kept to the greatest extent possible outside the Dispute Act. This applies not only to the special rules already placed elsewhere. The Law commission is of the opinion that also the special rules currently in chapters 28 and 29 (cases concerning marriages and descendants) should be wholly or partly moved to other laws.[38]

It does not seem that, in drafting the new chapter in the Dispute Act, the Ministry of Justice and Public Security made a real effort to follow this objective. The ministry proposed a new chapter in the Dispute Act on information orders and justified its proposal to include a new chapter in the Act by saying:

> The provisions apply thematically into the Dispute Act. The Dispute Act already contains certain specific provisions for certain types of cases.[39]

It is not clear why the provisions would apply 'thematically' into the Dispute Act, but the ministry was probably referring to the fact that the provisions contained procedural rules. Nor is it clear what 'specific provisions' the ministry was referring to, but it is commonly held that they referred to the rules in the Dispute Act for cases of administrative enforcement decisions in the health and social sector, as contained in chapter 36. This chapter is the only one in the Dispute Act that contains rules on a specific type of cases, aside from chapter 28 A on information orders. After all the other rules on specific cases were taken out in the drafting of the Dispute Act, the law commission left chapter 36 concerning administrative enforcement decisions. The reasoning behind this was that these

---

38 NOU 2001: 32, 509.

39 Prop. 81 L (2012–2013) 74.

rules would cover quite different types of measures, enshrined in different administrative laws, and that it therefore seemed that the best solution would be for them to be included in a separate chapter of the Dispute Act.[40] The law commission acknowledged that this legislative technique had its weaknesses, and gave examples, but nevertheless decided that this was the best solution.

The thorough assessments in the preparatory works to the Dispute Act contrast with the two sentences cited above from the preparatory works for chapter 28 A. Alternatives to implementing the Directive's procedural provisions in a separate chapter of the Dispute Act are in fact not discussed in the preparatory works. The result is a general civil procedure act with a chapter that both legislatively and in content stands out.

The incorporation of the Lugano Convention into Norwegian law is different from other adjustments resulting from EU law, primarily because it is a convention to which the EU is a party, rather than being secondary EU legislation. Instead of the Convention being considered as a change to Norwegian law, the adoption of the Lugano Convention of 2007 can also be seen as a continuation of the Lugano Convention of 1988, but in which the EU has gained a much larger and more significant position. It should be noted that the Convention was implemented in the same way as the Norwegian government would have implemented an EU regulation, i.e. through incorporation. On the other hand, this form of implementation has also been used for many other conventions. There are many examples of this. One act resulting from this type of implementation is the Human Rights Act of 21 May 1999 no. 30, through which five of the most central conventions in the field of human rights were implemented into Norwegian law through incorporation. The fact that the Norwegian authorities chose to follow the wording of the Convention in the Dispute Act instead of continuing to have a separate Norwegian law on the Lugano Convention was due to the fact that the ministry thought it was fundamentally not desirable to have a separate act containing only one operative paragraph. It was also considered unfortunate that procedural questions of such great practical significance had been governed outside the general procedural laws (the Dispute Act and the Enforcement Act).[41] Even though the Convention has merely been added on to the Dispute Act, this is acceptable in Norwegian legislation.

7. VOLUNTARY IMPLEMENTATION OF EU LAW

As a party to the EEA Agreement, Norway is obliged to make adjustments to Norwegian rules that conflict with the principle of free movement of goods,

40 NOU 2001:32, 522.

41 Ot.prp. no. 89 (2008–2009) 11.

persons, services and capital. The alignment of the rules on the right of lawyers from other EEA states to provide legal assistance and act as counsel in Norway and the rules on security for liability for costs is justified in order for the regulations to be in line with Norway's obligations under the EEA Agreement. Through these adjustments, the rules of the EFTA states are harmonised with those of the EU Member States, and such harmonisation helps to reduce the legal differences between the countries. Rules that are not covered by the EEA Agreement are not, as a matter of principle, affected by the agreement.

Even though Norway is not a member of the EU, the Norwegian authorities still seem to be concerned with having a regulatory framework that complies with EU law, even outside the scope of the EEA Agreement. In the preparatory works for chapter 28A of the Dispute Act, it is stated:

> The Directive is not a part of the EEA Agreement. Consideration for Norwegian industry nevertheless implies that Norway as part of the EEA market should have rules on enforcement of industrial property rights which at least meet the minimum requirements of the Directive. … It is important that the regulations are at least as beneficial for rights holders in Norway as for rights holders in the EU as regards enforcement.[42]

The desire for harmonisation is double-sided. In addition to the fact that similar rules facilitate activity between countries and thus are good for both individual EU citizens and the EU system as such, the statement shows that it may also benefit the individual country to harmonise its legislation. Whereas the EU has to actively remind Member States to implement EU directives, Norway, standing outside the EU, considers it most appropriate to voluntarily implement EU directives in order to comply with other European countries.

However, the desire to comply with EU rules can be met in many ways. Directives are implemented through transposition, by which process they become part of the national legislation. For EU Member States, it is up to each country how this transposition is accomplished, so long as the aims of the Directive are achieved. The goal is simply for the rules become national, with the authority and legitimacy that provides.[43] In implementing Directive 2004/48/EC, the Norwegian Ministry of Justice and Public Security, as described in section 4 of this chapter, determined that the provisions thematically applied into the Dispute Act and that there were already special provisions for certain types of cases in the Act.[44] Except for this relatively vague statement, no assessment was made of how the content of the Directive could be incorporated into existing

---

42 Prop. 81 L (2012–2013) 13.

43 Fredrik Sejersted, Finn Arnesen, Ole-Andreas Rognstad, Sten Foyn and Olav Kolstad, *EØS-rett* (4th edn, Universitetsforlaget 2014) 53.

44 Prop. 81 L (2012–2013) 74.

legislation. The Dispute Act already contains rules on access to evidence and, as mentioned above, rules on securing evidence prior to a lawsuit; the rules on information orders could have been incorporated into these two sets of rules in order to avoid the breach of legislative technique and legal tradition, and to make the rules appear as Norwegian. This option was not commented on or discussed in the preparatory works.

Another possibility could have been to make the rules general, as the Norwegian authorities did when implementing the rules on securing of evidence prior to a case in chapter 28 of the Dispute Act. Like Directive 2004/48/EC, the TRIPS Agreement's rules on the securing of evidence are limited to the protection of intellectual property rights.[45] However, the Norwegian authorities chose to make the rules general so that they can be used irrespective of the type of case. The reason was that the need for securing of evidence may be just as considerable in other cases as in cases of infringements of intellectual property rights. It was stated that a 'procedural special rule for the protection of intellectual property rights will appear as a poorly substantiated special protection of a particular category of rights'.[46] In addition, the benefit of avoiding difficult demarcation issues by making the rule general was noted. Similar assessments were not made in implementing Directive 2004/48/EC.

A third option could have been to place procedural rules relating to intellectual property rights in a single act. This solution was used by Sweden, for example, when it introduced rules on the securing of evidence based on Article 50 of the TRIPS Agreement.[47] Rules on intellectual property, trademarks, patents, designs, companies, circuits for semiconductor products and plant processing rights all received adjustments in relation to the securing of evidence. However, again this option was not discussed in Norway in the preparatory works for the chapter on information orders.

The outcome of the implementation of EU law differs for the adjustments in the Dispute Act. In relation to the rules on giving EEA lawyers access to Norway in order to provide legal assistance and act as counsel and the rules on security for liability for costs, only small adjustments were needed to the existing rules in order to fulfil Norway's obligations under the EEA Agreement. Surprisingly, the voluntary implementation of secondary EU law is what gives rise the most visible changes to Norwegian law. The rules on information orders, for instance, give the impression of being a foreign element in the Dispute Act, and the way they were implemented is unfortunate from the perspective of legislative technique.

---

45 The Agreement on Trade-Related Aspects of Intellectual Property Rights (the TRIPS Agreement) is part of the WTO Agreement (Agreement of 15 April 1994 on the establishment of the World Trade Organization).

46 Ot.prp. no. 33 (2003–2004), *Om lov om endringer i tvistemålsloven (bevisopptak utenfor rettssak)* 5.

47 Ot.prp. no. 33 (2003–2004) 3.

8. SUMMARY

In the preparatory works for the Dispute Act, the law commission expressed the view that the influence of the EU on Norwegian civil procedure was limited,[48] and it appears that the Norwegian authorities have chosen to hold on to this point of view. In the preparatory works for the changes in the rules on security for liability for costs and on information orders, it was emphasised that Norway has no obligation to amend its law in these areas. Having said that, the Norwegian authorities still chose to make adjustments and changes to Norwegian legislation to comply with the rules in other European countries.[49] The implementation was also not done subtly; on the contrary, by comparing chapter 28 A of the Norwegian Dispute Act with Directive 2004/48/EC, it is easy to see which of the Directive's articles has been implemented into Norwegian legislation.

However, a review of these amendments EU law shows that relatively few changes have been made to Norwegian civil procedural legislation. This may seem to confirm the general perception that Norwegian civil procedure is not particularly strongly influenced by the EU. Legislation is, however, just one of several legal sources, and a review of other legal sources will give a completely different picture.[50] However, such a review is beyond the scope of this chapter.

---

48 NOU 2001: 32, 154.

49 Prop. 81 L (2012–2013) 13; and Prop. 42 L (2016–2017) 7–8.

50 See, among others, Fredriksen (n 6); and Nylund (n 3).

CONSUMER PROTECTION AND EU-DRIVEN JUDICIAL ACTIVISM IN THE NETHERLANDS

Alain ANCERY and Bart KRANS

1. EU-DRIVEN JUDICIAL ACTIVISM

It is very likely that consumers are unaware of their rights in civil cases. Therefore, if a consumer is involved in a civil case before a court and is not represented by a legal professional, it is likely that he will not bring forward all the relevant legal aspects of the case. To take a simple example, say a company has delivered some form of good or service to a consumer and states afterwards that it follows from its general terms that a consumer has to pay a certain additional amount. The consumer refuses to pay the additional amount. If the company starts civil proceedings and files a claim against the consumer before a civil court, it is far from certain that during these proceedings the consumer will raise the issue of whether the general term on which the claim is based is valid.

The consumer may not be aware of his rights under the Unfair Terms Directive.[1] The court may be aware of the fact that the claim is perhaps based on an unfair term, but that issue is not brought forward in court by one of the parties. Will the court apply national rules that are based on the Directive on unfair terms *ex officio*? If so, the court will decide *ex officio* whether the general term at issue is unfair or not.

The vast amount of case law of the European Court of Justice (ECJ) on *ex officio* application of EU law has not gone unnoticed by Dutch courts. On the contrary, the numerous decisions the ECJ has issued on this topic in the field of consumer protection are studied carefully and taken seriously by Dutch courts.[2] Dutch courts try to comply with European case law on *ex officio* application of EU law, and there are many decisions on this topic by Dutch courts. Dutch courts are trying to fit this ECJ case law into the Dutch civil procedural system. The topic has several aspects and has led to several questions concerning the role of national (in this case Dutch) courts. Illustrating the importance of the topic, in 2000, as a consequence of ECJ case law, a working group of Dutch judges issued a report on *ex officio* application of EU consumer law and, in 2014, published an updated version.[3] In several cases, the Dutch Supreme Court has also ruled on the topic.[4] In addition, the matter has been the topic of a dissertation[5] and many other publications in the Netherlands.[6] Illustrating the impact of this topic in the Netherlands, a paper (in Dutch) was recently published on *ex officio* application of EU law in favour of representative organisations.[7]

It is obvious that the *ex officio* obligation raises several questions. In this chapter, we will limit ourselves to certain aspects of this topic. First, we will outline the basics of the Dutch procedural landscape for consumers

1 Directive 93/13/EEC of 5 April 1993 on unfair terms [1993] OJ L95/29.

2 See B. Krans, 'European Relief for Consumers. Procedural Challenges to the Fairness Test' in H. Peckanitez, N. Bolayir and C. Simil (eds), *XV. Dünya Us Hukukculari Kongresi/ XVth International Association of Procedural Law World Congress* (On Iki Levha Yayincilik 2016) 511–525, in particular §2.

3 Both versions can be found on the official website of the Judiciary in the Netherlands: <www. rechtspraak.nl> accessed October 2018. The name of the 2014 version of this report is *Ambtshalve toetsing II, Herzien rapport van de LOVCK-werkgroep*.

4 Supreme Court of the Netherlands, 13 September 2013, ECLI:NL:HR:2013:691; Supreme Court of the Netherlands, 26 February 2016, ECLI:NL:HR:2016:340; Supreme Court of the Netherlands, 29 April 2016, ECLI:NL:HR:2016:769; Supreme Court of the Netherlands, 21 April 2017, ECLI:NL:HR:2017:773.

5 A.G.F. Ancery, *Ambtshalve toepassing van EU-recht*, diss. University of Groningen (Kluwer 2012).

6 Most of them are in Dutch, obviously. See on the topic in English, *inter alia*, B. Krans, 'EU Law and National Civil Procedure Law: An Invisible Pillar', *ERPL* 2015 (4) 567–587, in particular §5; and earlier Ancery (n 5) 215–220.

7 F.E. Vermeulen and T.L. Schasfoort, 'Ambtshalve toetsing aan Unierecht ten gunste van belangenorganisaties?', *TCR* 2017, 89–99.

in section 2. In section 3, we will go into the rationale behind and the scope of the European case law. In sections 4 and 5, we will translate the ECJ case law to Dutch civil procedure, focusing on *ex officio* application by the courts of first instance (section 4) and appeal courts (section 5). Some remaining questions will be touched upon in section 6.

2. DUTCH PROCEDURAL LANDSCAPE FOR CONSUMERS

2.1. DISTRICT COURTS

To better understand the role of *ex officio* application in Dutch law, it is useful to give a brief overview of the position of consumers in the Dutch procedural landscape.

As far as civil cases at first instance before district courts are concerned, a general distinction between normal proceedings and proceedings involving a consumer must be made. In principle, all these cases have to be filed in a district court. These civil courts deal with a wide range of civil cases, for example on problems to do with sales, leases, property, tort or other unlawful acts.[8] There is no upper limit on the value of the claim. Legal representation by a lawyer is required in these types of cases.[9] Proceedings can be initiated on behalf of or against a consumer. The consumer will need legal representation. Although we do not have exact figures, we can safely state that this 'classic' route for civil cases is, however, not the most commonly used instrument to settle disputes where a consumer is involved. For consumer disputes, other options are more appropriate in the vast majority of cases.

First, there is the so-called *kantonrechter* (this judge is more or less comparable to a cantonal judge, local or regional judge or Justice of Peace). The *kantonrechter* has the authority to decide on, *inter alia*, civil cases with a maximum claim of €25,000.[10] The *kantonrechter* is part of the district court of first instance, but acts more or less as a special section of this court. One of the main differences between the *kantonrechter* and the other civil sections of the district court is that parties can appear before the *kantonrechter* without legal representation. As a result, in cases with a maximum claim of €25,000, parties are allowed to conduct the proceedings on their own. It is obvious that

---

8 Several types of cases at first instance have to be transferred to another court. We will not go into the details of these types.

9 Art 79 para 2 Dutch Code of Civil Procedure.

10 Art 93 Dutch Code of Civil Procedure. See for some information on the *kantonrechter* (sub-district judge) in English: <https://www.rechtspraak.nl/English/Judicial-system-and-legislation/Pages/District-courts.aspx> accessed October 2018.

this may involve consumers and that the absence of obligatory representation is relevant for the course of the proceedings before the *kantonrechter*.[11]

If a credit card company or a company that has sold a product or delivered services to a consumer files a claim against the consumer, for example for late payment, and the claim is for less than €25,000, the consumer is allowed to defend himself.[12] Given the costs of legal proceedings, consumers may very well use that right. However, it is very likely that a consumer without legal representation will not invoke all the legal grounds and rules that may be relevant for the case. As the ECJ has stated, for the *ex officio* application of the Unfair Terms Directive it is not relevant whether the consumer has legal representation or not.[13]

We do not have figures or a set of data, but we consider it very likely that consumers do not regularly start civil proceedings before the *kantonrechter* in the capacity as a claimant. If consumers are involved in proceedings before the *kantonrechter*, we consider it very likely that in the vast majority of cases the consumer acts as the defendant.

2.2. *GESCHILLENCOMMISSIE*

There is another important element of the Dutch landscape of consumer dispute settlement: the so-called *Geschillencommissie*, which is a private and independent consumer complaint board. According to its website, the *Geschillencommissie* (Dutch Foundation for Consumer Complaints Boards) offers complainants, whether they are a consumer or a business, alternative dispute schemes to help resolve their dispute out of court.[14] The complaints boards offer a quick and low-cost means of resolving a dispute. These alternative dispute schemes are, again according to the website, recognised by both the Dutch government and the European Commission. There are complaint boards on a wide variety of topics, such as for complaints concerning energy contracts, direct sales, public notaries, lawyers, recreation, travel, sports, telecommunications services, jewellery, taxis, private leases, public health and vehicles.

To file a claim on one of these areas before a complaint board, the company that the consumer has contracted with must fall within the scope of that complaint board. This is the case if the *Geschillencommissie* has authority to

---

11 The authority of the *kantonrechter* is not restricted to civil cases with a maximum value of €25,000. The *kantonrechter* is also competent to rule on cases concerning (in brief) lease and employment contracts.

12 The consumer is not allowed to defend himself before the court of appeal and thus requires a lawyer, although he is allowed to plead his own case in the courtroom (Art 134 para 3 Dutch Code of Civil Procedure).

13 Case C-429/05 *Max Rampion and Others v Franfinance SA and Others* [2006] ECR I-8017.

14 See: <https://www.degeschillencommissie.nl/english/> accessed October 2018.

rule on a consumer complaint against this company. The *Geschillencommissie*'s authority can result from a contractual clause, usually in the general terms. It may also be that the general terms used by a specific branch organisation states that companies that are affiliated with that organisation are subject to the authority of the *Geschillencommissie*. For example, the Dutch Association of Travel Agents and Tour Operators, which represents the travel industry and is not a consumer group[15] has travel and booking terms and conditions that state that, if a complaint by a traveller is not resolved satisfactorily in good time, the traveller can bring the dispute before the *Geschillencommissie Reizen*.[16]

Another example is the *Geschillencommissie Voertuigen* (Vehicles Complaint Board), which deals with disputes concerning car sales or repairs. If the company that has sold the car to the consumer or has repaired the consumer's car states in its general terms that a dispute can be filed with the *Geschillencommissie*, then the consumer is allowed to bring his there.

To file a claim before one of the *Geschillencommissie*, a fee must be paid.[17] Proceedings before a complaint board are usually faster and cheaper than proceedings before a district court. In practice, these complaint boards offer a relatively easy way for consumers to file a claim against a company (provided that the company has made itself subject to the authority of the *Geschillencommissie*).

If a consumer wants to bring a contract-related claim against a company that is subject to a *Geschillencommissie* according to its own general terms (or the terms of its branch organisation), it is very likely that the consumer will not commence ordinary proceedings before a district court, but rather turn to one of the complaint boards.

Given the international scope of this book, it is interesting to note that citizens of the EU, Norway and Iceland who do not live in the Netherlands and who would like to file a claim with one of the complaint boards can contact the European Consumer Centre (ECC) in their own country. The ECC cannot act on behalf of the consumer at the complaint boards, but it can assist.[18]

For consumers, it must be clear that the company will comply with the decision of the complaint board if it decides in favour of the consumer. These consumer complaint boards, sometimes also referred to as dispute committees,

---

15 The Dutch name of this organisation is *Algemene Nederlandse Vereniging van Reisondernemingen* (ANVR). More information can be found at: <https://www.anvr.nl/> accessed October 2018.

16 See Art 143 para 1 ANVR Consumer Terms and Conditions (Travel and Booking Terms and Conditions). These general terms may be found at: <https://www.anvr.nl/> accessed October 2018.

17 This amount is usually between €25 and €125, depending on the type of industry.

18 Information in English can be found at: <https://www.ecc.nederland.nl/en>.

give their decision in the form of a recommendation that is binding on the parties. To return to the example of booking and travel terms and conditions above, the *Algemene Nederlandse Vereniging van Reisondernemingen* (ANVR) guarantees compliance with the binding recommendations of the *Geschillencommissie Reizen* by its members.[19] Therefore, in these cases, consumers do not have to worry about whether the company will comply with the decision of the complaint board.

2.3. OTHER COMPLAINT BOARDS

Other consumer complaint boards exist other than those under the auspices of the *Geschillencommissie*. One of them is the *Kifid*, a complaint board for financial disputes,[20] also referred to as the financial services complaints tribunal.[21]

Another important complaint board for consumers is the *Stichting Klachten en Geschillen Zorgverzekeringen* (SKGZ). This complaint board decides health insurance-related disputes between consumers and insurance companies.

2.4. ADR ENTITIES UNDER THE CONSUMER ADR DIRECTIVE

The purpose of the Consumer ADR Directive is to contribute, by providing a high level of consumer protection, to the proper functioning of the internal market by ensuring that consumers can, on a voluntary basis, submit complaints against traders to entities offering independent, impartial, transparent, effective, fast and fair alternative dispute resolution procedures.[22] The Dutch *Implementatiewet buitengerechtelijke geschillenbeslechting consumenten* – the Act implementing the Consumer ADR Directive – formally designates the above-mentioned complaint boards (*Geschillencommissie, Kifid and SKGZ*) as ADR entities.[23]

---

19 See Art 14 ANVR Consumer Terms and Conditions (Travel and Booking Terms and Conditions). Article 14 also formulates some exceptions to this compliance guarantee.

20 *Kifid* is short for *Klachteninstituut Financiële Dienstverlening*. See for information on *Kifid* (in Dutch) see: <www.kifid.nl> accessed October 2018.

21 Information in English on the consumer complaints procedure before *Kifid* the website of the AFM, the Dutch Authority for the Financial Markets: <https://www.afm.nl/en/consumenten/themas/klacht/kifid> accessed October 2018.

22 Art 1 Directive 2013/11/EU of the European Parliament and of the Council of 21 May 2013 on alternative dispute resolution for consumer disputes and amending Regulation (EC) No 2006/2004 and Directive 2009/22/EC.

23 Staatscourant 7 July 2015, 19094 (concerning *SKGZ*); Staatscourant 8 July 2015, 19487 (concerning *Kifid*); and Staatscourant 17 December 2015, 45980 (concerning the *Stichting Geschillencommissies*).

So, to conclude this section, a consumer who wants to file a claim against a company arising from their contractual relationship often has the option of turning to a complaint board. As a result, consumers do not usually come before a district court as claimants. If a consumer is involved in proceedings before a district court, it is usually the capacity as a defendant. This is an important factor for the role of the judge in civil proceedings as far as the *ex officio* application of EU law is concerned.

3. *EX OFFICIO* APPLICATION AT THE EUROPEAN LEVEL

3.1. RATIONALE

The first judgments of the European Court on the *ex officio* application of EU consumer law date from the early 2000s.[24] Those cases, concerned a forum clause in the seller's general terms, stating that the competent court was the court of the place where the seller was located (*Océano*),[25] and a clause concerning a contractual interest rate and a penalty clause (*Cofidis*).[26] Both cases involved the Unfair Terms Directive. The ECJ ruled that the terms could potentially be unfair. Moreover, it ruled that the system of protection introduced by the Directive is based on the idea that the consumer is in a weak position *vis-à-vis* the seller or supplier, in terms of both his bargaining power and his level of knowledge. On the question as to into how much detail the national courts should go in determining whether the term at issue is unfair, the court ruled in the *Océano* case as follows:

> The aim of Article 6 of the Directive, which requires Member States to lay down that unfair terms are not binding on the consumer, would not be achieved if the consumer were himself obliged to raise the unfair nature of such terms. In disputes where the amounts involved are often limited, the lawyers' fees may be higher than the amount at stake, which may deter the consumer from contesting the application of an unfair term. While it is the case that, in a number of Member States, procedural rules enable individuals to defend themselves in such proceedings, there is a real risk that the consumer, particularly because of ignorance of the law, will not challenge the term pleaded against him on the grounds that it is unfair. It follows that effective protection of the consumer may be attained only if the national court acknowledges that it has power to evaluate terms of this kind of its own motion.

---

24 Case C-240–244/98 *Océano Grupo Editorial SA v Rocio Murciano Quintero and Others* [2005] ECR I-4941.

25 *Océano* (n 24).

26 Case C-473/00 *Cofidis SA v Jean-Louis Fredout* [2002] ECR I-10875.

The ECJ also ruled that Article 7 of the Directive, which requires Member States to implement adequate and effective means to prevent the continued use of unfair terms, requires a form of *ex officio* application. The court's power to determine of its own motion whether a term is unfair must be regarded as constituting a proper means of achieving the result sought, *inter alia*, by Article 6 of the Directive, namely preventing an individual consumer from being bound by an unfair term, according to the ECJ. The Court continued:

> It follows from the above that the protection provided for consumers by the Directive entails the national court being able to determine of its own motion whether a term of a contract before it is unfair when making its preliminary assessment as to whether a claim should be allowed to proceed before the national courts.[27]

The line of reasoning is also typical of the ECJ's case law in the years after the *Océano* judgment.[28] It is not the *ex officio* application of EU law by itself that has great importance for the ECJ, but rather the effectiveness of EU law. In order to ensure that consumers are afforded the protection given to them by EU directives – and thus to ensure the effectiveness of EU consumer law – a court should actively examine the case file, and if it finds arguments to do so, apply consumer-protective rules. The question is: why and to what extent?

To start with the first question, on a micro level, the obligation to apply consumer-protective rules *ex officio* intends to compensate for the inequality between consumers and professional parties. Unlike a professional party, a consumer is usually unaware of his rights or may experience financial difficulties in enforcing his rights before the court. Without such compensation, the consumer may be deprived of the rights he is afforded by the EU consumer protection directives.[29]

---

27 *Océano* (n 24) paras 25–29.

28 Cf *Cofidis* (n 26); Case C-168/05 *Elisa María Mostaza Claro v Centro Móvil Milenium SL* [2006] ECR I-10421; Case C-243/08 *Pannon GSM Zrt v Erzsébet Sustikné Győrfi* [2009] ECR I-4713; Case C-40/08 *Asturcom Telecomunicaciones SL v Christina Rodríguez Nogueira* [2009] ECR I-9579; Case C-137/08 *VB Pénzügyi Lízing Zrt v Ferenc Schneider* [2010] ECR I-10847; Case C-76/10 *Pohotovosť s.r.o. v Iveta Korčkovská* [2010] ECR I-11557; Case C-453/10 *Jana Pereničová and Vladislav Perenič v SOS financ spol. s.r.o.* ECLI:EU:C:2012:144; Case C-472/10 *Nemzeti Fogyasztóvédelmi Hatóság v Invitel Távközlési Zrt* ECLI:EU:C:2012:242; Case C-618/10 *Banco Español de Crédito SA v Joaquín Calderón Camino* ECLI:EU:C:2012:349; Case C-472/11 *Banif Plus Bank Zrt v Csaba Csipai and Viktória Csipai* ECLI:EU:C:2013:88; Case C-397/11 *Erika Jőrös v Aegon Magyarország Hitel Zrt* ECLI:EU:C:2013:340; Case C-488/11 *Dirk Frederik Asbeek Brusse and Others v Jahani BV* ECLI:EU:C:2013:341; Case C-169/14 *Juan Carlos Sánchez Morcillo and María del Carmen Abril García v Banco Bilbao Vizcaya Argentaria SA* ECLI:EU:C:2014:2099; Case C-567/13 *Nóra Baczó and János István Vizsnyiczai v Raiffeisen Bank Zrt* ECLI:EU:C:2015:88.

29 See on the rationale behind the ECJ case law of this topic in English: Krans (n 2) para 3. Previously Ancery has written extensively on the topic in his dissertation. Cf also A. Ancery and M. Wissink, 'ECJ 4 June 2009, Pannon GSM Zrt v Erzsébet Sustikné Györfi', *ERPL* 2010 (2) 307–316.

To make sure that the aim of the Unfair Terms Directive is achieved (namely that unfair terms in a contract concluded between a consumer and a seller or supplier are not binding on the consumer), the national court is not only allowed, but is indeed obliged, to apply this Directive *ex officio*.[30]

There is, however, also a macro level on which this problem should be considered. In the end, the aim of the required level of consumer protection is to encourage consumers to participate in the EU internal market. They are, after all, important members of the cross-border internal market and should not be discouraged from participating because of the fear that they may not be protected when doing so.[31]

3.2. SCOPE OF CASES

The case law of the ECJ is not limited to the Unfair Terms Directive, but also deals with European consumer law more generally.[32] After all, it is not just cases relating to the Unfair Terms Directive in which consumers are unaware of their rights or have difficulties in enforcing their rights before a court. It did not take long after the aforementioned *Océano* ruling before the first case on another consumer protection directive found its way to the ECJ. In the *Rampion* case,[33] the ECJ had to rule on the question whether the line of reasoning in the cases on the Unfair Terms Directive could be extended to consumer credit cases. The ECJ ruled that the aim of the Directive:

> could not be effectively achieved if the consumer were himself obliged to invoke the right to pursue remedies which he enjoys against the grantor of credit in accordance with the provisions of national law transposing Article 11(2) of Directive 87/102, in particular because of the real risk that the consumer may be unaware of his rights or may encounter difficulties in exercising them. As the Advocate General stated at point 107 of his Opinion, the fact that the main proceedings were brought by Mr and Mrs Rampion and that they are represented in those proceedings by a lawyer does not justify a different conclusion, as the issue must be settled independently of the specific circumstances of the case.[34]

It is not just the fact that the line of reasoning of *Océano* is extended to consumer credit that makes this judgment interesting. Contrary to most other comparable

---

30 See on this topic in English Ancery and Wissink (n 29); and Krans (n 2) para 4.

31 Cf A. Ancery and B. Krans, 'Ambtshalve toepassing van consumentenrecht: grensbepaling en praktische kwesties', *Ars Aequi* 2016 (11) 825.

32 Krans (n 6) §5.1.

33 Cf. *Rampion* (n 13).

34 *Rampion* (n 13) para 65.

cases, the consumer in the *Rampion* case was not the defendant but the plaintiff. And unlike to the other cases, the consumer was well represented by a lawyer and did not seem to have encountered financial difficulties on his way to court. The ECJ nevertheless affords the *Océano* protection to such consumers as well, pointing to the fact that the issue must be settled independently of the specific circumstances of the cases. Consumers are in a weaker position *vis-à-vis* professional parties and so courts should shift the balance slightly in favour of the consumer. That a consumer could in certain cases be in a stronger position *vis-à-vis* a professional party should therefore be disregarded. It is the court's task to *ex officio* apply consumer-protective provisions in those cases as well.[35]

After the *Rampion* ruling, the ECJ ruled in a similar way in cases on the Directive on contracts negotiated away from business premises[36] and the Consumer Sales Directive.

Among Dutch scholars, the question has been raised as to why this line of reasoning is restricted to European consumer cases.[37] Does it also apply to other relationships where one of the parties is weaker than the other? This may, for example, apply to the Directive on commercial agents.[38] The relationship between a commercial agent and a principal may not always be equal.

Returning to consumer law, the question has also been raised in the Netherlands why this duty for the court in civil proceedings is limited to cases that concern consumer law with a European background. Why should it matter to the consumer involved whether the applicable legal rule is purely domestic or has a European background?[39]

35 An example of a case where there was not a significant imbalance between the consumer and the professional party is the case that led to Supreme Court of the Netherlands, 13 September 2013, ECLI:NL:HR:2013:691.

36 Cf Case 227/08 *Eva Martín Martín v EDP Editores SL* [2009] ECR I-11939; Case C-32/12 *Soledad Duarte Hueros v Autociba SA and Automóviles Citroën España SA* ECLI:EU:C:2013:637; and Case C-497/13 *Froukje Faber v Autobedrijf Hazet Octhen BV* ECLI:EU:C:2014:2403. On these last two: A. Ancery and C. Pavillon, 'De rechterlijke lijdelijkheid in rook opgegaan? De ambtshalve toepassing van de consumentenkoopregels nader toegelicht', MvV 2015 (9) 243–254.

37 J.W. Rutgers, 'Ambtshalve toepassing van Europees recht in het civiele geding' in R. Flach et al (eds), *Amice. Liber amicorum Rutgers* (Kluwer 2005) 295–303; Krans (n 6) §5.1.

38 Directive 86/653 /EEC of 18 December 1986 on the coordination of the laws of the Member States relating to self-employed commercial agents.

39 A. Ancery and B. Krans, 'Ambtshalve toepassing van Europees consumentenrecht', *RM Themis* 2009 (5) 194–196; Krans (n 6); R. Steennot, 'Public and Private Enforcement in the Field of Unfair Contract Terms', *ERPL* 2015 (4) 589–620; A.M. Mancaleoni, 'The Obligation on Dutch and Italian Courts to Apply EU Law of Their Own Motion', ERPL 2016 (3–4) 553–578.

3.3. AMBIT OF THE DISPUTE

A more controversial aspect concerning the *ex officio* application, at least in the Netherlands, was tackled by the ECJ in its *Pannon* and *Pénzügyi* cases.[40] When a court is obliged to apply consumer-protective provisions *ex officio* and finds that the case file of the parties contains little to no factual information to facilitate that application, can it sit back or should it actively gather factual information?

In the *Pannon* case, the ECJ dealt with this question and ruled that a national court is required to examine, of its own motion, the unfairness of a contractual term where it has available to it the legal and factual elements necessary for that task. Where it considers such a term to be unfair, it must not apply it, except if the consumer opposes that non-application.[41] We cannot think of a reason why this should not be extended to other EU consumer protection directives. Thus, a court is obliged to apply consumer-protective provisions *ex officio* (or in the case of unfair terms we should perhaps say disregard the term) when it has available to it the necessary legal and factual elements. But when can a court conclude that it does not in fact have the necessary factual elements available to it? When these elements are contained in the case file but not referred to by the parties? When these elements are not even contained in the case file but could only be obtained if the court actively seeks them out? Or perhaps only then when a court can predict that even were it to try to actively seek out these elements, it would result in nothing?

The *Pénzügyi* case further clarified this matter. The ECJ ruled in that the required *ex officio* examination must be divided into two stages. At the first stage, the court must ascertain that the case falls within the scope of an EU consumer protection directive, and if so, it has to assess in the second stage, if necessary of its own motion, whether a consumer-protective provision should be applied.[42] *Ergo*, the burden placed upon the court at the first stage is heavier than at the second stage. At the first stage, the court has to actively investigate, whereas at the second stage, the court can more or less rely upon the parties. Does that mean that the parties have to actively refer to factual information necessary for the *ex officio* application of consumer-protective provisions? We are inclined to think not. After all, such a requirement could easily deprive the consumer of the protection granted to him by the EU directives. On the contrary, we are inclined to think that the obligation to apply consumer-protective provisions *ex officio* requires courts to actively

---

40 *Pannon* (n 28); and *Pénzügyi* (n 28).

41 Cf *Pannon* (n 28).

42 Cf *Pénzügyi* (n 28).

use their competences to obtain as much factual information as possible and necessary to support the application of a consumer-protective provision. However, the court only has to do so if it believes that it could lead to something. Obliging parties to produce evidence or answer questions is, after all, pointless if the court already feels this would bring the necessary information to light.

4. *EX OFFICIO* APPLICATION BY COURTS OF FIRST INSTANCE

The obligation for the court to apply consumer-protective rules *ex officio* whenever it has the necessary factual and legal elements available to it have led Dutch courts of first instance to believe that a fundamental change is required in the approach to cases between consumers and professional parties (so-called B2C cases). Where these courts would in the past have more or less awarded a claim in B2C cases if an appropriate defence was not put forward, they now realise that this approach might conflict with ECJ case law. In order to ensure the consistency of the case law of the different courts of first instance, they adopted a common approach in February 2010, which was later amended in November 2014, mainly due to ECJ case law.[43]

The courts state that *ex officio* application of EU consumer law is obligatory. In order to examine whether the court should apply a consumer-protective provision *ex officio*, it should firstly determine whether it is dealing with a B2C matter that falls within the scope of an EU directive. Unless there are signs to the contrary, a court can assume that the case concerns a B2C matter if one of the parties is a person and not a legal entity.[44]

If the court has determined that it is dealing with a B2C case that falls within the scope of an EU consumer protection directive, it has to determine whether it is relevant to apply a consumer-protective provision. There should, for example, be signs that a consumer-protective provision has been violated. Not all necessary factual information has to be available, but the court should have an indication that 'something is wrong'. If there is such an indication, the court should determine what factual information it has available to it. It should therefore examine the entire case file, regardless of whether parties have referred to all the information contained in the file. If the factual information is insufficient to apply the consumer-protective provision but the

43 Both reports (in Dutch) can be accessed at: <https://www.rechtspraak.nl/SiteCollectionDocuments/Eindrapport-LOVCK-werkgroep-ambtshalve-toetsing-17210.pdf> and <https://www.rechtspraak.nl/SiteCollectionDocuments/Rapport-ambtshalve-toetsing-II-versie-november-2014.pdf> both accessed October 2018.

44 Report *Ambtshalve toetsing II* (n 5) 13.

court has a clear indication that there is something wrong, it should actively seek to gather the necessary information by using its powers to request further information from the parties.[45]

If the court ultimately gathers enough information to apply a consumer-protective provision, then it should enable the parties to respond to its intention to apply this provision *ex officio*.

The Supreme Court of the Netherlands approved this common approach in its judgment of 13 September 2013 and rules more or less similarly.[46] The Supreme Court stresses that this active approach is not only intended to be applied when examining whether the case falls within the scope of an EU consumer protection directive, but also at the stage where the court has to examine of its own motion whether a consumer-protective provision has to be applied. This pertains to default cases as well. The court has to take the principle of hearing both sides into account and has to decide whether the claimant should be allowed to provide further information and, where necessary, to adjust his statements.[47]

5. *EX OFFICIO* APPLICATION BY COURTS OF APPEAL

It should not come as a surprise that the ECJ has already had to deal with the question of whether the obligation to apply consumer-protective provisions *ex officio* affects the appeal jurisdiction as well.[48] A Dutch court of appeal can go beyond the grounds of appeal as filed by the claimant in situations where the public order (or the *ordre public*) requires it to do so. However, it cannot make use of factual information that parties have not referred to, even in a situation in which the public order could potentially be violated and even if the factual information is contained in the case file.

In the Dutch *Asbeek Brusse* case, the ECJ ruled that provisions implemented as a result of an EU consumer protection directive are equal to public order provisions and should, therefore, be dealt with in the same manner. For Dutch courts of appeal, this would mean that they can overturn the judgment of the court of first instance based on consumer-protective provisions if the factual information referred to by the parties is sufficient to apply these provisions *ex officio*. The Supreme Court of the Netherlands approved this approach in its judgment of 13 September 2013.

45 Cf *Banif* (n 28) paras 25 ff.
46 Supreme Court of the Netherlands, 13 September 2013, ECLI:NL:HR:2013:691.
47 Supreme Court of the Netherlands, 13 September 2013, ECLI:NL:HR:2013:691, para 3.9.2.
48 Cf *Jőrös* (n 28); *Asbeek Brusse* (n 28).

In a judgment of 26 February 2016, the Supreme Court of the Netherlands further clarified how this *ex officio* application should take place in appeal proceedings. There were some inconsistencies in judgments of courts of appeal as to the difference between the grounds of appeal (where the court can go beyond) and the ambit of the dispute (where the court cannot go beyond). A court of appeal can only examine *ex officio* if the relevant part of the judgment of the court of first instance is appealed. For example, if a court of first instance applies a general term, but no ground of appeal is lodged in relation to this part of the decision, the court of appeal cannot annul the judgment *ex officio* based on the fact that this part of the decision is in violation of EU consumer law. It is not, however – and we cannot stress this enough – necessary for the ground of appeal lodged in relation to this part of the judgment to draw on EU consumer law.[49]

6. SOME REMAINING QUESTIONS

It took quite a number of cases on the *ex officio* application of EU consumer law for Dutch courts to generally accept that they should indeed, as far as possible, apply such provisions *ex officio* in order to ensure effective consumer protection. There remain, however, points of doubt.

One common question is whether a court of appeal should apply consumer-protective provisions *ex officio* if a claimant has appealed a judgment of the court of first instance but has not lodged any grounds of appeal. This would normally lead to the appeal being declared inadmissible. There are authors who believe that a shift in this approach is required to comply with EU law.[50] What they tend to overlook is that a court of appeal can only make use of the factual information that parties have referred to, and that without grounds of appeal, parties refer to nothing.

A situation where there is without a doubt too little factual information to apply EU consumer law *ex officio* is cassation proceedings. There has not yet been a ruling on whether the Supreme Court has to apply (parts of) consumer law *ex officio*. This may well be a difficult topic, because it may also be linked to the limitation of grounds for appeal to the Supreme Court. We consider it unlikely that the Dutch system for dealing with cases in cassation proceedings will have to change as a result of the European case law on this topic. Nevertheless, it will remain for the Supreme Court to rule on complaints that lower courts did not meet their obligations regarding the *ex officio* application of EU consumer law.

---

49 Cf Supreme Court of the Netherlands, 26 February 2016, ECLI:NL:HR:2016:340. On this judgment M. Nieuwenhuijs and M. Möhring, 'Vindt de consumentenbescherming haar grens in het appelprocesrecht', *TCR* 2016 (3) 87–92.

50 Nieuwenhuijs and Möhring (n 49) 90–91.

Another question that the Supreme Court of the Netherlands ruled on – although it could be argued that it should have been the ECJ to rule on this matter – is whether it is possible to apply supplementary provisions of the Dutch Civil Code whenever the *ex officio* application of EU consumer law leads to the annulment of a contractual term. According to the Supreme Court, this is possible.[51] Whether the ECJ agrees with this approach is something that future case law should clarify. Therefore, questions remain to be answered concerning the *ex officio* application of EU law, as has been the case ever since the *Océano* ruling in 2000.

Lastly, falling outside the scope of this chapter is the question of whether the rationale for the *ex officio* application should be extended to strictly B2B cases in which one of the parties is clearly in a weaker position *vis-à-vis* its counterparty. An example of this is cases on interest rate swaps between banks and SMEs (small to medium-sized enterprises).

7. CONCLUSION

Although several points of doubt remain, the trend is clear. It is fair to state that the role of Dutch courts in certain consumer cases has changed as a result of the ECJ case law on the *ex officio* application of EU consumer law. In general, Dutch courts seem to be aware of the European case law on *ex officio* application. The existence of the report (and its updated version) from the working group of Dutch judges on the topic illustrates the impact the ECJ case law has had on national courts. From this perspective, it is easy to conclude that judicial activism has increased – at first among district courts of first instance, but now having also reached the courts of appeal. The Supreme Court has also ruled on the topic, but 'only' concerning the role of courts of first instance and courts of appeal.

51 Supreme Court of the Netherlands, 21 April 2017, ECLI:NL:HR:2017:773.

THE ROLE OF THE JUDGE IN CONSUMER CASES

A German Perspective

Ivo Bach

1. INTRODUCTION

1.1. DICHOTOMY OF INTERESTS: IMPARTIALITY VS. CONSUMER PROTECTION

The position of judges in consumer cases is often inconvenient: they are torn in two different directions by two different sets of legal rules. On the one hand, procedural law requires them to be impartial: they must not grant any support to either one of the parties. On the other hand, substantive law itself is not impartial, but clearly sides with the consumer. The reason for this partiality is quite evident: it is an attempt to compensate for the at least potential imbalance in power and knowledge between a consumer and a professional.

It is not my intention in this chapter to question the premise that there is, normally, indeed such an imbalance in power. Instead, I focus on the question of what it means for the judges' role in consumer cases if we accept that premise. Is it sufficient for the substantive law to try to compensate for the imbalance so that the judge can stick to his role as an impartial entity? Or must the judge contribute to the goal of consumer protection and support the consumer in the proceedings, and if so, to what extent?

1.2. DICHOTOMY OF LEGAL SOURCES: EUROPEAN LAW AND NATIONAL LAW

In large part, these questions cannot be answered solely from a German perspective. This is simply because the German perspective is not crucial. Europe has taken over: consumer law is one of the core areas of EU legislative competence. Whenever substantive law is penned by the European legislator, the perspective of national procedural law suffers a certain decline in relevance. It must adhere to the targets set in Brussels (or in Luxembourg, where relevant). However, since my intention is to discuss not the European perspective but rather the German one, I have primarily restricted myself to the question of whether German rules of civil procedure[1] actually meet European targets. Having answered this question, however, I turn to those remaining areas of law that are not shaped by European targets (yet) and in which the domestic German perspective therefore remains crucial.

2. ECJ DECISIONS AND GERMAN LAW

2.1. *EX OFFICIO* EXAMINATION OF LEGAL QUESTIONS

The European Court of Justice (ECJ) has a quite clear position in the conflict between impartiality and consumer protection: it fights alongside the consumer. ECJ decisions always start with a harmless concession that – in general – questions of procedural law must not be answered by the ECJ but fall within the competence of the Member States.[2] However, there is always a reservation to this concession: the principle of the procedural autonomy of the Member States applies only on the condition that the national procedural rules 'are not less favourable than those governing similar domestic actions (principle of equivalence) and do not make it in practice impossible or excessively difficult to

---

1 In Germany, the vast majority of consumer cases are decided by state courts. Ombudsmen, conciliation boards or similar institutions are not (yet?) prevalent (except for in particular areas, such as banking and insurance cases, where the decision of the Ombudsman is binding for the bank/insurer, at least up to an amount of €10,000 in dispute). Only recently, in 2016, did German legislation establish a law on alternative dispute resolution in consumer cases.

2 Cf. e.g. Case C-78/98 *Shirley Preston and Others v Wolverhampton Healthcare NHS Trust and Others and Dorothy Fletcher and Others v Midland Bank plc* ECLI:EU:C:2000:247, para 31; Cases C-392/04 and C-422/04 *i-21 Germany GmbH and Arcor AG & Co. KG v Bundesrepublik Deutschland* ECLI:EU:C:2004:836, para 57.

exercise the rights conferred on consumers by European Union law (principle of effectiveness)'.[3]

Regarding the latter principle of effectiveness, the ECJ always points out that 'an imbalance between the consumer and the seller or supplier may only be corrected by positive action unconnected with the actual parties to the contract'.[4] In other words, European consumer protection directives are only effective if judges take action for the consumer.

In the first dozen or so cases,[5] the directive in question was the Directive on Unfair Terms in Consumer Contracts.[6] The 'positive action' that the ECJ required was simply 'that the national court is required to examine, of its own motion, the unfairness of a contractual term where it has available to it the legal and factual elements necessary for that task'.[7]

From a German perspective, this is quite natural. Under the principle of *iura novit curia*, it seems self-evident that courts must scrutinise all general terms in a contract in terms of their fairness – and that they must do so of their own motion, that is *ex officio*.[8]

The same seems to be true for all other Member States (at least all civil law Member States). Still, some Member States have rules that in certain situations provide exceptions from the principle of *iura novit curia* or even entirely prohibit courts from examining the legal situation. Interestingly, nearly all cases that have been referred to the ECJ on this subject come from Spain, Hungary and Slovakia. Apparently, German courts have not had any doubts yet with regard to the conformity of German procedural law with EU law.

Five years ago, however, the ECJ rendered a decision that has given rise to some doubts, at least amongst German academics: the *Banesto* decision.[9] A Spanish court had asked the ECJ whether the 'take action' principle applies in an order

---

3 Case C-168/05 *Mostaza Claro v Centro Móvil Milenium SL* ECLI:EU:C:2006:675, para 24; Case C-618/10 *Banco Español de Crédito v Joaquín Calderón Camino* ECLI:EU:C:2012:74, para 46.

4 *Mostaza Claro* (n 3), para 26; *Banco Español de Crédito* (n 3), para 41.

5 Cf. eg Cases C-240/98 to C-244/98 *Océano Grupo Editorial SA Roció Murciano Quintero and Others* ECLI:EU:C:2000:346; Case C-473/00 *Cofidis SA v Jean-Louis Fredout* ECLI:EU:2002:239; *Mostaza Claro* (n 3).

6 Council Directive 93/13/EEC of 5 April 1993 on unfair terms in consumer contracts [2002] OJ L95/29.

7 Case C-243/08 *Pannon GSM v Erzsébet Sustikné Győrfi* ECLI:EU:C:2009:350, para 35.

8 Thomas Rauscher in Wolfgang Krüger and others (eds), *Münchener Kommentar zur Zivilprozessordnung* (5th edn, CH Beck 2016) introduction para 344; Hans Prütting in Wolfgang Krüger and others (eds), *Münchener Kommentar zur Zivilprozessordnung* (5th edn, CH Beck 2016) §293 para 4; Ingo Saenger, *Handkommentar zur Zivilprozessordnung* (7th edn, CH Beck 2017) §293 para 1; with regard to foreign law, Ivo Bach and Urs Peter Gruber, 'National Report Austria and Germany' in Carlos Esplugues Mota and others (eds), *Application of Foreign Law* (Sellier European law publishers 2011) 101 ff; critically with regard to the question of whether courts, in fact, do know the law, Rüdiger Zuck, 'Iura novit curia' [2010] *ZRP* 272.

9 *Banco Español de Crédito* (n 3).

for payment procedure, and the ECJ answered the question in the affirmative. The German order for payment procedure, however, is automated:[10] it takes place without the input of a judge who could examine the claimant's general terms. The claimant fills out a form (which can be done online) and a computer issues the payment order on the basis of the claimant's particulars – be they true or false. What is more, the claimant is not even required to provide any details regarding his claim, let alone to turn in the relevant documents. The petition for a payment order must only contain information on what the claimant claims, but not why. If the Unfair Terms Directive did, in fact, require an *ex officio* examination of the relevant contract terms in every order for payment procedure, automated procedures would simply not be feasible at all in consumer cases.

Most likely, however, the Spanish question as well as the European answer were specially geared to the particularities of the Spanish order for payment procedure. In Spain, the order for payment procedure is apparently not automated, and the applicant must 'enclose with the application documents proving that the debt exists'.[11] That means the judge actually has to hand all the information necessary to identify whether or not the terms are unfair. In its judgment, the ECJ referred explicitly to this particular Spanish situation:

> In the light of those considerations, the answer to the first question is that Directive 93/13 must be interpreted as precluding legislation of a Member State, ... which does not allow the court before which an application for an order for payment has been brought to assess of its own motion ... *even though it already has the legal and factual elements necessary for that task available to it*, whether a term ... is unfair.[12]

In Germany, the bolded part of the ECJ's answer has triggered some sort of 'interpretation *e contrario*' – when the factual elements are *not* available, the court is *not* obliged to conduct an *ex officio* legal assessment.[13] Or, more

---

10 Cf. Stefan Schüler in Wolfgang Krüger and others (eds), *Münchener Kommentar zur Zivilprozessordnung* (5th edn, CH Beck 2016) §689 paras 2 ff.

11 *Banco Español de Crédito* (n 3), para 51.

12 *Banco Español de Crédito* (n 3), para 57.

13 Jürgen Basedow in Jürgen Säcker and others (eds), *Münchener Kommentar zum Bürgerlichen Gesetzbuch* (7th edn, CH Beck 2016) preliminary remark §305 para 41; Anatol Dutta, 'Nationales Mahnverfahren und die Effektivität des europäisches Verbraucherschutzes' [2013] *ZZP* no 226, 153, 166; Wolfgang Hau, 'EuGH vom 14.6.2012 – Banco Español de Crédito ./. Joaquín Calderón Camino (Prüfung missbräuchlicher Klauseln im Mahnverfahren)' [2012] *Juristenzeitung (JZ)* 964, 966; Michael Stürner, 'Amtsprüfung im Mahnverfahren und Unzulässigkeit der Vertragsanpassung bei missbräuchlicher Verzugszinsklausel, Anmerkung zu EuGH, Urteil vom 14.6.2012, Rs. C-681/10 – Banco Español de Crédito SA ./. Joaquín Calderón Camino' [2013] *ZEuP* 666, 676; Albrecht Wendenburg, 'Anmerkung zu Verbaucherrecht: Prüfung missbräuchlicher Klauseln im Mahnverfahren und geltungserhaltendende Reduktion' [2012] *EuZW* 758, 759.

concretely, when the claimant does not turn in the contract, the court cannot, and does not have to, examine whether or not the contractual terms are unfair.

In fact, this *e contrario* interpretation of the ECJ's ruling seems quite natural. It seems likely that the ECJ will approve of the German design of the order for payment procedure even in consumer cases. What we have learned in the past 60 years, however, is that ECJ rulings are often unpredictable. Therefore, in my opinion, the ECJ's reasoning in its *Banesto* decision does not constitute an *acte claire*[14] in favour of the German automated order for payment procedure. This means that a German reference to the ECJ is hence necessary – at least in theory. In practice, however, such a reference will obviously be a complex undertaking, given that the procedure is, in fact, automated.

2.2. *EX OFFICIO* EXAMINATION OF FACTS

2.2.1. European Standard

Instead of further elaborating on the question of what an automated reference to the ECJ might look like, I turn now to a more important issue – more important because it concerns a core principle of German (and certainly not only German) procedural law: the principle of party presentation in ordinary proceedings. *Iura novit curia*: the court knows the law. But it does not know the facts. Rather, it is for the parties to present their case: *da mihi facto, dabo tibi ius*.

The first set of ECJ decisions (including *Banesto*) did not affect this principle at all. As mentioned above, the ECJ merely require national courts to examine terms that had come to their knowledge. That has changed, however, in the recent *Faber* decision,[15] which dealt with another directive: the Consumer Sales Directive.[16] Although it was a Dutch court that referred the case to the ECJ, the decision is extraordinarily well known in Germany because the ECJ overturned settled German case law regarding the burden of proof in consumer sales contracts.[17] In the present context, however, it is not this burden-of-proof question that is of interest, but another aspect of the *Faber* decision.

---

14 Cf. regarding the *acte claire* Case C-283/81 *CILFIT v Ministero della Sanità* ECLI:EU:C:1982:335, paras 13 ff.

15 Case C-497/13 *Faber v Autobedrijf Hazet Ochten* ECLI:EU:C:2015:357.

16 Directive 1999/44/EC of the European Parliament and of the Council of 25 May 1999 on certain aspects of the sale of consumer goods and associated guarantees [1999] OJ L171/12.

17 German Federal Supreme Court (Bundesgerichtshof, BGH) 2 June 2004, VIII ZR 329/03 (*Zahnriemen*); subsequent BGH 22 November 2004, VIII ZR 21/04 (*Teichbecken*); BGH 21 December 2005, VIII ZR 49/05; BGH 14 September 2005, VIII ZR 363/04; BGH 23 November 2005, VIII ZR 43/05 (*Turbolader*); BGH 29 March 2006, VIII ZR 173/05; BGH 18 July 2007, XII ZR 259/06 (*Zylinderkopfdichtung*); BGH 15 January 2014, VIII ZR 70/13; observing the ECJ's ruling now BGH 12 October 2016, VIII ZR 103/15.

Here is a short summary of the facts. A Dutch lady (Froukje Faber) purchased a second-hand car at a Dutch garage (Hazet Autobedrijf). Less than half a year later – and while driving, no less – the car caught fire and was completely destroyed. For some reason, the car wreck was scrapped, meaning that there could be no investigation into the causes of the fire. Therefore, in the court proceedings that had been initiated by Ms Faber, the distribution of the burden of proof was the crucial question. Dutch law provides – in compliance with the standards set out in the Consumer Sales Directive – that the burden of proof in consumer sales lies with the seller if a defect becomes evident within six months on delivery.

However, the court apparently did not know whether the sales contract between the Hazet Garage and Ms Faber was actually a consumer contract. More precisely, Ms Faber had not submitted that she had bought the car for private purposes. The Dutch court therefore referred the following question to the ECJ: 'Is a national court … obliged to investigate of its own motion whether, in relation to a contract, the purchaser is a consumer within the meaning of Article 1(2)(a) of Directive 1999/44?'

The difference between this Dutch question in the *Faber* case and the Spanish question in the *Banesto* case is substantial: the *Banesto* question dealt with the legal evaluation of established facts, while the *Faber* question addressed an earlier stage of the proceedings – the examination of facts. Yet the ECJ's answer was the same in both cases – that national courts are indeed obliged to carry out an *ex officio* examination:

> [T]he principle of effectiveness requires a national court before which a dispute relating to a contract which may be covered by that directive has been brought to determine whether the purchaser may be classified as a consumer, even if the purchaser has not expressly claimed to have that status, as soon as that court has at its disposal the matters of law and of fact that are necessary for that purpose *or may have them at its disposal simply by making a request for clarification.*[18]

In other words, the court must take positive action to examine the facts of the case.[19]

---

18 *Faber* (n 15), para 46.

19 The same duty has in fact been established in Case C-137/08 *VB Pénzügyi Lizing ZRT v Ferenc Scheider* ECLI:EU:C:2010:401, para 49 ff; but see for a rather restrictive interpretation of this decision Jürgen Basedow in Jürgen Säcker and others (eds), *Münchener Kommentar zum Bürgerlichen Gesetzbuch* (7th edn, CH Beck 2016) preliminary remarks to §305 para 40; Kalev Saare and Karin Sein, 'Amtsermittlungspflicht der nationalen Gerichte ber der Kontrolle von missbräuchlichen Klauseln in Verbraucherverträgen' [2013] *J of Eur Consumer and Market L (EuVR)* 15.

2.2.2. *The Legal Situation in Germany*

This ruling touches upon an issue that has been discussed in German procedural law for decades. According to §139 of the German Code of Civil Procedure (Zivilprozessordnung, ZPO), courts are empowered – and indeed obliged – to direct the proceedings (*materielle Prozessleitung*):

> To the extent required, the court is to discuss with the parties the circumstances and facts as well as the relationship of the parties to the dispute, both in terms of the factual aspects of the matter and of its legal ramifications, and it is to ask questions. The court is to work towards ensuring that the parties to the dispute make declarations in due time and completely, regarding all significant facts, and in particular is to ensure that the parties amend by further information those facts that they have asserted only incompletely, that they designate the evidence, and that they file the relevant petitions.

The plain wording of this provision seems to grant courts a wide scope to 'take positive action'. However, German courts tend towards a rather narrow interpretation of §139 ZPO: the court's obligation to provide information ends where such information would be in conflict with the court's duty to treat both parties equally. Judges must not take over the role of legal advisors of either party. If they do, they may be challenged for lack of impartiality.[20] But where is the line between a good job in directing the proceedings and partiality towards one party? When does a judge merely comply with his obligation 'to work towards ensuring that the parties to the dispute make declarations in due time and completely' and when does he slip into the role of one party's lawyer?

The German Federal Supreme Court draws the line as follows. On the one hand, the court may and must give notice when the submissions of a party are incomplete, unsubstantiated or ambiguous. On the other hand, the court must not indicate that the claim may be successful on another legal basis. For instance, if the plaintiff claims damages for breach of contract, the court may and must indicate that the plaintiff has not yet submitted any facts that would allow the conclusion that a contract has been entered into between the parties; the court may not indicate, however, that a tort claim would have better prospects of success and that the plaintiff therefore should submit further facts to support such a claim.

When applying this standard, it seems likely that if a German court had decided the *Faber* case, it actually would have asked Ms Faber to submit the

[20] Cf. Jörn FRITSCHE in Wolfgang KRÜGER and others (eds), *Münchener Kommentar zur Zivilprozessordnung* (5th edn, CH Beck 2016) §139 para 8; Astrid STADLER in Hans Joachim MUSIELAK and Wolfgang VOIT (eds), *Zivilprozessordnung* (14th edn, CH Beck 2017) §139 ZPO para 5.

relevant facts, i.e. the facts regarding the purpose of her purchase.[21] It at least seems safe to say that §139 ZPO is broad enough to smoothly implement the ECJ's aims in proceedings before German courts.

In a nutshell, German procedural law seems fairly EU-proof. It is only in relation to the automated order for payment procedure that it may be desirable – but at the same time complex in practice – to ask the ECJ for approval.[22]

3. AUTONOMOUS GERMAN PERSPECTIVE

In the following, I will narrow the focus and concentrate on a purely German perspective on the judges' role. As already mentioned, from the Federal Supreme Court's perspective the line between good and bad information, between directing the proceedings and being biased, is quite a fine one: information is admissible (and even required) when the plaintiff's submissions regarding his concrete claims are incomplete or ambiguous, but information is inadmissible when it concerns new, independent legal grounds for the claim. Likewise, giving the defendant information is admissible so long as the court only informs him that his previous submissions are not substantiated enough; it is inadmissible, however, when the court alludes to new, independent means of defence. For instance, a court may not point out to the defendant that he might have the right to avoid the contract for mistake.

This fine line between good and bad information becomes even finer when it is considered against the background of a peculiarity of German law, where a distinction is made between two forms of defences: the so-called *Einwendung* and the so-called *Einrede*. The difference between these two forms of defence is that courts will consider an *Einwendung ex officio*, but will consider an *Einrede* only when the defendant relies on it.[23] To be clear, in the context of an *Einwendung, ex officio* consideration does not mean that the court will ascertain the facts of its own motion. It merely means that if the facts are clear, the court

21 Note: if the case had been governed by German substantive law, such a request would not have been necessary in the first place: §13 BGB contains a legal assumption according to which a natural person concludes a contract for private purposes. Therefore, the burden of submitting and proving the opposite lies with the professional.

22 See section 2.1 above.

23 Cf. Peter Gröschler, 'Zur Wirkungsweise und zur Frage der Geltendmachung von Einrede und Einwendung im materiellen Zivilrecht' [2001] *AcP* no 201, 48 ff; Caroline Meller-Hannich, 'Die Einrede der Verjährung der Verjährung' [2005] *JZ* 656, 658; Günther Jahr, 'Die Einrede des bürgerlichen Rechts' [1964] *JuS* 125, 128 ff; critically: Matthias Fervers, 'Dispositions- und Verhandlungsgrundsatz im Spannungsverhältnis zum (europäisierten) materiellen Recht' in Daniel Effer-Uhe and others (eds), *Einheit der Prozessrechtswissenschaft?* (Richard Boorberg Verlag 2016) 85 ff; Ivo Bach in Beate Gsell and others (eds), *Beck'scher Online-Großkommentar* (edn 01.02.2018, CH Beck 2018) §214 BGB para 3.1.

will apply the legal consequences *ex officio*. While this seems fairly self-evident given that German procedural law follows the principle of *iura novit curia*, the opposite is true for the *Einrede* – courts consider it only if the defendant relies on it.

The most important example of an *Einrede* is the statute of limitation. §214 of the German Civil Code (Bürgerliches Gesetzbuch, BGB) provides: 'After limitation occurs, the obligor is entitled to refuse performance'. The German Supreme Court has ruled, however, that when refusing performance the obligor must do so with reference to the claim's limitation. In other words, he must more or less 'declare' limitation, just like he would have to declare avoidance for mistake. The mere lapse of a limitation period has no legal consequence in and of itself. A court does not *ex officio* reject a claim for being time-barred. Even if it is obvious that the limitation period has long since lapsed, the court will ignore it.

What is more, the court will not even inform the defendant that he must rely on the claim's limitation in order to make it legally relevant. The statute of limitation constitutes an independent means of defence and, therefore, courts must not provide the defendant with any information in relation to it.

As a matter of fact, when a judge at the Lower Court of Dessau did pass this information on to the defendant, the plaintiff recused himself for being biased – and the Federal Supreme Court ruled that he (the plaintiff) was right in doing so.[24] In its reasoning, the Supreme Court held that by informing the defendant about the limitation, the judge had departed from his position of equal distance from both parties and had taken on the role of a legal adviser to the defendant.[25]

The majority of German legal writers seem to agree.[26] Personally, I belong to the sceptical minority.[27] In my opinion, the Dessau judge laudably fulfilled his obligation to direct the proceedings, for two reasons.

---

24 BGH 2 October 2003, V ZB 22/03.

25 BGH 2 October 2003, V ZB 22/03.

26 Ekkehart Becker-Eberhard, 'Besorgnis der Befangenheit durch Hinweis auf die Möglichkeit der Verjährungseinrede' [2004] *Lindenmaier-Möhring Kommentierte BGH-Rechtsprechung (LMK)* 32; Meller-Hannich (n 23), 662; Hartmut Rensen, 'Richterlicher Hinweis auf Verjährung als Ablehnungsgrund?' [2004] *MDR* 489, 490; Christoph Kern in Friedrich Stein and Martin Jonas (eds), *Kommentar zur Zivilprozessordnung* (23th edn, Mohr 2016) §139 para 54; Stadler (n 20), §139 ZPO para 9; Reinhard Greger in Richard Zöller and others (eds) *Kommentar zur Zivilprozessordnung* (32 edn, Dr. Otto Schmidt 2017) §139 ZPO para 17; Hans Prütting, 'Die Grundlagen des Zivilprozesses im Wandel der Gesetzgebung' [1980] *NJW* 361, 364 ff; Klaus Reischl, 'Der Umfang der richterlichen Instruktionstätigkeit' [2003] *ZZP* no 116, 81, 111 ff; dissenting, Andreas Wacke and Horst Seelig, 'Richterablehung wegen Hinweis auf Möglichkeit der Verjährungseinrede' [1980] *NJW* 1170; Egon Schneider, 'Befangenheit des auf Verjährungsablauf hinweisenden Richters?' [1979] *MDR* 974; Rolf Bender, 'Nochmals – Zivilprozeß und Ideologie' [1982] *JZ* 709, 710; Wolfgang Grunsky, 'Rezension zu Horst Seelig – Die prozessuale Behandlung materiellrechtlicher Einreden' [1981] *AcP* no 181, 564, 566.

27 Bach (n 23), §214 para 57.

The first reason relates to the requirement of invoking limitation. In reading the relevant provision (§214 BGB), there is not the slightest hint that limitation must be invoked in order to become legally relevant. Nevertheless, all German courts and nearly all German academics accept this requirement. They argue, *inter alia*, that since the plaintiff's claim is actually justified, the defendant can freely decide whether or not to rely on the limitation. The defendant has the opportunity to act as a 'man of honour' and fulfil his obligations even after a long time has passed.[28]

However, I have not yet understood why a man of honour should be barred from fulfilling his obligation when courts consider the statute of limitation *ex officio*. The man of honour may simply pay his debts even if a court has ruled that he does not have to do so anymore. A judgment in his favour will not effectively stop him from doing so. What is more, the defendant may simply waive his limitation defence. By doing so, he would prevent the court from rejecting the claim on the basis of limitation; the court would have to decide on the merits of the claim. Therefore, in my opinion, §214 should be interpreted in line with its plain wording: after limitation has occurred, an obligor must not be ordered to fulfil his obligations – irrespective of whether he has relied on the limitation defence or not.

However – and this is my second point – having realised that limitation has occurred, courts should at least be allowed (and probably even obliged) to inform the defendant that he needs to rely on the *Einrede* of limitation. The defendant must have the opportunity to decide freely whether he wants to be a man of honour – and to make this decision, he needs to know that he actually has a choice. Ignorance of the law is simply not the same as honour.

What is more, court proceedings are not a legal competition: it is not the smartest party that should win, but rather the party that has the law on his side. A naïve party must be able to win a lawsuit. This is in particular true when that party is a consumer. It goes seriously against my notion of justice if a court must render a judgment in favour of the plaintiff even though it clearly sees that the defendant is equipped with the best defence available – but that he simply does not realise it because he is an inexperienced consumer.

Therefore, what the ECJ has held in relation to European consumer law should apply in the context of national law as well: it should be considered to be the court's most urgent task to ensure that substantive law is effective. What we need is a domestic principle of effectiveness. Remarkably, establishing the principle of effectiveness in a national context would have a positive effect on the judge's position: the strain upon him would decrease – at least to a certain extent.

---

28 Sahm, 'Die außergerichtliche Geltendmachung der Verjährungseinrede' [1905] *Jehrings Jahrbücher für die Dogmatik des Bürgerlichen Rechts* no 49, 59, 90; Jahr (n 23), 296; Meller-Hannich (n 23), 658.

4. SUMMARY

European substantive law on consumer protection has a strong influence on national law of procedure: the latter must ensure that the former is effective. National courts, therefore, must take action for the consumer: they must *ex officio* consider the European substantive rules and they must even *ex officio* examine the facts of the case (at least regarding the question of whether or not European consumer protection rules in fact apply). Judges, therefore, must not lean back and rely on the parties' own initiative: they must play an active role. To a certain extent, they must support and advise consumers.

German procedural law has a procedural means that allows courts to carry out this task: the obligation of *materielle Prozessleitung* (§139 ZPO). However, settled case law on this obligation is rather averse to courts giving legal advice to one party. In order to meet European targets, the German Federal Supreme Court might have to lessen its restrictions in this regard. It should do so, however, not only where it is forced to by the ECJ, but also in a purely domestic context. Consumer protection rules need to be effective irrespective of their legal source. The European principle of effectiveness, therefore, should be a role model for German domestic law.

EX OFFICIO APPLICATION OF THE UNFAIR TERMS DIRECTIVE CASES AGAINST CONSUMERS

A Swedish Perspective

Torbjörn ANDERSSON*

1. INTRODUCTION

This chapter deals with the *ex officio* application before Swedish courts of the Unfair Terms Directive.[1] The Directive contains two related, but different, means of providing consumer protection before domestic courts and other public enforcement mechanisms (in the wide sense). One of the means concerns consumer protection in individual cases[2] and the other aims at consumer protection as a public interest.[3] The former draws on the traditional tools and objectives of civil procedure (individual compensation with a retrospective focus on the circumstances in the individual case), while the latter is designed to allow for public interference with sellers and suppliers for the prospective

* I would like to thank Aleš Galič, Ljubljana, for valuable comments and input on a draft of this chapter.
1 Directive 93/13/EU on Unfair Terms in Consumer Contracts.
2 Article 6 of the Unfair Terms Directive.
3 Article 7 of the Unfair Terms Directive.

objective of correcting individual abusers, but primarily to clarify the law and deter future abuses.[4]

The following will be limited not only to one aspect of the general subject but also to one part of that aspect: the obligation on Swedish courts to act of their own motion to safeguard consumer interests in individual cases where consumers are defendants. First, the public enforcement of consumer protection will be dealt with only insofar as it concerns individual disputes where unfair terms in consumer relations are of relevance. Second, situations where consumer protection emerges in cases where the consumer acts as claimant will be left out. This delimitation may be surprising since recently the EU legislature has been particularly active in relation to public enforcement and devising mechanisms for conflict resolution where consumers are initiators.[5] Still, I would say that the most frequent way in which an unfair term under a consumer contract comes to be tried before a court or a quasi-court (or to be settled without the involvement of the judiciary) is where the seller/supplier directs a claim for payment against the consumer. Hence, I have considered it relevant to use that angle in a discussion on the practical implementation in Sweden of the requirements of consumer protection before the courts.

The focus will be on the requirements of the Directive, as revealed through the case law of the European Court of Justice (ECJ), in relation to the obligation on national courts to protect consumer interests *ex officio*. In the main, I will concentrate on two types of potential infringements of consumer protection in which that obligation is typically triggered and presumably may conflict with the principle of party autonomy of Swedish civil procedure. One is where a dispute concerns a contract that is clearly or possibly substantively unfair, but where the consumer does not object that the term is unfair. The other concerns forum issues (like unfair prorogation clauses), which are procedural questions.

---

4 In Sweden, the obligations under Article 7 of the Unfair Terms Directive are met by giving a public body, *Konsumentombudsmannen* (the Consumer Ombudsman), the power to bring applications for injunctions (prohibitions of future use of an unfair term) before a special court, the Patents and Market Court. In cases where the Consumer Ombudsman chooses not to bring such a claim, organisations of undertakings, consumers or employees may make an application before the same court. This follows from the Swedish Act on Unfair Terms in Consumer Relations, section 4.

5 Directive 2013/11/EU on alternative dispute resolution for consumer disputes does not apply where consumers are subject to proceedings commenced by traders: Article 2(2)(g). Still, it is worth mentioning that in Sweden this Directive is implemented by the Act on Alternative Dispute Resolution in Consumer Relations (Lag (2015:671) om alternativ tvistlösning i konsumentförhållanden), under which appointment of alternative dispute resolution boards, as stipulated by the Directive, is entrusted to the Legal, Financial and Administrative Services Agency (*Kammarkollegiet*) as the competent authority. Only public authorities may be appointed, the most important of which is the National Board for Consumer Disputes (*Allmänna reklamationsnämnden*, ARN).

My discussion of these issues will be structured in the following manner. First, I describe EU law – the Directive and some relevant case law of the ECJ regarding *ex officio* application before national courts, with particular focus on the questions mentioned above (section 2). Since the case law of the ECJ is, and has been, under development in this area, the exact content of the requirements submitted is evolving and remains somewhat unclear. Therefore, it is necessary to deal with most of the cases where the questions have been addressed. I then describe the relevant aspects of the content of Swedish civil procedural law (section 3). I also discuss whether Swedish law meets the requirements of the ECJ. This section is divided into two parts. First, I deal with the highly unusual situation where the seller commences litigation before an ordinary court (section 3.1). Next, I deal with the situation where the seller takes action by way of summary proceedings (section 3.2). I conclude with a brief analysis and some remarks (section 4).

2. THE UNFAIR TERMS DIRECTIVE

In essence, Article 3 of the Unfair Terms Directive means that the Directive applies in situations where there is a contract between a seller/supplier and where that contract has not been individually negotiated. Where a contract has been drafted in advance, it is generally regarded as not individually negotiated. Individual negotiation of aspects of a term or one specific term does not exclude application of the Directive for the rest of the contract.

Article 6 stipulates that Member States should establish that unfair terms, under the Directive, shall not be binding on the consumer. The annex blacklists typically unfair terms in consumer contracts (1.a–1.q), the last of which covers:

> terms which have the effect of excluding or hindering the consumer's right to take legal action or exercise any other legal remedy, particularly by requiring the consumer to take disputes exclusively to arbitration not covered by legal provisions, unduly restricting the evidence available to him or imposing on him a burden of proof which, according to the applicable law, should lie with another party to the contract.

From the ECJ's *Océano*[6] judgment in 2000 it is clear that the effectiveness of consumer protection can only be ensured where domestic courts are able to consider unfair terms *ex officio*, and that prorogation clauses are covered

[6] Case C-240–244/98 *Océano Grupo Editorial SA v Rocio Murciano Quintero and Others* [2005] ECR I-494.

by 1.q of the blacklist of the annex to the Directive.[7] In *Cofidis*,[8] the ECJ held that consumer protection covers the situation where the consumer refrains from claiming that a specific term is unfair.[9]

In *Mostaza Claro*,[10] the Court held that domestic courts must determine in actions of annulment of arbitration awards whether the arbitration awards are void as a consequence of arbitration agreements containing unfair terms, even where the consumer has not pleaded invalidity in arbitration proceedings but only in the actions for annulment.[11] The Court also held that Article 6(1) is a mandatory provision that aims to replace the formal balance that the contract establishes between the rights and obligations of the parties with an effective balance that re-establishes equality between them.[12] Furthermore, it was held that the Directive constitutes a measure that is essential to this, and ultimately to accomplishing the tasks entrusted to the community and to raising the standard of living and the quality of life in its territory. The nature and importance of the public interest underlying consumer protection justify the fact that domestic courts are required to assess of their own motion whether contractual terms are unfair.[13] In *Asturcom*,[14] the ECJ went further, submitting that in view of the nature and importance of the public interest underlying the protection that the Directive confers on individuals, Article 6 must be regarded as a provision with equal standing to national rules that rank, within the domestic legal system, as rules of public policy.[15]

In *Pannon GSM*,[16] the ECJ repeatedly emphasised the *ex officio* obligation, holding that the domestic court must, of its own motion, consider whether a term is unfair as soon as the court has become aware of the legal and factual circumstances necessary. In that case, the ECJ added that where the court finds a term unfair, it should not apply that term unless the consumer objects to it not being applied.[17]

In *VB Pénzügyi Lízing*,[18] the ECJ again held that the national court must ascertain whether a contractual term that is the subject of the dispute falls

7 For an analysis from a Swedish perspective of this case, see Torbjörn Andersson, 'EG-domstolens avgörande i Océano-målet samt konsumenträtt och forumregler i Sverige' (2001) *Europarättslig tidskrift* 565.

8 Case C-473/00 *Cofidis SA v Jean-Louis Fredout* [2002] ECR I-10875.

9 *Cofidis* (n 8), para 34.

10 Case C-168/05 *Elisa Maria Mostaza Claro v Centro Movil Milenium SL* [2006] ECR I-10421.

11 *Mostaza Claro* (n 10), para 39.

12 *Mostaza Claro* (n 10), para 36. See also Case C-40/08 *Asturcom Telecomunicaciones SL v Christina Rodríguez Nogueira* [2009] ECR I-9579, para 30.

13 *Mostaza Claro* (n 10), paras 37–38.

14 *Asturcom* (n 12).

15 *Asturcom* (n 12), para 52.

16 Case C-243/08 *Pannon GSM Zrt v Erzsébet Sustikné Győrfi* [2009] ECR I-4713.

17 *Pannon* (n 16), para 35.

18 Case C-137/08 *VB Pénzügyi Lízing Zr. v Ferenc Schneider* [2010] ECR I-10847.

within the scope of the Directive and assess that term, if necessary of its own motion, in the light of the requirements of consumer protection laid down in the Directive. In *Banif Plus Bank Zrt*,[19] the ECJ held that a national court that has found a contractual term unfair of its own motion is not obliged, in order to carry out the consequences, to wait for the consumer, who will have been informed, to make a request for invalidity. Furthermore, the Court held that the principle of *audi alteram partem* requires a court to inform the parties and invite them to give their views, in accordance with the formal requirements under domestic law.[20] Affording the consumer this opportunity also fulfils the national court's obligation to take into account the intention expressed by the consumer that he/she is opposed to the unfair term being disregarded.[21]

In *Erika Jörös*,[22] a domestic court of appeal had discovered that the underlying contract was unfair, although the consumer had not addressed that issue. The ECJ held that where a national court on appeal has the power, under domestic law, to examine any grounds for invalidity apparent from the elements submitted at first instance and, if necessary, to redefine, depending on the facts determined, the legal basis relied upon to establish that those terms are invalid, it must assess of its own motion or by redefining the legal basis of the application whether those terms are unfair in the light of the criteria of the Directive.[23]

The obligation of *ex officio* consumer protection also applies to domestic courts at the stage of enforcement of an arbitration award or another title of execution given in respect of consumer contracts. In *Asturcom*,[24] the ECJ found that the Directive must be interpreted as meaning that in a national court or tribunal hearing an action for enforcement of an arbitration award that has become final and made in the absence of the consumer requires the court or tribunal, where it has available to it the legal and factual elements necessary for that task, to assess of its own motion whether an arbitration clause in a consumer contract is unfair, insofar as, under national rules of procedure, it can carry out such an assessment in similar actions of a domestic nature.[25] This is a consequence that arises where enforcement might be rejected due to domestic public policy, since Article 6 is considered EU public policy.[26]

---

19 Case C-472/11 *Banif Plus Bank Zrt v Csaba Csipai, Viktória Csipai* ECLI:EU:C:2013:88.

20 *Banif* (n 19), para 36.

21 *Banif* (n 19), para 35.

22 Case C-397/11 *Erika Jőrös v Aegon Magyarország Hitel Zrt* ECLI:EU:C:2013:340.

23 *Erika Jőrös* (n 22), para 38.

24 *Asturcom* (n 12).

25 *Asturcom* (n 12), para 59.

26 See *Mostaza Claro* (n 10).

In the recent *Finanmadrid EFC*[27] case, the ECJ held that the Directive precludes all national legislation that does not permit the court ruling on the enforcement of an order for payment to assess of its own motion whether a term concluded between a seller or a supplier and a consumer is unfair, when the authority hearing the application for an order for payment does not have the power to make such an assessment.

Thus, the obligation on domestic courts to act of their own motion contains the requirements detailed below.

Where the case contains the factual and legal elements necessary for an assessment, the court must *ex officio* assess whether the claim against the consumer is unfair and invalid under the Directive. This goes for first instance courts and appellate courts.[28] When seised with a case involving an unfair claim, the court, having determined that the claim is unfair, must inform the parties and allow them to give their views. This includes meeting the requirement that the court allow the consumer to ask the court to stick with the unfair term. If the consumer says nothing and the seller's view does not alter the court's assessment, the court must rule that the term is invalid and carry out all the consequences that follow from such a determination under domestic law (for example, potentially invalidating the entire contract, etc.).

Even where there is a final arbitration award or payment order with the force of *res judicata* and where no court has been involved in deciding the case, a court responsible for the enforcement of the execution title must assess whether the underlying claim is based on an unfair term in a consumer contract, since enforcement of the execution title would be in breach of EU public policy.

All elements of the obligation mentioned above are conditional, in the sense that any required court motion must be allowed under domestic procedural law in domestic claims. Still, where courts are obliged to act *ex officio* but domestic rules do not permit it, the courts must assess whether applicable domestic procedural rules render the protection of individual consumer rights impossible or exceedingly difficult (the principle of effectiveness). It is not perfectly clear whether the principle of effectiveness would apply at the enforcement stage in jurisdictions where domestic courts have no power to refuse enforcement due to public policy considerations – typically when applying the *van Schijndel* formula.[29] The ECJ has been keen to give much weight to the procedural principle of *res judicata* and the objective of finality

---

27 See Case C-49/14 *Finanmadrid EFC SA v Jesús Vicente Albán Zambrano and Others* ECLI:EU:C:2016:98.

28 At least when that is possible under domestic procedural rules regarding similar domestic claims.

29 See e.g. Case C-430/93 *Jeroen van Schijndel and Johannes Nicolaas Cornelis van Veen v Stichting Pensioenfonds voor Fysiotherapeuten* [1995] ECR I-470.

of proceedings and limit the requirements on domestic courts to what is possible under domestic procedural law.

3. SWEDISH PROCEDURAL LAW

As submitted in the introduction, the discussion in this chapter is limited to the *ex officio* obligation on Swedish courts in individual cases, where a claim is brought by the seller against the consumer. The most common way in which a seller enforces (in the wide sense) a claim against a consumer is by a payment order (*betalningsföreläggande*), which is a type of summary proceeding designed to promote speed and efficiency in dealing with mass claims. But in order to provide a view of the Swedish procedural system as regards the principle of autonomy and rules on forum, I will begin by considering the leeway for Swedish courts to comply with EU requirements in situations where a seller makes a claim for payment against a consumer (based on a contract containing an unfair term) before an ordinary court.

At the outset, it should be noted that Swedish consumer law (of which there exists a lot) is traditionally considered to be *semi-mandatory*. That means that a consumer is not bound by an agreement on an unfair term, but may agree on it subsequently when there has been a dispute on the contract.[30] A consequence of this is that when there is a consumer dispute before a Swedish court, the principle of party autonomy applies, although the court may exercise a more extensive *prozessleitung* than normal.[31] When implementing the Unfair Terms Directive, the Swedish legislator made the assessment that this way of handling consumer disputes should be maintained. After the emergence of a dispute, the consumer is subject to the normal requirements of parties in relation to formulating claims, submitting facts and making objections.[32]

3.1. PROCEEDINGS COMMENCED BEFORE A COURT

I will now take as an example a situation where a consumer has concluded a contract on goods and services based on a standard form including two unfair

30 A similar semi-mandatory provision may be found in Article 19(1) of the Brussels I *bis* Regulation.

31 In Sweden, *prozessleitung* means the possibility and obligation on the court to be active during proceedings when necessary, i.e. asking the parties to clarify what is unclear and draw the attention of the parties to aspects of the case they may have missed or misunderstood. It does not mean that the court has a right to include facts or extend claims where the parties are passive, at least not in cases where the principle of party autonomy applies. The need for court activity in this sense is, of course, bigger where one of the parties is in a weaker position, e.g. in consumer cases.

32 Governmental bill 1994/95:17 21.

terms. One term obliges the consumer to fulfil all his/her obligations even if the seller does not perform his/hers,[33] and another term states that the domicile of the seller is the exclusive forum for litigation arising from the contract.[34]

Proceedings begin when the seller files a statement of claim ('originating summons'). It must contain a claim and grounds for the claim. Say the seller claims a sum of money due to be paid under the contact and submits the contract as evidence of the obligation to pay. The contract also contains a prorogation clause conferring jurisdiction on the court where the case was filed, but the seller does not have to prove that the court has jurisdiction. The general rule in Sweden is that all rules on the forum are default rules, except where the jurisdiction is explicitly exclusive, such as in disputes over real estate and family matters. Thus, although the rule states that a contract dispute should be brought with the defendant's domicile as the forum,[35] the court cannot reject the case without summoning the consumer. The consumer must, in his/her statement of defence, object to the jurisdiction of the court or else lose his/her right to object.[36] Loss of the right to object will also occur where the defendant fails to respond or is not present at the first court hearing.[37]

Where the consumer objects in proper time, the court need not use the Directive as a basis for rejection. In the event that the seller invokes the prorogation clause as the basis for the court's jurisdiction, the court must assess its validity[38] and may then comply with EU requirements by informing the parties of its decision and by giving them opportunity to present their views (including giving the defendant the possibility to waive his/her objection). Then the court may reject the case, even if the consumer fails to respond.[39]

---

33 See term 1(o) of the annex to the Directive.

34 See term 1(q) of the annex, which has been considered to contain a prohibition on prorogation clauses by the CJEU in a number of cases.

35 This is subject to some exceptions of no relevance in this context.

36 Under the Swedish Code of Procedure, Ch 10 section 19, the court must not reject a case when it lacks jurisdiction. The absence of an objection in proper time will confer jurisdiction on the court. Ch 34 section 2 sets the relevant time limit.

37 It is debatable whether in a situation where there are no detectably unfair clauses in a consumer contract but the seller still files a statement of claim before the court at his/her domicile, the court should inform the consumer/defendant that he/she must object or else the objection will be precluded. It would be extremely hard to claim that the court is under an obligation to protect the consumer's right. The argument would have to be that it is unfair for the consumer to have to enter into a legal dispute at a forum that is not convenient and that the forum itself is an obstacle to the protection of the consumer's rights.

38 It is also now established under Swedish that prorogation clauses in consumer agreements are unfair; this has been held on a number of occasions by the Swedish Market Court in public interest proceedings.

39 The court has no option to transfer the case to the court of the defendant's domicile. Although there is a rule on transfer of cases between courts (Code of Procedure, Ch 10 section 20a), it only applies where the first court lacks jurisdiction due to the rules on exclusive jurisdiction and a transfer must only be made before the order to summons has been issued and with the consent of the claimant.

The time limits for the defendant to object to the jurisdiction of the court are harsh. What happens if the defendant does not respond at all to the court's information initially, but at a later stage wants to object to the prorogation clause? Does the preclusion rule, which has a tough time limit, make it 'exceedingly difficult' for the consumer to enforce her/his rights? In view of the ECJ's case law on domestic time limits precluding individual claims under EU law,[40] it may well be that, at least where a consumer is the defendant, the deadline for objecting must be extended.[41]

It may even be the case that the obligation on the defendant to object should be set aside in cases where the defendant is a consumer. The ECJ's formulation of the requirement of *ex officio* activity seems to mean that passivity on the part of the consumer triggers the court to act of its own motion on behalf of the consumer. Only the consumer's explicit request that an unfair term remain binding relieves the court of its obligation to act of its own motion.

However, under Swedish law, the burden to object is clearly laid down in statutory law. It cannot easily be spirited away by interpretation. Similarly, as when extending a time limit set in statutory law, it would be necessary to read the ECJ's case law into the Swedish Act implementing the Directive and set aside the rule in the Chapter 10 section 18 of the Code of Procedure (CoP). Since Chapter 10 is subsidiary to rules on jurisdiction laid down in specific legislation, it would be possible to use the Act on Unfair Terms in Consumer Relations[42] to achieve that result. Still, as will be clear below, such an act would require a great deal of constructive interpretation.

Now, if the obligation to object were to be set aside, would that apply only where the seller invokes an (unfair) prorogation clause, or should it apply generally for contracts containing unfair terms? If the contract in the example above only contained the term on lack of reciprocity in performance, the contract would not contain any elements hindering the consumer's right to take legal action. The procedural difficulties for the consumer would arise not from the contract, but from Swedish law. Since all legal subjects have to comply with

40 See e.g. Case C-312/93 *Peterbroeck, Van Campenhout & Cie SCS v Belgian State* [1995] ECR I-4599; see also Torbjörn Andersson, *Rättsskyddsprincipen* (Iustus förlag 1997) 123 ff for a slightly outdated analysis of the ECJ's case law on time limits and procedural autonomy of the Member States.

41 Under CoP Ch 10 section 18, the defendant must make an objection in time. The time limit ('when the defendant makes a claim for the first time') is set in CoP Ch 34 section 2. Deviating from CoP Ch 34 section 2 and extending the time limit requires a heavily constructive interpretation. The act implementing the Directive is as laconic as the Directive itself – for example, the blacklist is not set out in statutory writing. By way of interpretation, it will be necessary to insert prorogation terms into the concept of unfair terms and also any procedural norms necessary to effectively protect the rights of the consumer. It could then be said that the implementing act establishes an exception to the time limit set in CoP Ch 34 section 2.

42 Lag (1994:1512) om avtalsvillkor i konsumentförhållanden.

the burden to object where they are sued before the 'wrong' court, it would be hard to make an exception in situations where the defendant is a consumer, whether or not the court finds that the contract contains unfair terms. Consequently, since a prorogation clause will matter only after the defendant has objected to the court's jurisdiction, there will be no real reason to relieve the consumer of the burden to object, even where such a clause is part of the contract used as a ground for the substantive claim.

Thus, the obligation to act *ex officio* with respect to an unfair prorogation clause will only be effective where the claimant has invoked it as a basis for the jurisdiction of the court, which presupposes an objection by the consumer.

To conclude, it seems that Swedish procedural law is reconcilable with the requirements laid down by the ECJ, insofar as *ex officio* activity regarding prorogation clauses is concerned. The same goes for *ex officio* activity regarding substantive terms, such as the one above. With regard to the latter, the Code of Procedure makes a distinction between substantive questions governed by default rules and substantive questions governed by mandatory law. Although the requirement of the ECJ that domestic courts should act *ex officio* where the consumer is passive but be bound where the consumer makes an explicit request to the contrary contains elements of both mandatory and party autonomous character, the Swedish Code provides enough leeway for courts to meet that requirement in individual proceedings.

Still, it is clear that the Swedish obligation to object as a necessary element for rejecting a case is a general obstacle to EU consumer protection, and not just in cases where unfair terms are at issue. That obstacle could be removed by instead making the consumer's domicile the exclusive forum for litigation in consumer cases. That would make it impossible to give the consumer the choice to have the case tried elsewhere. Promoting consumer policy in general is not part of the requirements the ECJ makes of domestic courts in terms of safeguarding consumers' rights when they are infringed by unfair terms.

3.2. PROCEEDINGS INITIATED BY A PAYMENT ORDER

The Act on Payment Orders (APO) regulates payment orders.[43] Payment orders are decided and issued by the *Kronofogdemyndigheten* (Swedish Enforcement Authority, EA). The procedure is strictly written and structured as provided below.

A case is initiated when one party files an application claiming that another party must pay a certain sum of money. The application must contain a specific amount, the due date and the interest claimed. The basis for the claim does not need to be included in the application. Only undisputed claims are subject to

43 Lag (1990:746) om betalningsföreläggande och handräckning.

payment orders. The EA orders the defendant to reply within a specified period of time, generally not exceeding two weeks. Thus, the defendant is informed that the case may be decided even if he/she does not reply. If the defendant contests the claim, he/she is required to submit reasons.

The claimant is notified if the defendant contests the claim (which must be done in writing). The claimant may then within four weeks of the notification ask that the case be handed over to a court. This request must contain the circumstances and proof the claimant wants to bring before the court. The EA hands over the case to the court of first instance that, according to the documents, has jurisdiction. Of course, the claimant may also commence proceedings before an ordinary court after the expiry of the four-week period.

In the event that the claim is not contested (in time), the EA issues a payment order on the claim. A payment order is enforceable as a judgment. Still, the defendant may, within one month from the date the order was issued, apply for recovery, which means that the EA must hand over the case to an ordinary court for continued proceedings. The EA determines which court from the case documents.

The EA may reject an application where it can be assumed that the claim is unfounded. The claim is then handled as if the defendant had contested it.

It can be assumed that most claims from Swedish sellers to Swedish consumers that are not paid without involvement of the judiciary and enforcement machinery will be enforced via the system of payment orders, and only exceptionally via the ordinary courts under the procedure described above.

In order to demonstrate how the system could work for consumer contracts containing unfair terms of the kind discussed above under section 3.1 (a prorogation clause and a term on non-reciprocal performance of the consumer), I will use the example of a seller using those terms in a standard contract for the sale of a sound system. Furthermore, I will, without any hard statistics but only my subjective and rough estimations as a basis, illustrate the hypothetical effects of enforcement or non-enforcement of the Directive in a situation where the seller sells his/her products to 1,000 customers. The example will also be used to illustrate the ways in which consumer protection via *ex officio* application by Swedish courts and quasi-courts may materialise.

Say that the product, the sound system and a commitment to support it, is sold on an instalment basis to 1,000 consumers. Of those, 100 consumers experience a malfunction and ask for support to upgrade their system, requests which the seller repeatedly leaves unattended. Let us say 45 of these 100 consumers pay the next instalment, even though the seller has not honoured his/her commitment to provide support. Another 25 pay when they get a notice from a debt collecting company to which the debt has been assigned, and another 15 pay when they receive a notice from the EA that there is a claim against them and an order to submit reasons in the event they want to *contest* the claim. Only eight (8/1,000 of those subject to the unfair contract term) contest the claim. Five might apply for *recovery* after the payment order has been issued, while three will be subject to the payment order without applying for recovery and must either pay or be subject to coercive *enforcement*.

When a claim is *contested*, the seller may choose to drop the claim or take action under normal rules (see section 3.1 above) before or after the expiry of the time limit. The seller may also ask that the claim be handed over to a court and, as was mentioned above, the EA determines from the documents in the case before it which court seems to have jurisdiction to hear it. At this stage, the case file attached to the application may include the written contract with the unfair prorogation clause. When deciding which court to hand over the claim to, the EA will probably notice the prorogation clause. The EA may then, of its own motion, find the clause unfair under European and Swedish law. If it does, the EA should then hand over the case to the courts where the consumer is domiciled (which will also happen in the event that the EA does not notice the clause). On the hand, it is not unlikely (since the proceedings before the EA are summary and involve multitudes of cases) that the EA, having noticed the clause but not received an objection from the consumer in relation to the forum, will hand over the case to the court provided with jurisdiction by the prorogation clause.

As to the five who apply for *recovery*, the claims will be handled in the same way: the EA will use the case documents to determine which court has jurisdiction and will hand the case over to that court.

Under APO section 61, in cases that have been handed over to courts from the EA due to contested claims or applications for recovery, the court receiving the case may, in turn, in cases where it finds that the documents do not indicate that it has jurisdiction, hand it over to another court that may have jurisdiction. This rule applies not only in respect of forum rules that the parties have no choice over, but also when the court receiving the case has no jurisdiction under default rules.[44] Therefore, a court to which one of the eight plus five claims from our example above are handed over may make an *ex officio* assessment of the prorogation clause, set it aside and hand the case to, for example, the forum of the domicile of the consumer. Ideally, the court should inform both parties of its finding that the court's jurisdiction rests on an invalid contract term and ask the consumer if he/she would still like to have it try the case. In the event that the consumer does not respond, the court would hand over the case to the other court.[45] Thus, the Swedish system provides opportunities

---

[44] A similar rule is provided in the CoP, but that only applies where a claim is made before a court that does not have jurisdiction under mandatory rules: see CoP Ch 10 section 20a. Thus, Swedish civil procedure contains a rule on *forum non conveniens*.

[45] I would think that passing the case on without informing the parties would not be in breach of EU law. If the parties prefer to stick to the prorogation clause, they could have that settled before the court to which the case is passed on. Still, it would cause delay and be inconvenient.

for courts to meet the requirements on *ex officio* application as laid down by the ECJ.

Still, it must be remembered that where the court is not alert but allows proceedings to commence, the consumer's right to object will be precluded. Moreover, the consumer will possibly have the case decided at a place that is not convenient. It is debatable whether this is in line with the requirements of the ECJ, but it is clear that domestic procedural rules do not unconditionally allow objections to the forum after proceedings have commenced. The situation where a court receives a case arising from an unfair prorogation clause and fails to make enquiries with the parties as to the clause's validity and/or reject the case *ex officio* should not be treated differently from the situation where a seller makes a claim against the consumer before the 'wrong' court.

What about the three consumers in our example above who have remained passive and become subjects of enforceable payment orders? Since a payment order is a title for execution and since the Swedish system, apparently unlike the Spanish,[46] does not make execution dependent on a court decision, there is no leeway for *ex officio* assessments by courts. The case law of the ECJ is addressed to domestic courts only.

Having said that, it could be argued, particularly in cross-border situations, that the requirements laid down for domestic courts also apply to the EA. Under Article 3(b) Brussels I *bis*,[47] the EA shall be considered a court with respect to its role in summary proceedings concerning orders to pay, which is exactly the situation under discussion here. The EA has the same status under Article 4(7) of the European Enforcement Order Regulation.[48] Although European enforcement orders only are relevant in cross-border situations, the fact that when issuing payment orders the EA is considered to be a court under Brussels I in practice means that the ECJ requirements must be understood to also apply to the EA. When a payment order is issued for an uncontested claim, it will not yet be known to anyone, and especially not to the EA, whether the applicant will try to have the order enforced abroad in the EU. Therefore, the requirements of the ECJ must reasonably be understood to mean that the EA will act *ex officio* when the authority can deduce from the legal and factual elements of the case that it concerns the enforcement of an unfair term in a consumer contract.

Within what limits, then, may the EA act *ex officio* to protect the individual consumer before issuing a payment order? Since summary proceedings of payment orders are a procedural mechanism set up to deal with a mass of

---

46 *Finanmadrid* (n 27).

47 Regulation (EU) 1215/2012 on jurisdiction and the recognition and enforcement of judgments in civil and commercial matters (recast) [2012] OJ L351/1.

48 Regulation (EC) 805/2004 creating a European Enforcement Order for uncontested claims [2004] OJ L143/15.

uncontested claims quickly and efficiently, the individual case will probably not provide much material for an assessment. Moreover, there will probably not be much time for careful examination either. The following must be seen in light of that.

When a claim can be assumed to be *unfounded*, the EA shall consider it contested, i.e. leave it up to the applicant to apply for the EA to hand it over to a court.[49] In a case as in the example above, the application would need to have the contract attached (which is not required – see above) and the receiving official would need sufficient time and knowledge to examine the terms. It would be unlikely that the applicant would attach the contract in a typical case, and it would be unlikely that even a thorough official of the EA would act before notifying the consumer of the claim. However, that is basically the only legal ground for the EA to comply with the requirements of the ECJ in consumer cases.[50] Consequently, the protection afforded to consumers who are entirely passive when confronted by payment orders is very limited.

3.3. ENFORCEMENT

When the EA acts in its capacity as the enforcement authority of execution titles, it is not subject to the requirements of the ECJ, since the case law explicitly concerns courts. The *Finanmadrid* case, where the ECJ was concerned with the protection of consumers at the enforcement stage, explicitly addressed what was required from the domestic court involved in the enforcement proceedings. Furthermore, as an entity entrusted with enforcement, the EA is not subject to any particular requirements under Brussels I *bis*; it is not a requirement that the enforcement of foreign claims be scrutinised by a court. Therefore, the requirements of *ex officio* assessment do not apply where the EA acts as the enforcer of foreign judgments against consumers.[51]

49 APO section 23 para 1.

50 Under APO section 42, the EA shall immediately issue an order on the claim if the defendant has not responded in due time.

51 Still, it must be noted that in a situation as in the example above, but where a foreign judgment is being enforced in Sweden under Brussels I *bis*, it is submitted that where judgment is given against the consumer (Articles 46 and 45(1)(e)) and the jurisdiction of the court giving judgment was based on a prorogation clause set out in a standard contract and not agreed upon after the dispute had arisen (cf. Article 19(1)), there is ground for refusal to enforce the judgment. The EA's jurisdiction to enforce such a judgment in Sweden rests on a Swedish act (2014:912) with supplementing provisions on the jurisdiction of courts and on recognition and international enforcement of certain decisions, which submits that a foreign judgment must be enforced like an enforceable Swedish judgment where the requirements of Brussels I are met, unless something different follows from the Brussels I. Even if this may create an obstacle to enforcement, it does not create an obligation on the EA to make

Thus, the requirements of *ex officio* application do not seem to apply to the EA when it enforces foreign judgments against consumers in cross-border situations under EU law; the same rules apply as when the EA enforces Swedish judgments or payment orders. In fact, when it comes to *ex officio* activity for contract terms that are substantively unfair, it seems impossible even for Member State courts to meet the ECJ's requirements at the stage of enforcement. Article 52 Brussels I *bis* provides that under 'no circumstances may a judgment given in a Member State be reviewed as to its substance in the Member State addressed'. Still, it is quite important to find out what powers the EA has under Swedish law to consider the Directive when enforcing judgments and payments orders relating to claims that may infringe consumer rights under the Directive.

Under the Swedish Code of Execution,[52] there is an obstacle to enforcement where the defendant makes an objection that some 'circumstances concerning the relation between the parties constitute an obstacle to enforcement and such objection cannot be disregarded'. It is possible, or at least (with some effort) arguable, that the EA may be convinced not to enforce the judgment or payment where the consumer objects that enforcement would be contrary to EU *ordre public* – but it is far from certain. In any event, that provision does not provide a basis for the EA to stop enforcement *ex officio*.

4. CONCLUDING REMARKS

From a Swedish perspective, considered from the angle of both civil procedure and substantive private law, the requirements placed on domestic courts regarding consumer protection before courts may be characterised as paternalistic. The requirements seem to build on the perception that consumers are in general not fully capable legal subjects, able to meet the ordinary conditions to defend one's rights before the court. It is one thing to have semi-mandatory consumer law, protecting the consumer at the time a contract is concluded, but still making the consumer subject to the ordinary conditions of private and procedural law; that is, after a dispute has arisen, the consumer has the responsibility and the right to determine whether it is worthwhile to accept a term which the consumer could lawfully object to. It is quite another thing to go beyond the limits of the ordinary rules and, for example, enforce

an *ex officio* assessment, since refusal to enforce requires that the person against whom enforcement is sought must make an application to the court appointed by Sweden to hear matters concerning refusals to enforce judgments under the Regulation (see governmental ordinance 2014:1517 on courts; the competent court for dealing with the issue in the scenario above will be the court of the domicile of the applicant/consumer).

52 Ch 3 section 21 para 2.

consumer rights where the individual consumer is completely passive in court proceedings, which would normally have the effect that the defendant will have his/her options (for example, to object to the court's jurisdiction, invoke counterfactual circumstances, to contradict the facts, etc.) precluded at different stages of procedure.

Moreover, the requirements under the Directive seem a bit hard to reconcile with the development of civil procedure by the EU legislature in relation to the handling of mass claims in cross-border cases. The European Enforcement Order Regulation[53] and the European Order for Payment Regulation[54] do not leave much room for *ex officio* assessments by the courts deciding uncontested claims. A court may perhaps notice that a prorogation clause that is taken to be the basis for assigning it jurisdiction (cf. European Order for Payment Regulation Article 8) is unfair and invalid, and this may also be the case when the EA applies the Regulation.[55] However, I find it improbable that, in summary proceedings, any court (or the EA) could find sufficient legal and factual elements in a claim to make an *ex officio* assessment of unfairness in the substance of a contract. In view of the objective behind the Regulations – efficient and speedy enforcement of uncontested claims in cross-border cases – that is not surprising. But it is also at odds with the court's obligation to protect consumers who are passive in proceedings.

Furthermore, it is a bit hard to digest the ECJ's finding that consumer protection in individual cases is part of EU public policy and requires *ex officio* protection by courts. The Swedish view on consumer protection would be that, since there is a parallel system of public legal intervention, which safeguards the general – public – interest of consumers,[56] there is no need to deviate from ordinary rules of procedure in individual consumer disputes. In public litigation, the general interest is at stake, but in individual disputes, only the subjective interest of the individual consumer is at stake. Thus, from a Swedish perspective, it is entirely incomprehensible that the interests of an individual should qualify as public policy. The same goes for other areas with mixed procedural mechanisms and substantive law, such as labour law, competition

53 Regulation 805/2004/EU creating a European Enforcement Order for uncontested claims.

54 Regulation 1896/2006/EU creating a European order for payment procedure.

55 The Regulation refers to Brussels I *bis* in in relation which organs should be considered competent as courts, see Article 6. Furthermore, it is submitted that jurisdiction in cases where the defendant is a consumer may only be conferred courts in the consumer's domicile. Since the EA is also entrusted with European payment orders under Swedish law, an application for such an order relating to a cross-border contract will be decided by the EA. The conditions for issuing an order are somewhat more demanding in comparison to issuing a Swedish payment order. Brussels I *bis* also requires that a judgment by a foreign court against a consumer, where the consumer has acted as defendant, may only be enforced where the consumer has agreed to depart from his/her domicile jurisdiction by an agreement entered into after the dispute has arisen.

56 See (n 4) above.

law and environmental law.[57] Furthermore, I find it a bit depressing to attribute to the consumption of goods and services such a fundamental value that any consumer should be relieved of his/her responsibility to behave as a fully capable individual in proceedings relating to his/her consumption. Semi-mandatory rules are definitely needed in this field of standard forms and click-wrap agreements, but to elevate the protection of the individual consumer to one of the central pillars of society would go too far. But it is hard to argue with the case law of the ECJ on this point.

The requirements the ECJ places on domestic courts follow the pattern of the principle of procedural autonomy in that the requirements apply when domestic procedural rules allow the courts to act. Still, following the same pattern, when domestic procedural rules create obstacles to the protection of individual rights under EU law, they must be measured against the *Van Schijndel* criteria. If they do not pass the test, they must be set aside in individual cases. There is no reason to believe that this does not also apply to the requirements regarding *ex officio* application under the Unfair Terms Directive. It should be noted, however, that in its case law the ECJ has given the principle of *res judicata* great weight in the balancing test, and it generally outweighs the individual right that it impairs. Accordingly, the requirements placed on domestic courts regarding *ex officio* application at the enforcement stage would be conditional on existing legal avenues under domestic law for those courts to act *ex officio*, for example in the event of a breach of *ordre public*.

One of the lessons to be learnt for Sweden would be that the defendant's obligation to object in his/her first reply should be mitigated. When the court issues the summons, it should attach information that the defendant may reject the venue, where that is possible. This ought to be standard procedure where the defendant could be expected to be the weaker party. This practice would not be in breach of the rules of Swedish civil procedure, but may be an additional administrative burden to bear. It could be supplemented by an option to extend the time limit for making an objection, but that would require a change to the existing rules if it were to apply generally in cases where the defendants are in a weaker position. It would also be in conflict with the objective of determining the jurisdiction of the court as soon as possible in order to avoid unnecessary work. Since CoP Chapter 10 is subsidiary, such a change in consumer cases could be easily achieved by adding a paragraph to the Act on Unfair Terms in Consumer Relations. It should be pointed out that such an alteration is not necessary in order to comply with requirements of the ECJ, but would be in line with the objective of the Directive.

---

[57] Still, it should be observed that in private litigation on competition law, the prohibition on anti-competitive agreements between undertakings must be considered as in the public interest, which the parties must not be given a choice over.

Additionally, the Swedish Act on Unfair Terms in Consumer Relations should definitely be amended to include the blacklist of the Directive and requirements following from the case law of the ECJ. A court must act *ex officio* in the interests of the consumer when the legal and factual elements of the case make an assessment possible. Further, silence on the part of the consumer as to whether he or she agrees to depart from the Directive should not count as tacit agreement, independent of the content of the applicable procedural rules. Although we may not like many of the elements of these requirements for structural or political reasons, they are nevertheless an expression of the law exclusively interpreted by the ECJ.

Another thing to examine would be the conditions for issuing payment orders. There should perhaps be some opening or duty for the EA to assess consumer claims before issuing payment orders when the consumer has remained entirely passive. On the other hand, the objectives of summary proceedings are efficiency and speed, and any requirements of further assessments or possibilities of objections at the enforcement stage are bound to make summary proceedings a blunt tool to achieve these objectives.

To conclude, the difficulties connected with *ex officio* application in cases where consumers act as defendants before Swedish courts have been recognised since the *Océano* case was decided in 2000. Apart from an article in 2001,[58] and a report by the *Domstolsverket* (Board of Swedish Courts),[59] these difficulties have not been addressed by the legislature or in academic writing. This is surprising, in view of the fact that the majority of cases in which individual consumer rights may be at issue are initiated by a claim directed by the seller against the consumer.

58 Andersson, (n 7) above.

59 *DV-rapport 2003:4 Forum i tvistemål.* Promemoria V från Domstolsverkets arbetsgrupp för processrättsliga frågor.

EX OFFICIO APPLICATION OF EU CONSUMER PROTECTION LAW IN NORWEGIAN COURTS

Halvard HAUKELAND FREDRIKSEN and Magne STRANDBERG

1. INTRODUCTION: THE STATUS OF EU CONSUMER PROTECTION LAW IN NORWAY

On numerous occasions the Court of Justice of the European Union (ECJ) has concluded that national courts of European Union Member States have an obligation to protect EU consumer rights of their own motion (so-called *ex officio*). The starting point was Directive 93/13/EEC on unfair terms in consumer contracts,[1] but over the years this obligation has been extended to

[1] See, e.g., Joined Cases C-240–244/98 *Océano Grupo Editorial v Quintero and Salvat Editores v Prades and Others* [2000] ECR I-4941; Case C-473/00 *Cofidis* EU:C:2002:705; Case C-168/05 *Mostaza Claro v Centro Móvil Milenium* [2006] ECR I-10421; Case C-137/08 *Pénzügyi v Schneider* [2010] ECR I-10847; Case C-243/08 *Pannon v Erzsébet Sustikne Győrfi* [2009] ECR I-4713; Case C-453/10 *Pereničová and Perenič v SOS financ spol.* ECLI:EU:C:2010:144; Case C-618/10 *Banco Español v Camino* ECLI:EU:C:2012:349; Case C-415/11 *Aziz v Catalunyacaixa* ECLI:EU:C:2013:164; Case C-280/13 *Barclays Bank v García and Barrera* ECLI:EU:C:2014:279; Case C-421/14 *Banco Primus v García* ECLI:EU:C:2017:60; Case C-598/15 *Banco Santander v López* ECLI:EU:C:2017:945.

other parts of EU consumer protection law, such as Directive 1999/44/EC on consumer sale contracts,[2] and Directives 87/102/EEC and now 2008/48/EC on consumer credit contracts.[3] The ECJ has justified these inroads into national procedural law primarily by the need to compensate for the imbalance that generally exists between the consumer and the seller or supplier.[4]

Through the Agreement on the European Economic Area (EEA Agreement), EU consumer protection law is also applicable in Norway. On the basis of Article 72 of the Main Part of the EEA Agreement, the EEA Joint Committee has incorporated the entire body of EU consumer contract law into the Agreement's Annex XIX.[5] Among the EU legal acts found in this Annex are the above-mentioned Directives on unfair terms in consumer contracts,[6] consumer sale contracts[7] and consumer credit contracts.[8]

The object and purpose of the EEA Agreement is to extend the EU internal market to the participating EFTA States (Iceland, Liechtenstein and Norway).[9] The only way to achieve this is through uniform interpretation and application of the common rules of EU and EEA law.[10] Based on this 'principle of homogeneity', it may be safely assumed that the ECJ's deduction of procedural obligations from the consumer contract directives is also applicable in an EEA law context.[11]

---

2 Case C-32/12 *Hueros v Autociba and Citroën España* ECLI:EU:C:2013:637; Case C-497/13 *Faber v Hazet Ochten* ECLI:EU:C:2015:357.

3 Case C-429/05 *Rampion and Godard v Franfinance and K par K SAS* [2007] ECR I-8017; Case C-377/14 *Radlinger and Radlingerová v Finway* ECLI:EU:C:2016:283.

4 e.g. *Pannon* (n 1) paras 22–23; *Faber* (n 2) para 37.

5 For an overview, see Berte-Elen R. Konow's extensive comments on Article 72 EEA in Finn Arnesen, Halvard H. Fredriksen, Hans Petter Graver, Ola Mestad and Christoph Vedder (eds), *The Agreement on the European Economic Area – a Commentary* (Beck, Hart, Nomos and Universitetsforlaget 2018).

6 Incorporated into the EEA Agreement by decision of the EEA Joint Committee No 7/94 of 21 March 1994.

7 Incorporated into the EEA Agreement by decision of the EEA Joint Committee No 12/2000 of 28 January 2000.

8 Directive 2008/48/EC on credit agreements for consumers [2008] OJ L133/66 was incorporated into the EEA Agreement by decision of the EEA Joint Committee No 16/2009 of 5 February 2009. It replaced Directive 87/102/EEC concerning consumer credits [1986] OJ L42/48, which was part of the EEA Agreement from the very beginning.

9 As explained by the ECJ in Case C-452/01 *Ospelt and Weissenberg v the Verwaltungsgerichtshof* [2003] ECR I-9743, para 29.

10 See, e.g., Arts 1, 6 and 105 in the Agreement on the European Economic Area [1994] OJ L1/3 (EEA Agreement), as well as the recital 15 of the Preamble. For an extensive analysis of the homogeneity principle, see P. Wennerås' comments on Article 6 EEA in Arnesen, Fredriksen, Graver, Mestad and Vedder (n 5).

11 See, in English, e.g., Konow (n 5); Halvard H. Fredriksen and Magne Strandberg, 'Norwegian Civil Procedure Under the Influence of EU Law' in Alan Uzelac and C.H. van Rhee (eds), *Transformation of Civil Justice. Unity and Diversity*, (Springer 2018) 41–62.

The EFTA Court confirmed this is in *Engilbertsson*. Paraphrasing ECJ case law, the EFTA Court noted that:

> Given the nature and significance of the public interest which constitutes the basis of the protection guaranteed to consumers, who are in a weak position *vis-à-vis* sellers or suppliers, Directive 93/13/EEC requires EEA States to provide for adequate and effective means to prevent the continued use of unfair terms in contracts concluded with consumers by sellers or suppliers.[12]

In accordance with ECJ case law, the EFTA Court followed up by explaining the consequences for the national courts:

> As follows from settled case law, the national court is required, where it has available to it the legal and factual elements necessary for that task, to assess of its own motion whether a contractual term falling within the scope of the Directive is unfair, compensating in this way for the imbalance which exists between the consumer and the seller or supplier.[13]

Under the principle of homogeneity, there is no reason to believe that this will be any different for the other consumer contract directives that the ECJ has interpreted in the same manner.

Even though the obligation on the national courts to apply EU consumer protection law of their own motion is generally accepted in Norwegian legal literature,[14] it is far from clear how this obligation can or ought to be fulfilled in Norwegian law.

One of the reasons for the uncertainty is the Norwegian legislator's general lack of interest in the impact of EU law on Norwegian civil procedure. Although the current Norwegian code of civil procedure – the 2005 Dispute Act[15] – represents

---

12 Case E-25/13 *Gunnar V. Engilbertsson v Íslandsbanki* [2014] EFTA Ct Rep 524, para 158.

13 *Engilbertsson* (n 12) para 162. The EFTA Court referred to the ECJ's decisions in *Barclays Bank* (n 1) para 34; *Aziz* (n 1) para 46.

14 See, e.g., Inge Lorange Backer, *Sivilprosess* (Universitetsforlaget 2015) 269; Erik Eldjarn, *Materiell prosessledelse* (Cappelen akademisk 2016) 237 ff; Halvard H. Fredriksen, 'Tvisteloven og EØS-avtalen' [2008] *TfR* 290–359, 321 ff; Johan Giertsen, *Avtaler* (3rd edn, Universitetsforlaget 2014) 215–216; Erlend Haaskjold, *Kontraktsforpliktelser* (2nd edn, Cappelen akademisk 2013) 437; Anne Robberstad, 'Norske dommeres plikt til å veilede om EØS-retten' [2002] *LoR* 195–223; Jens Edvin A. Skoghøy, *Tvisteløsning* (3rd edn, Universitetsforlaget 2017) 600–604; Geir Woxholth, *Avtalerett* (10th edn, Gyldendal 2017) 325; Marie Natland Wabakken, 'Om standardiseringen av en rettslig standard. En analyse av forbrukeravtaledirektivet og forholdet til avtaleloven §36' [2017] 494 *MarIus* 53–55.

15 Act of 17 June 2005 no 90, in force since 1 January 2008. The Act is regularly referred to in English as 'the Dispute Act' despite the fact that it is a full-blown Code of Civil Procedure in the continental tradition. Somewhat reluctantly, we too will refer to it as the Dispute Act in this chapter. An English translation of the Act can be found by searching for 'tvisteloven' at <http://app.uio.no/ub/ujur/oversatte-lover/english.shtml> accessed 18 April 2018. Note that

a complete overhaul of the former code from 1915, the EEA law obligation of *ex officio* application of EU consumer protection law was not considered by either the expert committee that prepared the reform, the Ministry of Justice or Parliament.[16] The developments in the case law of the ECJ since the enactment of the Dispute Act have not caught the attention of the legislator either.

In Norwegian legal literature, however, the national court's obligation to apply EU consumer protection law *ex officio* has been the subject of several contributions, both from a civil procedure perspective and from a contract law perspective.[17] Thus far, no consensus has emerged as to how the ECJ's demands ought to be adhered to. Whereas some authors argue that EU consumer protection law has to be regarded as a matter where public policy limits the parties' rights of disposition in the legal action (so-called non-dispositive elements),[18] others argue that active guidance (*materiell prosessledelse*) will have to suffice.[19] The crux of the matter is whether the obligation to apply EU consumer protection law prevails even in situations where the consumer himself/herself is reluctant to invoke his/her EU law rights.

When we enter this debate and consider how Norwegian civil procedure ought to implement the ECJ's demands, we will do so based on the following premise: if the obligations flowing from EU/EEA law can be fulfilled in different ways, the option that fits best with the existing principles of Norwegian civil procedure law should be preferred.

2. THE *IURA NOVIT CURIA* PRINCIPLE IN NORWEGIAN CIVIL PROCEDURAL LAW

The courts' duty to apply matters of law of their own motion is well known in Norwegian law. The *iura novit curia* principle has been a cornerstone

---

the translation has not been updated, but so far, the number of amendments is fairly limited. For an informative introduction in the English language, see Inge Lorange Backer, 'The Norwegian Reform of Civil Procedure' [2007] 51 *Scandinavian Studies in Law* 41 and several of the contributions in Halvard H. Fredriksen and Volker Lipp (eds), *Reforms of Civil Procedure in Germany and Norway* (Mohr Siebeck 2007).

16 The general limitations of national procedural law brought about by the EU law principles of equivalence and effectiveness were recognised by the Expert Committee, but the committee (and later on in the process also the Ministry of Justice) clearly regarded the practical implications for Norwegian civil procedural law as very limited and did not go into any details, cf the Expert Committee's final report (NOU 2001: 32 *Rett på sak*, 154–155; the Ministry's subsequent White Paper to Parliament (Ot.prp. no 51 *Om lov om mekling og rettergang i sivile tvister* (2004–2005)) 32.

17 See the literature listed in (n 14).

18 Haaskjold (n 14) 437; Skoghøy (n 14) 600–604.

19 Giertsen (n 14) 216; Woxholt (n 14) 325.

of Norwegian civil procedural law from even before the 1915 code of civil procedure.[20] The principle was left unchanged by the 2005 reform,[21] and is now found in section 11-3 of the Dispute Act:

> The court shall on its own motion apply current law within the scope of section 11-2(1).

As a general principle of Norwegian civil procedure, the courts' responsibility to apply the law extends to all applicable law in all cases. Consequently, Norwegian judges are never bound by the parties' pleadings on matters of law. Even if the parties agree on a matter of law, the court is obliged to apply the law as the court finds it. In the fulfilment of this obligation, the court shall take into account any relevant source of law, including sources not introduced by the parties. If the court's understanding of the law so requires, then a case may have to be decided based on another legal rule than the one(s) relied upon by the parties.[22]

Usually, the parties get the chance to argue on matters of law at several stages of the proceedings. From the outset, the parties' introductory documents may disclose their view; the statement of case must include the basic legal arguments for the plaintiff's claim,[23] and the reply ought to include the defendants' view.[24] In most cases, the parties will be invited to argue on matters of law towards the end of the main hearing where any relevant sources of law are often discussed in detail.

It has been argued that the parties' argumentation on matters of law affects the court's competence to apply substantive law. The expert committee that prepared the draft for the Dispute Act suggested that the parties should have a right to be heard before the court is able to apply other substantive rules than those introduced by the parties.[25] However, the Ministry of Justice disagreed, arguing that such a right could lead to disproportional costs in situations where the judges discover new legal solutions after the main hearing.[26] As Parliament agreed with the view taken by the Ministry of Justice, the right to be heard in section 11-1 (3) of the Dispute Act relates to matters of fact only. Hence, Norwegian judges may apply legal rules that none of the parties relied upon in the proceedings.

As a general principle of civil procedural law, the *iura novit curia* principle also applies to Norwegian law originating from the EU. Thus, at first sight, the

20 Jon Skeie, *Den norske civilprosess*, vol 1 (1939) 411.
21 See NOU 2001: 32, 137.
22 See Backer (n 14) 312–315; Skoghøy (n 14) 968–972.
23 Section 9-2 (2) (d) of the Dispute Act.
24 Section 9-3 (3) (b) of the Dispute Act.
25 NOU 2001: 32, 137.
26 Ot.prp. no 51 (2004–2005) 167–169.

duty to apply EU/EEA consumer protection law does not add any additional duties for Norwegian judges.

However, a Norwegian court's duty to apply the law is restricted by the equally fundamental adversary principle now found in section 11-2 (1) of the Dispute Act:

> The court may only rule on the claims that are made in the case. The ruling must fall within the scope of the parties' prayers for relief and the court may only base its ruling on the grounds for the prayers for relief that have been invoked. The grounds for the prayers for relief are the material facts upon which a party bases its prayer for relief.

Thus, the court's duty to apply the law of its own motion is restricted to legal rules that are relevant to the claims introduced by the parties and, furthermore, applicable to the material facts introduced by the parties.

Obviously, a consumer unaware of his/her EU law rights may fail to invoke all of the material facts necessary for the court to be able to apply EU consumer protection law. The *iura novit curia* principle, therefore, is not as such sufficient to enable Norwegian courts to compensate for the imbalance between the consumer and the seller or supplier, as required by the ECJ. On the contrary, effective judicial protection of consumers may require the introduction of new material facts, reformulation of the relief sought or even introduction of a new claim.

According to the adversary principle of Norwegian civil procedure law, all of these procedural actions concerning claims, reliefs and facts are for the parties to take. However, the Dispute Act provides the courts with powers to actively handle situations where a party's procedural actions seem to be incomplete or misguided. These powers constitute the natural starting point for a discussion of how Norwegian judges may deal with their duty to apply EU consumer law of their own motion.

3. THE COURT'S DUTY TO GIVE GUIDANCE

Norwegian civil procedural law has long recognised the need for guidance from the court. A few rules to this effect already existed in the old Dispute Act of 1915,[27] and more general ones were gradually developed through court practice.[28] These rules on guidance were codified and further developed by the 2005 Dispute Act.

The contemporary Norwegian rules on guidance are a mix of duties and discretionary powers. According to section 11-5 (1) of the Dispute Act, the court

---

27 Sections 86 and 87.

28 Skoghøy (n 14) 964.

is under a general duty to give the parties such guidance on procedural rules and routines and other formalities as is necessary to enable them to safeguard their interests in the case. If a party has made a procedural error, the court must give such guidance as is necessary to enable it to be rectified.[29] Under section 16-5 (2), rectification can only be denied if the party can be strongly reproached and no weighty reasons suggest that it must nonetheless be allowed to rectify the error. It may safely be assumed that the average consumer will be allowed to rectify deficient procedural steps. Guidance on procedural matters and rectification of errors may, of course, also be relevant in cases of EU consumer law. In some cases, guidance on procedural rules and routines may be all that it takes to put the court in a position to apply certain aspects of EU consumer protection law.

Concerning the judge's guidance on matters of substantive law, Norwegian law distinguishes between clarification of the parties' positions and the encouragement to take a position on new factual and legal issues that appear to be important to the case.

Under section 11-5 (3) of the Dispute Act, Norwegian judges are under a general duty to contribute to the clarification of the parties' positions:

> The court shall endeavour to clarify disputed issues and ensure that the parties' prayers for relief and their positions regarding factual and legal issues are clarified.

The duty to clarify the parties' positions applies where the meaning of a procedural step taken is unclear. Thus, it does not extend to suggestions concerning *new procedural steps*. In consumer cases, questions from the court in order to clarify the parties' claims, their prayers for relief and their positions regarding factual and legal issues may fulfil the requirements set by the ECJ, but only if the consumer's claims, prayers for relief and the material facts upon which the latter are based can reasonably be interpreted as allowing for the application of relevant parts of EU consumer protection law. In cases where the consumer is unaware of his/her EU law rights, there will often be a need to add new procedural steps to those already taken.

The court's ability to offer guidance on such new procedural steps is dealt with in section 11-5 (4) and (5) of the Dispute Act:

> The court may encourage a party to take a position on factual and legal issues that appear to be important to the case.
>
> The court may encourage a party to offer evidence.

Inherent in the court's power to ask for a party's stance on material facts or legal questions and to encourage a party to present evidence is a right to remind or

29 The right to rectify errors is regulated in section 16-5 of the Dispute Act.

inform a party of procedural steps that could be added to those already taken. However, the established view in Norwegian legal literature is that such guidance is merely an option for the court, not an obligation.[30] Although the German rules on substantive guidance (*materielle Prozessleitung*), which served as inspiration for the Norwegian rules, contain duties on the court,[31] the Norwegian legal sources clearly point in the direction of this being merely an option. Neither the wording of section 11-5 (4) and (5) of the Dispute Act, nor the preparatory works to that provision,[32] nor the jurisprudence of the Norwegian Supreme Court, supports the view that a court may be under an obligation to provide such guidance. Thus, a Norwegian judge who does not encourage a party to take a position on new factual or legal issues that appear to be important to the case has not committed an error. Consequently, lack of guidance on such matters cannot be a reason for appeal.

Nevertheless, section 11-5 (4) and (5) of the Dispute Act is the natural starting point for a discussion of how Norwegian courts may fulfil their EU/EEA law duty to apply consumer law of their own motion. These rules on guidance are a well-established part of Norwegian procedural law, they apply in all cases and all Norwegian judges are familiar with them.

Importantly, use of the possibilities enshrined in section 11-5 (4) and (5) of the Dispute Act appears sufficient to comply with the ECJ's requirements. It is not perfectly clear what ECJ requires of the national courts, but there are several reasons why we believe that use of the well-established Norwegian rules on substantive guidance suffices.

Firstly, the national courts' duty to apply EU consumer protection law of their own motion is not a duty to apply, or investigate whether one can apply, any potentially relevant part of law. It is a duty to apply such law if most parts necessary for its application are already available to the court – see, for instance, the ECJ's judgment in *Pannon*:

> The court seised of the action is … required to ensure the effectiveness of the protection intended to be given by the provisions of the Directive. Consequently, the role thus attributed to the national court by Community law in this area is not limited to a mere power to rule on the possible unfairness of a contractual term, but also consist of the obligation to examine that issue of its own motion, *where it has available to it the legal and factual elements necessary for that task*, including when it is assessing whether it has territorial jurisdiction.[33]

---

30 Backer (n 14) 276–277; Skoghøy (n 14) 964.

31 See U. Haas, 'The Relationship between the Judge and the Parties under German Law' in Fredriksen and Lipp (n 15) 87–114, at 101; Ivo Bach, in this volume, section 2.2.2.

32 NOU 2001: 32, 709; Ot.prp. no 51 (2004–2005) 406–407.

33 *Pannon* (n 1) para 32 (emphasis added). *Camino* (n 1) para 43; *Barclays Bank* (n 1) para 34; *Aziz* (n 1) para 46. From the EFTA Court, *Engilbertsson* (n 12) para 162.

The Norwegian rules on substantive guidance are based on a similar understanding of the court's role in civil cases. Under Norwegian law, a judge is neither expected nor entitled to guide on all matters of law or fact that may have relevance for the dispute in question. The expectations on the judge are limited by the way the parties have chosen to present their case.[34] A judge may suggest the inclusion of matters of facts that the parties have not explicitly invoked, but only if those new facts are related to the facts that a party has based his/her case on or at least brought to the court's attention. In practice, substantive guidance will only deal with matters that are quite closely connected to the factual and legal issues already introduced.[35] A Norwegian court cannot – and will not – enter into a more general investigation of whatever facts may be relevant to the dispute before it.

Secondly, the ECJ's justification for the establishment of the national courts' duty to apply EU consumer law of their own motion is to compensate for the imbalance that typically exists between a consumer and a seller or supplier.[36] An active court is particularly important in cases where the consumer appear to be unaware of his/her rights, as highlighted by the ECJ, for example in *Cofidis*:

> That power of the court has been regarded as necessary for ensuring that the consumer enjoys effective protection, in view of the real risk that he is unaware of his rights or encounters difficulties in enforcing them.[37]

This reasoning is similar to that underlying the Norwegian rules on substantive guidance. Whilst the overarching goal of these Norwegian rules is to secure a materially correct ruling in the case based on the facts and the applicable rules,[38] the Dispute Act seeks to achieve this through communication between the judge and the parties. The basic idea is that guidance will cause the parties to take the procedural steps necessary to enable the court to come to a materially correct ruling, so that there is no need to vest the court with the power to take procedural steps on behalf of the parties (or ignore procedural steps actually taken by them).

Thirdly, the Norwegian rules on guidance apply irrespective of whether a party is self-represented or represented by a lawyer, but section 11-5 (6) of the Dispute Act obliges the court to show particular consideration for the need

---

[34] Eldjarn (n 14) 238.

[35] Ot.prp. no 51 (2004–2005) 406–407; Eldjarn (n 14) 107.

[36] e.g. *Océano* (n 1) para 25; *Mostaza Claro* (n 1) paras 25–27; Case C-40/08 *Asturcom Telecommunicaciones v Nogueira* [2009] ECR I-9579, para 29; *Pénzügyi* (n 1) para 46; *Pannon* (n 1) paras 23 and 31; *Camino* (n 1) para 42; *Faber* (n 2) para 42.

[37] *Cofidis* (n 1) para 33. See also *Mostaza Claro* (n 1) para 28.

[38] Section 11-5 (2) of the Dispute Act: 'The court shall, in accordance with subsections (3) to (7), give guidance that contributes to a correct ruling in the case based on the facts and the applicable rules'. See further Eldjarn (n 14) 75–79.

for guidance of parties not represented by counsel.[39] This is fully in line with the ECJ's approach in consumer cases: a national court has a duty to apply EU consumer protection law irrespective of whether the consumer is represented by counsel or not,[40] but the need for an active judge is particularly important in the latter cases.[41]

However, there is one crucial difference between the Norwegian rules on guidance and the requirements developed by the ECJ for consumer cases: whereas the ECJ has in numerous judgments underlined the national courts' *duty* to apply consumer law,[42] Norwegian law only provides judges with a *discretionary competence* to guide on substantive matters whenever the guidance needed exceeds mere clarification of procedural steps already taken.

Acknowledging the important difference between a procedural duty and a procedural power, we are of the opinion that the Norwegian rules on guidance should still be regarded as the natural starting point for the fulfilment of the EU/EEA law obligations established by the ECJ: in cases concerning EU consumer protection law, a Norwegian court will simply be under an obligation to make use of the discretionary powers enshrined in section 11-5 of the Dispute Act. Such a transformation of a discretionary competence into a duty was also suggested by the ECJ as early as in *Océano*, where the ECJ stated that the national court was obliged to interpret national law in compliance with the EU directive in question and was thus obliged, if at all possible, to choose an interpretation that would allow the court to apply the directive of its own motion.[43]

Although the wording of section 11-5 (4) and (5) of the Dispute Act points clearly in direction of a mere power, thereby leaving little room for the deduction of an obligation, a duty to guide on new factual and/or legal issues has indeed been recognised by the Norwegian Supreme Court in extraordinary cases where a party's vital social interests are at stake and the party in question clearly lacks the resources necessary to provide the court with the relevant facts. For instance, the Supreme Court found that there was an obligation to offer guidance in a case where a defendant risked being forced out of his home and lacked the economic and intellectual resources to argue his case.[44] The preparatory works to the 2005 Dispute Act acknowledged and confirmed this unwritten obligation to provide guidance in extraordinary cases, even though this is not reflected in the wording of section 11-5.[45]

---

39 See, e.g., Tore Schei et al, *Tvisteloven kommentarutgave* (2nd edn, Universitetsforlaget 2013) 417; Eldjarn (n 14) 293 ff.

40 e.g. *Rampion* (n 3) para 65.

41 e.g. *Faber* (n 2) paras 44 and 47.

42 e.g. *Mostaza Claro* (n 1) para 38; *Pénzügyi* (n 1); *Pannon* (n 1) para 44; *Faber* (n 2) para 56.

43 *Océano* (n 1) paras 30–32.

44 Rt. 1950, 981.

45 NOU 2001: 32, 709. See also Schei et al (n 39) 416; Eldjarn (n 14) 104.

Admittedly, most consumer cases will not meet the threshold so far established by the Supreme Court – neither regarding the importance of the dispute for the consumer, nor regarding the economic and intellectual resources of the average consumer. However, the development of Norwegian civil procedural law clearly suggests that the threshold for the courts' obligation to offer guidance is decreasing.[46] Thus, it could be argued that such a transformation from discretionary to obligatory guidance in all consumer cases would be the natural next step even in a purely domestic legal development. Be that as it may, the acknowledgement of a duty to provide guidance in cases concerning EU consumer protection law requires no more than the continuation of an already ongoing development.

For these reasons, an interpretation of section 11-5 (4) and (5) to the effect that the courts are under an obligation to provide guidance to the consumer in all cases involving EU consumer protection law is a natural way for Norwegian civil procedural law to fulfil the requirements flowing from the ECJ case law.

Against this background, it may further be argued that an obligation to provide guidance ought to be recognised in all consumer cases – in other words, also in cases outside the reach of EU consumer protection law. Such a development is, of course, not required by the EEA Agreement, but the underlying reasoning of the ECJ – the imbalance between the consumer and the seller or supplier – has general appeal. Furthermore, the coherence of this part of Norwegian civil procedure law can only be maintained if one embraces this kind of 'spill-over effect'. Particularly in consumer cases where some questions are regulated by EU consumer protection law whereas others are not, an attempt to limit the court's obligation to offer guidance to the former category seems untenable.

4. EU CONSUMER PROTECTION LAW AS NON-DISPOSITIVE ELEMENTS OF NORWEGIAN LAW?

As explained above, the Norwegian rules on guidance rest on the assumption that guidance will cause the parties to take the procedural steps necessary to enable the court to come to a materially correct ruling, so that there is no need to vest the court with the power to take procedural steps on behalf of the parties (or ignore procedural steps actually taken by them). Thus, the rules on guidance do not limit the principle of party autonomy; they only allow the court to make sure that the decisions taken by the parties are well informed. However, even though most consumers will probably act on questions and encouragements from the court, this may not always be the case. Thus, there may be cases where

46 See e.g. Backer (n 14) 274–275.

we might ask whether guidance from the court will suffice to fulfil Norway's EEA law obligation to ensure the effectiveness of EU consumer protection law.

In Norwegian legal literature, it has been argued that the requirements flowing from the ECJ case law will only be fulfilled if EU consumer protection law is regarded as a matter where public policy limits the parties' rights of disposition in the legal action (so-called non-dispositive elements of law).[47]

The category of 'non-dispositive elements' in Norwegian civil procedural law is derived from a distinction between dispositive and non-dispositive cases. This distinction was developed well before the 2005 Dispute Act. Non-dispositive cases are cases where the parties' autonomy is reduced and the competences (and duties) of the court are increased correspondingly. Usually, this is a procedural side-effect of such restrictions being placed on the parties' rights of disposition outside the courtroom. Thus, it is the applicable substantive law that decides whether a case is considered to be wholly or partially non-dispositive.[48] Pursuant to section 11-4 of the Dispute Act, the general principle of party autonomy enshrined in section 11-2 only applies within the restrictions required by public policy (emphasis added):

> In cases relating to matters of personal status and legal capacity, the legal status of children pursuant to the Children's Act, administrative decisions on coercive measures pursuant to Chapter 36 and *other cases where public policy limits the parties' rights of disposition in the legal action*, the court is only bound by the parties' procedural steps to the extent that these are compatible with public policy. However, the court may only rule on the claims that are made in the case.

As a starting point, all contract cases are considered to be dispositive, including cases where the validity of a contract is in dispute. However, dispositive contract law disputes may involve *non-dispositive elements*. One example is Article 5-1-2 of the Norwegian Code of 1687, after which a contract with illegal or amoral content is exempted from the *pacta sunt servanda* rule. The courts' obligation to apply this provision of their own motion is based on the idea that the judicial system ought not to contribute to the enforcement of contracts that violate law or basic morals. The prevailing view is that section 2 of the 1993 Price Policy Act,[49] according to which it is prohibited to 'take, demand or agree on prices that are unreasonable', also constitutes a non-dispositive element.[50] Another example is section 10 of the 2004 Competition Act, according to which all agreements between undertakings, decisions by associations of undertakings and concerted

47 Skoghøy (n 14) 600–602; Eldjarn (n 14) 192; Haaskjold (n 14) 437.
48 Eldjarn (n 14) 186–187.
49 Act of 11 June 1993 no 66.
50 Skoghøy (n 14) 600; Eldjarn (n 14) 193.

practices that have as their object or effect the prevention, restriction or distortion of competition must be automatically void.[51] The courts' obligation under Norwegian law to apply this provision of their own motion is closely connected to their EEA law obligation to apply the equivalent provision found in Article 53 of the EEA Agreement, which again mirrors what is now Article 101 TFEU.[52]

In cases where public policy limits the parties' rights of disposition in the legal action, the court is only bound by the parties' procedural steps to the extent that these are compatible with the applicable part of public policy. By way of an example, a court shall not accept a contract which violates Article 5-1-2 of the Norwegian Code of 1687, even if none of the parties have argued for such a solution and even if the parties agree before the court that the contract is valid. Nor is the court bound by relief sought by the parties. Pursuant to section 21-3 (2) of the Dispute Act, the court also has a duty to gather and present evidence or at least to make sure that the evidence provided by the parties provides a sound factual basis for the ruling:

> In cases where for reasons of public policy the right of disposition of the parties is limited, cf. section 11-4, the court has a duty to ensure that the presentation of evidence provides a sound factual basis for the ruling.

However, an important limitation follows from the last sentence of section 11-4 of the Dispute Act: even in cases where public policy limits the parties' rights of disposition in the legal action, the court may only rule on the claims that are made in the case.

If the entire body of EU consumer protection law is to be considered a non-dispositive element of Norwegian law, the role of the court will be fundamentally changed. This is especially so with regard to the factual basis for the ruling, as the presentation of evidence is left almost entirely to the parties in all dispositive cases.[53] From the perspective of the parties, the principle of party autonomy will be significantly reduced, with far-reaching consequences for their ability, for example, to end the dispute through an in-court settlement.

In our opinion, such a radical change to Norwegian civil procedure law is not necessary to meet the national courts' obligation to ensure the effectiveness of EU consumer protection law. As was underlined in the section on substantial

---

51 Act of 5 March 2004 no 12.

52 See the ECJ's judgment in Case C-126/97 *ECO Swiss v Benetton* [1999] ECR I-3055, para 36.

53 After section 21-3 (2) of the Dispute Act, the court may take charge of the presentation of evidence also in dispositive cases, but only if none of the parties object. In practice, this power is hardly ever used, leaving substantive guidance in accordance with section 11-5 (5) as the preferred tool to ensure that the presentation of evidence provides a sound factual basis for the ruling.

guidance above, the ECJ's leading argument in establishing and developing the duty to apply consumer law *ex officio* appears to be the imbalance that exists between the consumer and the seller or supplier, in particular in cases where the consumer is unaware of his/her rights. Thus, the ECJ does not seem to be of the opinion that EU consumer protection law has a moral or societal value of the kind that cannot, as a matter of principle, be left to the parties' autonomy.

Admittedly, references to public interest are included in some of the ECJ decisions, such as *Pannon*:

> It should also be pointed out that the Court has held, in *Mostaza Claro*, paragraph 38, that *the nature and importance of the public interest underlying the protection which the Directive confers on consumers* justify the national court being required to assess of its own motion whether a contractual term is unfair, compensating in this way for the imbalance which exist between the consumer and the seller or supplier.[54]

It is submitted, however, that this statement supports rather than contradicts our view that the courts' duty to apply EU consumer law of their own motion is first and foremost justified by the imbalance that exists between the parties. Indeed, in *Pannon* the ECJ seems to be of the opinion that the consumer will have the final word:

> In carrying out that obligation, the national court is not, however, required under the Directive to exclude the possibility that the term in question may be applicable, if the consumer, after having been informed of it by that court, does not intend to assert its unfair or non-binding status.[55]

Hence, the essence of the ECJ's ruling in *Pannon* is that the national courts are *not* required to apply the relevant parts of EU consumer protection law of their own motion if this contradicts the informed will of the consumer.[56]

As far as Norwegian law is concerned, this suggests that guidance of the parties will suffice to meet the EEA law obligation to secure the effectiveness of EU consumer protection law. Through substantive guidance, the court will be able to compensate for the imbalance that exists between the consumer and the seller or supplier and make sure that the consumer is aware of his/her rights. There is thus no need for limitations on the parties' rights of disposition in the legal action.

Still, it may be argued that the EU law *principle of equivalence* requires that EU consumer protection law is regarded as a non-dispositive element of

---

[54] *Pannon* (n 1) para 31 (emphasis added). See also *Camino* (n 1) para 68 and, from the EFTA Court, *Engilbertsson* (n 12) para 158.

[55] *Pannon* (n 1) para 33.

[56] *Pannon* (n 1).

Norwegian law. As is well known to EU-law lawyers, the principle of equivalence restricts the procedural autonomy of the EU Member States by extending the general principle of equality to the law of remedies: national procedural law cannot treat actions to defend rights that consumers derive from EU law less favourably than similar domestic actions.[57] Based on the principle of homogeneity between EU and EEA law, the EFTA Court has confirmed that the case law of the ECJ concerning the principle of equivalence (and that of effectiveness) applies *mutatis mutandis* in the EEA context.[58]

In *Froukje Faber*, the ECJ held the principle of equivalence to require that Directive 1999/44/EC on consumer sales contracts be regarded as a matter of public policy in Dutch law:

> In those circumstances ... Article 5(3) of Directive 1999/44 must be interpreted as meaning that it must be regarded as a provision of equal standing to a national rule which ranks, within the domestic legal system, as a rule of public policy and that the national court must of its own motion apply any provision which transposes it into domestic law.[59]

While acknowledging that the Dutch rules on public policy seem to have similarities with the Norwegian rules on non-dispositive elements, we will nevertheless argue that the principle of equivalence cannot be understood such that EU consumer protection law must be regarded as a non-dispositive element of Norwegian law.

When applying the principle of equivalence, one must start by identifying the elements of national law that form the best grounds for comparison with the EU rules in question. In our opinion, most EU consumer protection law is better compared with Norwegian consumer law in general than with, for example, the morally charged Article 5-1-2 of the Norwegian Code of 1687 or, albeit perhaps to a lesser extent, section 2 of the Price Policy Act. The duty to apply section 10 of the 2004 Competition Act *ex officio* is itself a result of EEA law obligations and is, in any event, characterised by the fact that it is easy to envisage a contract law dispute in which neither of the parties has any interest in arguing that the contract is in breach of competition rules.

As long as EU consumer protection law is not handled less favourably by the courts than 'original' Norwegian consumer protection law, it is hard to accept that there is a violation of the principle of equivalence. Since nearly all aspects of

57 e.g. Cases C-222–225/05 *Van der Weerd and Others v Minister van Landbouw* [2007] ECR I-4233, para 28, *Radlinger* (n 3) para 48.

58 See, e.g., Case E-11/12 *Koch, Hummel and Müller v Swiss Life* [2013] EFTA Ct Rep 272, paras 121 ff. See further Fredriksen and Strandberg (n 11) 53–57.

59 *Faber* (n 2) para 57.

Norwegian consumer law are regarded as dispositive elements of law, it should be acceptable to handle EU consumer protection law in the same manner.

5. *EX OFFICIO* APPLICATION OF JURISDICTION CLAUSES

A contract between a consumer and a seller or supplier may include clauses concerning procedural matters. Under Norwegian law, the above-mentioned rules on guidance found in section 11-5 of the Dispute Act are important to ensuring that such clauses do not undermine the EU law rights of consumers. However, certain judgments from the ECJ suggest that this may not be enough to satisfy the obligation to secure the effect of EU consumer protection law.

Particular attention has been paid to jurisdiction clauses, which were at the centre of the famous *Océano* judgment.[60] The case concerned five consumers who had bought encyclopaedias from a Spanish seller on deferred payment terms. The contract included a non-individually negotiated term stating that an action could be lodged with a first instance court in Barcelona, where the seller had its headquarters but none of the defendants had their residence. When some of the consumers did not pay what they should have paid under the contract, the seller initiated proceedings in Barcelona. Even before the defendants were notified of the action, the court in Barcelona requested a preliminary ruling from the ECJ on whether the jurisdiction clause violated Article 3(1) of Directive 93/13/EEC. As is well known, the ECJ not only found the jurisdiction clause to be unfair and thus void, it also stated that a court seised of a dispute concerning such a contract might apply the Directive of its own motion.

In later cases such as *Pannon* and *Pènzügyi*, the ECJ clarified that national courts not only can, but indeed must, determine the unfairness of a clause concerning exclusive jurisdiction in a consumer contract of their own motion.[61]

Now, what effect do these cases have on Norwegian civil procedure? The main rule on territorial jurisdiction (venue) is found in section 4-4 of the Dispute Act, after which an action may be filed with the court of the ordinary venue of the defendant. For natural persons, that is the place of their habitual residence: see section 4-4(2). However, a special venue for contractual relations follows from section 4-5 (2) of the Dispute Act:

> Actions relating to contractual relationships may be brought at the place where the obligation upon which the action is based has been performed or is to be performed.

---

60 *Océano* (n 1).

61 *Pannon* (n 1); *Pénzügyi* (n 1).

> This does not apply to claims for the payment of money if the defendant has an ordinary venue in Norway pursuant to section 4-4.[62]

Furthermore, a special venue applies in consumer cases – see section 4-5 (7) of the Dispute Act:

> A consumer who has entered into an agreement with a tradesperson with respect to goods or services for personal use may bring an action against such tradesperson at his own ordinary venue. This does not apply if the agreement has been entered into by the consumer in person at the tradesperson's permanent place of business.

Finally, an action may also be filed with the court agreed upon by the parties: see section 4-6 (1) of the Dispute Act. Pursuant to the third paragraph of this section, however, the freedom of contract is highly restricted in consumer cases:

> An agreement between a consumer and a tradesperson that limits the right to bring an action beyond what is provided in sections 4-4 and 4-5 shall be made in writing. The agreement is not binding on the consumer if it was concluded before the dispute arose.

Thus, when proceedings are initiated before a court that has jurisdiction according to the consumer contract in question, but not according to sections 4-4 and 4-5 of the Dispute Act, the consumer may choose to accept that clause, but they are not obliged to do so.

Unfortunately, the wording of section 4-6 (1) only covers *limitations* of the right to bring an action. A clause like the one in *Océano*, where the seller got a *new* venue in addition to the ones entailed by Spanish law, is thus not covered by the wording of section 4-6. However, the whole *raison d'être* of section 4-6 (3) is to protect consumers from procedural arrangements that are less attractive to him/her (and, conversely, more attractive to the seller). Therefore, a teleological interpretation strongly suggests that a clause giving the seller an additional venue for an action against the consumer will also be caught by section 4-6 (3). If this interpretation is accepted, all jurisdiction clauses that put the consumer in a less favourable position *vis-à-vis* the seller will be dealt with by the Dispute Act, thus leaving no need for recourse to, for example, the provision transposing Article 3 of Directive 93/13/EEC into Norwegian law.[63]

---

62 As EU lawyers will notice, this provision mirrors Article 5(1) of the Convention on jurisdiction and the enforcement of judgments in civil and commercial matters [2007] OJ L 339/3 (the Lugano Convention), which again mirrors the provision now found in Article 7(1) of the Regulation (EU) 1215/2012 on jurisdiction and the recognition and enforcement of judgments in civil and commercial matters [2012] OJ L351/1.

63 Section 37 of Act of 31 May 1918 no 4 on Conclusion of Agreements.

Under section 36 of the 1915 Courts of Justice Act, Norwegian courts are obliged to consider of their own motion whether they are competent to handle a case.[64] However, this provision does not oblige the court to investigate the facts of the case. On the contrary, pursuant to the second paragraph of that section, the court shall base its assessment on the plaintiff's submission, 'provided that it has not been demonstrated that the submission is erroneous'.[65] This is in line with the general rule of Norwegian procedural law that it is for the parties to present the facts upon which the court is to base its decisions, which also applies to procedural matters.[66] It is also linked to the first paragraph of section 9-2(3) of the Dispute Act, according to which the writ of summons shall give the court a basis for assessing its jurisdiction.

However, it is doubtful whether the approach set out in section 36 of the 1915 Courts of Justice Act is in line with the ECJ's expectations. In *Pénzügyi*, the ECJ concluded that the court must *investigate* whether a jurisdiction clause violates EU consumer protection law:

> The national court must investigate of its own motion whether a term conferring exclusive territorial jurisdiction in a contract concluded between a seller or supplier and a consumer, which is the subject of a dispute before it, falls within the scope of Directive 93/13 and, if it does, assess of its own motion whether such a term is unfair.[67]

This requirement appears go further than the established understanding of a court's duty under section 36 of the Courts of Justice Act. However, it is not entirely clear how the investigation demanded by the ECJ in *Pénzügyi* relates to the statements in other cases that the national courts' obligation to apply EU consumer protection law of their own motion is limited to situations where they have available to them the factual elements necessary for that task.[68] The ECJ's wording in *Pénzügyi* suggests that the obligation to investigate is limited to whether the jurisdiction clause falls within the scope EU consumer protection law (*in casu:* Directive 93/13/EEC) – in other words, whether the case before the court is a consumer case or not.

If the consumer does not question the court's competence, we may ask whether he/she must be considered to have lost his/her right to do so. According to the wording of section 9-6 (2) of the Dispute Act, a party must raise any objection

---

64 Act of 13 August 1915 no 5. The Act applies in both criminal cases and civil cases.

65 Unofficial translation provided by the Norwegian Courts Administration, available at: <http://app.uio.no/ub/ujur/oversatte-lover/english.shtml> accessed 18 April 2018.

66 Sections 11-2 (2) and 21-3 (1) of the Dispute Act.

67 *Pénzügyi* (n 1) third point of the operative part.

68 *Pannon* (n 1) para 32; *Camino* (n 1) para 43; *Barclays Bank* (n 1) para 34; *Aziz* (n 1) para 46; and, from the EFTA Court, *Engilbertsson* (n 12) para 162.

to procedural steps as soon as possible. This obligation clearly also covers the claimant's choice of venue. However, the absence of any objection from the consumer does not exempt the court from its duty to consider its competence of its own motion.[69] This applies even if the consumer, from the very beginning of the court proceedings, was well aware of his/her right to object to the venue chosen. The situation was different under the 1915 Dispute Act, where section 92 made clear that a defendant was considered to have agreed to the venue chosen by the claimant if he/she entered into argument about the merits of the case. The absence of a similar provision in the 2005 Dispute Act suggests that a consumer will not lose his/her right to object that the court's jurisdiction is based on an unfair jurisdictional clause, even if it is clear that that objection could have been raised at a much earlier stage of the proceedings.

6. *EX OFFICIO* APPLICATION OF ARBITRATION CLAUSES

Consumer contracts sometimes contain *arbitration clauses*. A prominent example from ECJ case law is *Mostaza Claro*,[70] which concerned a mobile telephone contract concluded between a Spanish telecommunications company and Ms Mostaza Claro. The contract contained an arbitration clause under which any dispute arising from the contract were to be referred for arbitration to the European Association of Arbitration in Law and in Equity (AEADE). As Ms Claro did not comply with the minimum subscription period, the telecommunications company initiated arbitration proceedings before the AEADE. The AEADE granted Ms Claro a period of 10 days in which to refuse arbitration proceedings. Ms Claro presented arguments on the merits of the dispute, but did not object to the arbitration proceedings or claim that the arbitration agreement was void. The arbitration proceedings subsequently took place and the arbitrator found against her. The ECJ found the following:

> Council Directive 93/13/EEC of 5 April 1993 on unfair terms in consumer contracts must be interpreted as meaning that a national court seised of an action for annulment of an arbitration award must determine whether the arbitration agreement is void and annul that award where that agreement contains an unfair term, even though the consumer has not pleaded that invalidity in the course of the arbitration proceedings, but only in that of the action for annulment.[71]

---

69 NOU 2001: 32, 248 and Skoghøy (n 14) 248.

70 *Mostaza Claro* (n 1).

71 *Mostaza Claro* (n 1) para 39.

In Norway, section 11 of the 2004 Arbitration Act makes clear that an arbitration agreement is not binding on a consumer if entered into before the dispute arose.[72] The second subsection of that provision states that an arbitration agreement to which a consumer is a party must be made in a separate document and be signed by both parties. The third subsection makes clear that a consumer who enters into proceedings before an arbitral tribunal without being aware that the arbitration agreement is not binding on him/her pursuant to the provisions of subsections 1 and 2 can plead that the arbitration agreement is null and void at any stage of the proceedings.

In a hypothetical Norwegian parallel to *Mostaza Claro*, in which a consumer fails to object that the arbitral tribunal does not have jurisdiction and the conditions in section 11 (3) are not fulfilled, the consumer will be able to plead the invalidity of the award before the courts. According to section 43 (1) of the Arbitration Act, an award may be set aside by the courts if, for example, the arbitration agreement is invalid under the law to which the parties have agreed to subject it or, failing such agreement, under Norwegian law. Violation of the requirement for consumer arbitration contracts in section 11 is one such ground for invalidity.[73] If the consumer has started proceedings before the arbitration court even though he has been made aware of the invalidity of the arbitration clause, the right to claim invalidity will be lost according to section 11-3 (3). Because of the requirements set out by the ECJ, especially in *Mostaza Claro*, the consumer must still be able to claim that the arbitration clause violates Directive 93/13/EEC.[74]

7. CONCLUDING REMARKS

In our view, the courts' duty to apply EU consumer law of their own motion can be taken care of by the Norwegian version of the *iura novit curia* principle combined with the rules on guidance found in section 11-5 of the Dispute Act. The rules on guidance provide judges with the tools necessary to adjust what may otherwise be an imbalanced situation between the parties, and proper guidance should leave consumers in situations where they may apply their autonomy as a party in a well-informed and rational fashion.

If, however, one takes the view that guidance will not suffice, and thus that EU consumer protection law has to be regarded as a non-dispositive element of Norwegian law, it becomes important to clarify what consequences this will have

---

72 Act of 14 May 2004 no 25, available in an unofficial English translation at: <http://app.uio.no/ub/ujur/oversatte-lover/english.shtml> accessed 18 April 2018.

73 Borgar Høgetveit Berg (ed), *Voldgiftsloven med kommentarer* (Gyldendal 2006) 319.

74 Geir Woxholth, *Voldgift* (Gyldendal 2013) 260–261.

for the court's obligation to make sure that the factual basis for the application of EU rules in question is sound. As both the ECJ and the EFTA Court have stated that the national courts' obligation to apply EU/EEA consumer protection law of their own motion is limited to situations where they have available to them the factual elements necessary for that task,[75] it is clear that the duties of a Norwegian court in a case with non-dispositive elements go beyond the minimum requirements of EU/EEA law. If it is the national court's duty to investigate, for instance, whether a party is a consumer, in Norwegian law that duty is better handled as a further development of the court's power to conduct evidence under the last sentence of section 21-3 of the Dispute Act.

The most surprising element of the Norwegian experience, however, is the total lack of cases concerning the courts' duty to apply EU consumer law of their own motion. Part of the explanation for this is that consumer claims are rarely taken to court in Norway. Most consumer cases are dealt with by different complaints boards, which are practically free of charge and, therefore, much more attractive than the quite expensive Norwegian court system. Other cases, typically those brought by a seller when the consumer has not paid, will normally go directly to enforcement as long as the claim is not contested by the consumer. An important question in Norwegian law, then, is whether the complaints boards or the enforcement authorities are obliged to apply EU consumer law of their own motion. We will not try to answer this challenging question; however, putting such duties on those actors would be of far greater importance in Norway than the duties or obligations of the court.

75 *Pannon* (n 1) para 32; *Camino* (n 1) para 43; *Barclays Bank* (n 1) para 34; *Aziz* (n 1) para 46; and, from the EFTA Court, *Engilbertsson* (n 12) para 162.

MAINTENANCE AND MULTI-LEVEL HARMONISATION

A European Union Perspective

Volker Lipp

1. CROSS-BORDER MAINTENANCE CASES WITHIN AND OUTSIDE THE EU

Family law issues are often seen as being culturally more sensitive than other areas of the law and, therefore, less apt for harmonisation either within the EU or on an international level outside of it. However, family law cases in general, and maintenance cases in particular, are becoming more and more transnational due to the increasing mobility of people. Despite the diversity of national laws on family maintenance and its cultural sensitivity, the need for coherent rules in cross-border maintenance cases and international co-operation has been recognised since the 1950s by the UN[1] and the Hague Conference on Private International Law (Hague Conference).[2]

The EU, on the other hand, did not pay much attention, generally speaking, to the field of family law, or to family maintenance in particular, for a long time, even where it had the power to legislate, namely in relation to cross-border cases in the field of international civil procedure and private international law. The old Brussels I regime[3] and most of its accompanying instruments,[4] as well as the Lugano Conventions,[5] do cover maintenance cases, but apart from a special rule on jurisdiction,[6] these instruments do not take into account the vulnerable situation of the maintenance creditor and the 'need for speed' in these cases. Moreover, they do not address international co-operation as a means to provide support, but instead leave this completely to the 1956 New York Convention.

This old system is now being replaced by a new system. The EU, with its Tampere program of 1999, set out to simplify and accelerate, *inter alia*, maintenance proceedings.[7] As the Hague Conference also planned to overhaul their conventions on maintenance, both projects were being worked on in a co-ordinated manner. It helped that the EU as such had become a member of the Hague Conference.[8] The EU now is a party to the two new Hague

1 New York Convention of 20 June 1956 on the Recovery Abroad of Maintenance (the 1956 New York Convention).

2 Cf the Convention of 24 October 1956 on the Law Applicable to Maintenance Obligations (the 1956 Hague Convention) and the Convention of 15 April 1958 on Recognition and Enforcement of Maintenance Obligations (the 1958 Hague Convention).

3 The term 'Brussels I regime' refers collectively to the Convention on jurisdiction and the enforcement of civil and commercial matters of 27 September 1968 (the Brussels Convention) and its later versions when new Member States of the European Communities, as it was then, acceded to the Convention; and to Regulation (EC) 44/2001 on jurisdiction and the recognition and enforcement of judgments in civil and commercial matters (the Brussels I Regulation) [2001] OJ L12/1. It has been replaced by the Regulation (EC) 1215/2012 on jurisdiction and the recognition and enforcement in civil and commercial matters (the Brussels I *bis* Regulation) [2012] OJ L351/1.

4 E.g. Directive 2002/8/EC of 27 January 2003 to improve access to justice in cross-border disputes by establishing minimum common rules relating to legal aid for such disputes (Directive on legal aid in cross-border cases) [2003] OJ L26/41; Regulation (EC) 805/2004 of the European Parliament and of the Council of 21 April 2004 creating a European Enforcement Order for uncontested claims (European Enforcement Order Regulation) [2004] OJ L143/15.

5 Convention of 13 October 2007 on jurisdiction and the recognition and enforcement of judgments in civil and commercial matters (the 2007 Lugano Convention) [2007] OJ L339/3. The 2007 Lugano Convention replaced the Convention on jurisdiction and the enforcement of judgments in civil and commercial matters of 19 September 1988 (the 1988 Lugano Convention).

6 Cf Art 5(2) Brussels Convention; Art 5(2) Brussels I Regulation; Art 5(2) 1998 Lugano Convention; Art 5(2) 2007 Lugano Convention.

7 Tampere European Council, 15–16 October 1999, Presidency conclusions, nos 30, 34 <http://www.europarl.europa.eu/summits/tam_en.htm> accessed 18 July 2018.

8 Paul Beaumont, 'International Family Law in Europe – the Maintenance Project, the Hague conference and the EC: a triumph of reverse subsidiarity' (2009) 73 *RabelsZ* 509.

instruments of 2007[9] dealing with international maintenance cases, and enacted the EU Maintenance Regulation in 2009[10] for maintenance cases inside the EU. Together, these instruments make up a new system for cross-border maintenance cases within and outside of the EU. Consequently, the new Brussels I *bis* Regulation, by virtue of its Article 1 (2) (e), does not cover maintenance cases anymore.

This chapter analyses the new system for cross-border maintenance cases and explores the interplay between the Hague Convention of 2007, the Hague Protocol of 2007, and the EU Maintenance Regulation of 2009. The focus is on the achievements and the shortcomings of this multi-level approach to cross-border maintenance cases with instruments that partly overlap. The instruments will be discussed in this context but not dealt with in detail, as the aim is to outline and explore the new system, rather than to analyse the instruments as such.

Section 2 will outline some characteristics of (international) maintenance cases that need to be taken into account by law-makers. The work of the UN and the Hague Conference is then discussed in section 3, the work of the EU in section 4, and the outlines of the new system inside and outside the EU in section 5. Some observations and conclusions on the multi-level harmonisation are drawn in the final section 6.

2. BACKGROUND

Maintenance, from a comparative perspective, is about financial support to cover a person's needs. It is provided for children by parents, for family members within families and after divorce. Maintenance cases are, therefore, about financial obligations, but based on family relations like parentage, marriage or affinity. Frequently they are part of a complex family case, for example in the event of a divorce or a paternity dispute. Family laws in general, and maintenance laws in particular, show great diversity and fundamental differences on all levels, in substantive law as well as in procedural law. It adds to the complexity of maintenance cases that the family relationship on which a maintenance claim is based may not always be universally recognised, like a parent–child relationship,

---

9 Convention of 23 November 2007 on the International Recovery of Child Support and other Forms of Family Maintenance (the 2007 Hague Convention); Protocol of 23 November 2007 (the 2007 Hague Protocol).

10 Regulation (EC) 4/2009 on jurisdiction, applicable law, recognition and enforcement of decisions and co-operation in matters relating to maintenance obligations (the Maintenance Regulation) [2009] OJ L7/1.

but rather only be recognised by some states and rejected outright by others, like same-sex marriage.[11]

The parties in a maintenance case may be the person claiming maintenance (creditor) and the person who is supposed to pay it (debtor) in proceedings either for maintenance or for re-payment of maintenance that was received without a legal basis. However, one party may also be a third party who provided maintenance instead of the debtor and is now claiming reimbursement.

Unlike in other civil cases, maintenance cases frequently involve a public authority or public body. That public body may help an individual to claim money from a family member who is primarily responsible for providing financial support. Sometimes the public body covers the person's needs itself and then claims reimbursement. A claim for reimbursement may be based on the original maintenance obligation that has been subrogated to the public body, or it may be based on the powers of the public body under public law. Sometimes the state may even pay financial support to a person in need without reclaiming that money from anybody else; in that situation, we are definitely outside the scope of family and maintenance law and within the realm of social law and public law.[12]

Since the creditor needs maintenance in order to cover his living expenses, his position *vis-à-vis* the debtor is an unequal and weak one. The accessibility and duration of proceedings, including enforcement, are important to any creditor, but even more so to a maintenance creditor, particularly in cross-border cases where legal issues are more complicated, and proceedings lengthier, than in purely national cases. In effect, a maintenance creditor is without doubt in a more vulnerable position than a consumer.[13]

International instruments have addressed these particular challenges of cross-border maintenance cases in various ways.

3. INTERNATIONAL INSTRUMENTS

3.1. THE 1956 NEW YORK CONVENTION

The 1956 New York Convention was drafted within the framework of the United Nations following the model of the US Uniform Reciprocal Enforcement of

---

11 Cf Anna Nylund, in this volume, section 2; Volker Lipp, 'Europäisches Unterhaltsrecht' in Martin Ahrens, Volker Lipp and István Varga (eds), *Europäisches Zivilprozessrecht – Einfluss auf Deutschland und Ungarn* (Universitätsverlag Göttingen 2011) 167 et seq.

12 Cf Volker Lipp 'EG-UntVO' in Thomas Rauscher (ed), *Münchener Kommentar zum FamFG* (2nd ed, C.H. Beck 2013) Art 1 nos 53 et seq, Art 64.

13 Volker Lipp, 'Parteiautonomie im internationalen Unterhaltsrecht' in Alain-Laurent Verbeke, Jens M. Scherpe, Charlotte Declerck, Tobias Helms and Patrick Senaeve (eds), *Confronting the Frontiers of Family and Succession Law. Liber Amicorum Walter Pintens* (Intersentia 2012) 855.

Support Act. Its purpose is to facilitate the recovery of maintenance in cross-border cases by judicial and administrative co-operation between Member States. In order to achieve this aim, the Convention established a network of Central Authorities in Member States entrusted with this task.[14]

The 1956 New York Convention requires Member States to support a creditor when he pursues his claim for maintenance against a debtor in another Member State either through judicial proceedings or extra-judicially. He may apply to the Central Agency in his country of residence, which will transfer the application to the Central Agency of the Member State where the debtor is situated. The receiving Central Authority will then take all appropriate steps to recover maintenance from the debtor.[15] This support is in addition to, not as a substitute for, other remedies that are available for the parties.

Unlike the Hague Conventions,[16] the 1956 New York Convention does not apply only to a specific category of maintenance claims, such as for child support, but is applicable in all maintenance claims. It is not clear, however, if a debtor asking for an adjustment of a maintenance order or for a re-payment of maintenance that the creditor received without a valid legal basis may also receive support from the Central Agencies.[17]

3.2. THE HAGUE CONVENTIONS UNTIL 2007

Work in the Hague Conference started in parallel with the work of the UN on the 1956 New York Convention. It resulted in two conventions, the procedural convention of 1958 on the recognition and enforcement of maintenance decisions[18] and the convention of 1956 on the applicable law.[19] Both Conventions apply to child support only, a 'child' being defined by the Conventions as a person under the age of 21,[20] at that time the age of majority in many participating countries.

This narrow scope of application of the 1958 and 1956 Hague Conventions was criticised as being too limited. Hence, two new Conventions were drawn

---

[14] 1956 New York Convention, Preamble and Art 1.

[15] 1956 New York Convention, Arts 2–8.

[16] Cf section 3.2.

[17] Volker Lipp, 'New Yorker UN-Übereinkommen über die Geltendmachung von Unterhaltsansprüchen im Ausland (UNUÜ 1956)' in Thomas Rauscher (ed), *Münchener Kommentar zum FamFG* (2nd ed, C.H. Beck 2013) Art 1 nos 1, 2, 10–12.

[18] Convention of 15 April 1958 on Recognition and Enforcement of Maintenance Obligations (the 1958 Hague Convention).

[19] Convention of 24 October 1956 on the Law Applicable to Maintenance Obligations (the 1956 Hague Convention).

[20] 1958 Hague Convention, Art 1(1); 1956 Hague Convention, Art 1(4).

up in 1973, once again a procedural one[21] and another one on the applicable law.[22] They apply to all forms of maintenance based on a family relationship and explicitly include proceedings where a public body claims reimbursement of benefits given to a maintenance creditor from a maintenance debtor.[23] The 1973 Hague Conventions replaced the 1958 and 1956 Hague Conventions almost completely.

However, the 1973 Hague Conventions also had some shortcomings. First, Member States can declare various reservations, limiting the scope of application effectively to support for children until the age of 21 and for spouses and former spouses.[24] Second, there are no uniform rules on direct jurisdiction, as the 1973 Hague Convention on Recognition and Enforcement deals with recognition and enforcement only. Third, and probably most important, the 1973 Hague Conventions, as well as their predecessors, were almost exclusively ratified by European states, except for Australia, which ratified the 1973 Hague Convention on Recognition and Enforcement as late as 2002, and Japan, which ratified the 1973 Hague Convention on Applicable Law in 1986. They cannot even be called true European conventions, as neither all the Member States of the EU nor all the Member States of the EEA, the EFTA or the Council of Europe have ratified them.

3.3. THE 2007 HAGUE CONVENTION AND THE 2007 HAGUE PROTOCOL

The shortcomings of the 1973 Hague Conventions and of the 1956 New York Convention led the Hague Conference to prepare a new convention in order to improve co-operation between states in relation to the international recovery of child support and other forms of family maintenance and to provide parties with procedures that are accessible, prompt, efficient, cost-effective, responsive and fair. Obviously, work on this new convention did not have to start from scratch but could build upon the best features of the existing Hague Conventions and the 1956 New York Convention. The idea was to establish a comprehensive system of co-operation between the authorities of the Member States, and

---

21 Convention of 2 October 1973 on the Recognition and Enforcement of Decisions Relating to Maintenance Obligations (the 1973 Hague Convention on Recognition and Enforcement).

22 Convention of 2 October 1973 on the Law Applicable to Maintenance Obligations (the 1973 Hague Convention on Applicable Law).

23 1973 Hague Convention on Recognition and Enforcement, Arts 1, 18 and 20; 1973 Hague Convention on Applicable Law, Arts 1 and 9.

24 1973 Hague Convention on Recognition and Enforcement, Art 26; 1973 Hague Convention on Applicable Law, Arts 13 and 14.

to create uniform rules on applications to Central Authorities for support in maintenance cases, on the law applicable to family maintenance obligations, on jurisdiction in maintenance cases, and on the recognition and enforcement of maintenance decisions, and also to introduce measures for the prompt enforcement of maintenance decisions.[25]

Whereas the Hague Conference succeeded in integrating the 1956 New York Convention into the new convention, it failed to do so with the rules on jurisdiction and applicable law. As it turned out, no consensus could be reached regarding the rules on direct jurisdiction. What could be done was regulating jurisdiction indirectly by setting out grounds for recognition or non-recognition respectively, as the previous Hague Conventions did.[26] Not all participants agreed that it was necessary to harmonise the rules on applicable law and to integrate them into the new convention. In the end, two conventions were drafted, the 2007 Hague Convention dealing with administrative and judicial co-operation and with recognition and enforcement of maintenance decisions,[27] and the 2007 Hague Protocol on the law applicable to maintenance obligations.[28]

The 2007 Hague Convention regulates recognition and enforcement of maintenance decisions but has also taken up the system of administrative and judicial co-operation set up by the 1956 New York Convention and improved it considerably. It applies to child support for children until the age of 21 and to maintenance for spouses and former spouses if combined with child support. Otherwise, parties in cases of spousal support will not be supported by the Central Authorities, but decisions on spousal support can be recognised and enforced under the 2007 Hague Convention. This is but the basic set of rules. There are many ways in which Member States can either limit or extend the scope of application of the 2007 Hague Convention, either generally or only a particular part of it. For example, a Member State can limit the scope of application with respect to child support for children until the age of 18, and it can extend it to other forms of family maintenance.[29] The 2007 Hague Protocol, in contrast, applies to all family maintenance obligations, and its

---

25 William Duncan, 'The New Hague Child Support Convention: Goals and Outcomes of the Negotiations' (2009) 43 *FamLQ* 1.

26 Duncan (n 25) 14–15; Anna Nylund, in this volume, section 4.2.

27 Convention of 23 November 2007 on the International Recovery of Child Support and Other Forms of Family Maintenance (the 2007 Hague Convention).

28 Protocol of 23 November 2007 on the Law Applicable to Maintenance Obligations (the 2007 Hague Protocol).

29 2007 Hague Convention, Art 2. The background of this article is explained by Alegria Borrás and Jennifer Degeling, *Explanatory Report. Convention of 23 November 2007 on the International Recovery of Child Support and Other Forms of Family Maintenance* (Hague Conference on Private International Law 2013) nos 45–57.

scope of application cannot be restricted.[30] The EU currently applies the 2007 Hague Convention to spousal support without exceptions, and is willing to examine the possibility of extending the application of the Convention to all maintenance obligations arising from a family relationship, parentage, marriage or affinity in the future.[31] Both conventions will then have roughly the same material scope of application for EU Member States.

This variation in the material scope of application might seem odd at first glance. If one looks at the status tables of the two conventions,[32] the reasons may become clearer. The EU (for its Member States, except for Denmark and the United Kingdom), Serbia, Kazakhstan and Brazil have ratified both conventions. In contrast, the 2007 Hague Convention also applies to Albania, Belarus, Bosnia-Herzegovina, Montenegro, Norway, Turkey, Ukraine, the United Kingdom and, most importantly, the United States. Therefore, whereas the 2007 Hague Protocol is mainly an instrument harmonising private international law rules within the EU, the 2007 Hague Convention is a truly international instrument that needs to bridge the differences between larger numbers of legal systems.[33]

4. HARMONISATION WITHIN THE EUROPEAN UNION

4.1. THE BRUSSELS REGIME

The Brussels regime – from its early days shaped by the original 1968 Brussels Convention until the Brussels I Regulation – regulated jurisdiction, recognition and enforcement in civil and commercial matters. Family matters and succession fell outside the Brussels regime, except for maintenance obligations, which were included but treated mainly as financial obligations. In general, maintenance cases followed the common rules for civil and commercial cases. Parties could therefore enter into an agreement on jurisdiction with respect to child support under the same liberal rules as they could in any commercial transaction.[34] Later amendments to the Brussels regime, like the European

30 2007 Hague Protocol, Arts 1, 27 and 28.

31 The declaration of the EU can be found via the status table for the 2007 Hague Convention on the website of the Hague Conference for child support and other forms of family maintenance: <https://www.hcch.net/en/instruments/conventions/specialised-sections/child-support>.

32 See the website of the Hague Conference for child support and other forms of family maintenance: <https://www.hcch.net/en/instruments/conventions/specialised-sections/child-support>.

33 Borrás and Degeling (n 29) nos 48, 51 and 57.

34 Art 17 Brussels Convention; Art 23 Brussels I Regulation.

Enforcement Order Regulation[35] or the Directive on legal aid in cross-border cases,[36] were also applicable in maintenance cases.

The only rules especially designed for maintenance cases under the Brussels regime were the special grounds in Article 5(2) Brussels Convention/Brussels I Regulation for jurisdiction where the maintenance creditor is habitually resident, or where maintenance is claimed as an annex to status proceedings. However, these fora were not available for public bodies claiming reimbursement from the debtor, even when based on the original maintenance obligation subrogated to them, since the rationale behind these grounds for jurisdiction was, according to the European Court of Justice, protecting the creditor as the weaker party.[37]

Support was provided to the creditor in the process of recovering maintenance by the network of Central Authorities established under the 1956 New York Convention.[38] This international system of judicial and administrative co-operation indirectly harmonised judicial and administrative co-operation within the EU, as most of the EU Member States were also parties to the 1956 New York Convention; despite this, it remained completely outside the Brussels regime and the EU legal order.

There was also indirect, but only very limited, harmonisation of the rules on applicable law as some Member States of the EU were also parties to the 1973 Hague Convention on Applicable Law, the latest figures being 11 out of 28 Member States.[39]

4.2. THE TWO-LEVEL REFORM PROCESS

The EU started its reform process with the European Council of Tampere in 1999. It decided to establish minimum standards ensuring an adequate level of legal aid in cross-border cases throughout the EU, as well as special common procedural rules for simplified and accelerated cross-border litigation, *inter alia*

---

35 Regulation (EC) 805/2004 of the European Parliament and of the Council of 21 April 2004 creating a European Enforcement Order for uncontested claims (European Enforcement Order Regulation) [2004] OJ L143/15.

36 Directive 2002/8/EC of 27 January 2003 to improve access to justice in cross-border disputes by establishing minimum common rules relating to legal aid for such disputes (Directive on legal aid in cross-border cases) [2003] OJ L26/41.

37 Case C-433/01 *Freistaat Bayern v Jan Blidjenstein* ECLI:EU:C:2004:21, para 34. For Art 5(2) Lugano Convention which has a similar provision see Anna Nylund, in this volume, section 3.2.

38 Cf section 3.1.

39 See the status table for the 1973 Hague Convention on Applicable Law on the website of the Hague Conference for child support and other forms of family maintenance: <https://www.hcch.net/en/instruments/conventions/specialised-sections/child-support>.

on maintenance claims. It also decided that alternative extra-judicial procedures should be made available. In addition, exequatur proceedings to enable the recognition and enforcement of a decision or judgment in another state, which were required under the Brussels I Regulation and Lugano Convention, as well as under the 1973 Hague Convention on Recognition and Enforcement and the 1958 Hague Convention, should be abolished in favour of titles in respect of, *inter alia*, maintenance claims. Such decisions should not only be automatically recognised but also be automatically enforceable throughout the EU without any intermediate proceedings or grounds for refusal of enforcement. This could be accompanied by the setting of minimum standards on specific aspects of civil procedural law.[40]

Initially, the idea was to draft a comprehensive regulation covering all aspects of cross-border maintenance cases, ranging from jurisdiction, recognition and enforcement, legal aid, support for parties by and legal and administrative co-operation between Central Authorities, to rules on applicable law. The new regulation would replace not only the Brussels I Regulation but also the Directive 2002/8/EC on legal aid in cross-border cases, the 1956 New York Convention, and the 1973 Hague Convention on Applicable Law.[41]

At the same time and with similar motives, the Hague Conference had begun to work on a new convention on family maintenance.[42] The EU, as a member of the Hague Conference since 3 April 2007, took an active part in these negotiations. As the new Hague convention was intended, at least in the beginning, to cover most, if not all, of the areas envisaged for the new EU regulation, there was obviously a need to co-ordinate work undertaken in the Hague Conference with the work being carried out within the EU. Whereas some argued for the EU to wait for the outcome of the debates at the Hague Conference, the European Commission decided to continue with preparing a new regulation.[43] This approach brought about a complex set of parallel and interwoven negotiations on the EU level and at the Hague Conference, and between a multitude of state actors ranging from EU Member States to the US and Latin American countries, but also including the European Commission.[44]

In this process, the EU decided not include the private international law rules on the law applicable to maintenance obligations in the new regulation but to discuss them exclusively at the Hague Conference. The EU was then the first party to ratify the 2007 Hague Protocol and even to apply it unilaterally

---

40 Cf (n 7).

41 Beaumont (n 8) 513–516.

42 See section 3.3.

43 Cf European Commission, 'Proposal for a Council Regulation on jurisdiction, applicable law, recognition and enforcement of decisions and cooperation in matters relating to maintenance obligations' and 'Impact Assessment' in the annex thereto, SEC(2005) 1629.

44 Beaumont (n 8) 513–516 and 543–546.

from 18 June 2011 onwards in all its Member States, except Denmark and the UK,[45] thus harmonising the rules on applicable law within the EU and also, albeit depending of course on the ratification or accession of other states, internationally. It is noteworthy that the 2007 Hague Protocol has become part of the law of the EU because the EU ratified it and decided to apply it provisionally and not by virtue of Article 15 of the Maintenance Regulation, which instead merely points towards the 2007 Hague Protocol.[46] In other words, the EU achieved its objective of harmonising the rules on applicable law within the EU through international negotiations at the Hague Conference and through an international convention, namely the 2007 Hague Protocol.[47]

All other aspects of cross-border maintenance cases – i.e. jurisdiction, recognition and enforcement, legal aid, and support for parties by and legal and administrative co-operation between Central Authorities – were to be covered by the new regulation. It was obviously necessary to co-ordinate the work on the new regulation with the work undertaken at the Hague Conference, as this also addressed recognition and enforcement, legal aid, and support for parties by and legal and administrative co-operation between Central Authorities. Although the Hague Conference had decided to leave out direct jurisdiction at an early stage and to concentrate on recognition and enforcement,[48] its jurisdictional rules in the context of recognition would determine whether a judgment from an EU Member State could be recognised outside of the EU. In order to ensure that an EU maintenance judgment could also be enforced outside of the EU, the rules on direct jurisdiction in the new regulation had to match the Hague rules on indirect jurisdiction. It was therefore also necessary to co-ordinate the work in this field on both levels.

4.3. THE MAINTENANCE REGULATION

The Maintenance Regulation is not in the end quite as comprehensive as had been intended at the outset, but it still covers most of the aspects relevant in cross-border maintenance cases: Chapter II deals with jurisdiction, Chapter IV with recognition and enforcement of judgments, Chapter VI with recognition and enforcement of court settlements and authentic instruments, Chapter V with access to justice and legal aid, and Chapter VII with support for parties by and legal and administrative co-operation between Central Authorities. As said before, the law applicable to maintenance obligations has to be ascertained

---

45 Cf text at (n 31) in section 3.3.
46 Lipp (n 12) Art 15 no 6.
47 Beaumont (n 8) 544.
48 Cf section 3.3.

according to the rules of the 2007 Hague Protocol in all Member States, except in Denmark and the UK. Article 15, the sole provision of Chapter III, references the 2007 Hague Protocol, but is purely declaratory in nature.[49] The Maintenance Regulation thus replaces not only the Brussels I Regulation and the Enforcement Order Regulation (Articles 68(1) and (2) Maintenance Regulation), but also in principle the Directive 2002/8/EC on legal aid in cross-border cases (Article 68(3) Maintenance Regulation) and, between the Member States, the Hague Conventions on recognition and enforcement of 1973 and 1958, as well as the 1956 New York Convention (Art 69(1) Maintenance Regulation).

Jurisdiction is regulated in Chapter II in basically the same way as in the Brussels I Regulation and the 2007 Lugano Convention. It is based on the appearance of the defendant unless the defendant contests the jurisdiction of the court (Article 5 Maintenance Regulation). Then the statutory rules of jurisdiction come into play. In addition to the general rule of *actor sequitur forum rei* (Article 3(a) Maintenance Regulation), the Maintenance Regulation allows the creditor to sue in his own forum (Article 3(b) Maintenance Regulation). The plaintiff can also claim maintenance in the forum of status proceedings if maintenance is an annex to the status (Article 3(c) and (d) Maintenance Regulation).[50] It is noteworthy that the rules on jurisdiction differ to some extent from the Brussels regime. First, jurisdiction is based on the habitual residence, rather than the domicile, of the defendant or the creditor respectively. Second, there is also jurisdiction under these rules when the defendant is habitually resident or domiciled outside of the EU. Third, Article 4 Maintenance Regulation has limited the choice of court by a prorogation agreement considerably compared to the Brussels regime. Fourth, as the jurisdictional rules should be comprehensive, the Maintenance Regulation provides subsidiary jurisdiction in Articles 6 and 7.

There are two paths for recognition and enforcement of judgments in another Member State in Chapter IV, one for judgments from the UK and Denmark, which are not bound by the 2007 Hague Protocol, another one for judgments from other Member States that are bound by it (Article 16 Maintenance Regulation). The same two paths are available for court settlements and authentic instruments under Chapter VI (Art 48(1) Maintenance Regulation). For judgments from the UK and Denmark, the rules of the Brussels I Regulation or the 2007 Lugano Convention, respectively, were transplanted into the Maintenance Regulation (Chapter IV, section 2). For judgments from other Member States, the Maintenance Regulation provides a new system (Chapter IV, section 1), which also applies if judgments *from* other Member States are to be

---

49 Cf text at (n 46) in section 4.2.

50 According to the European Court of Justice (Case C-184/14 *A/B* ECLI:EU:C:2015:479) there has to be a substantive connection between the maintenance claim and the status proceedings.

enforced *in* Denmark or in the UK. These judgments are not only recognised but also enforceable *ex lege* in all other Member States, i.e. without exequatur proceedings in the state of enforcement (Articles 17(1) and (2) Maintenance Regulation). Moreover, the grounds for refusing to enforce such a judgment were limited considerably (Article 21 Maintenance Regulation). The only ground of non-recognition from the old system still available under the new system is to be found in Article 21(2)(2) Maintenance Regulation, i.e. if a judgment is irreconcilable with a decision given in the Member State of enforcement or with a decision given in another state that meets the conditions necessary for its recognition in the state of enforcement.

The Maintenance Regulation, in Chapter VII, establishes a system of co-operation between Central Authorities in Member States in order to facilitate cross-border recovery of maintenance claims. Its features were designed in parallel to the provisions of the 2007 Hague Convention on support by, and legal and administrative co-operation between, Central Authorities.[51] They shall assist maintenance creditors and debtors in asserting their rights in another Member State by submitting applications for recognition, enforceability and enforcement of existing decisions, for the modification of such decisions or for the establishment of a decision. They shall also exchange information in order to locate debtors and creditors, and identify their income and assets as necessary. This system applies to all EU Member States, including the UK, with Denmark being the only exception.

As to the costs of proceedings, the Maintenance Regulation adds specific rules to the existing rules on legal aid under Directive 2003/8/EC, thus setting up a special legal aid scheme for maintenance obligations. The most notable provision was drafted on the model of Article 15 of the 2007 Hague Convention.[52] Article 46 Maintenance Regulation provides for full coverage of the costs relating to proceedings concerning maintenance obligations in respect of children under the age of 21 initiated via the Central Authorities. For other maintenance obligations, all parties are guaranteed the same treatment in terms of legal aid at the time of enforcement of a decision in another Member State by Article 47 Maintenance Regulation. Once again, this system applies to all EU Member States, including the UK, but not Denmark.

5. THE NEW SYSTEM – INSIDE AND OUTSIDE OF THE EU

The Maintenance Regulation entered into force on 18 June 2011 for all Member States of the EU except Denmark. On the same day, the 2007 Hague

[51] Beaumont (n 8) 516 and 625.
[52] Beaumont (n 8) 530–531.

Protocol also became applicable in the EU except for Denmark and the UK.[53] These two instruments are now the pillars of the new system for cross-border maintenance cases within the EU.

Whereas the UK is, until Brexit, a Member State of the EU for the purposes of the Maintenance Regulation as well as the 2007 Hague Convention, Denmark has a different position. It participates in the Maintenance Regulation only insofar it replaces the Brussels I Regulation, i.e. with respect to jurisdiction, recognition and enforcement. It remains completely outside the new system of support by, and legal and administrative co-operation between, Central Authorities, as neither Chapter VII of the Maintenance Regulation nor the 2007 Hague Convention are applicable in Denmark. Instead, the old system of the 1956 New York Convention still applies for Denmark.[54]As Denmark is neither a party to the 2007 Hague Convention nor participates in Chapter V of the Maintenance Regulation or the Directive 2003/8/EC on legal aid,[55] it also remains outside the legal aid scheme provided for by these instruments.

With respect to Iceland, Norway and Switzerland, the 2007 Lugano Convention remains applicable not only in these countries but also in the EU (Article 69(1) and 69(2) Maintenance Regulation). It is unclear, however, whether it is the 2007 Lugano Convention, or instead the Maintenance Regulation, that regulates jurisdiction of an EU court if the defendant is domiciled in one of the Lugano countries.[56] In any event, courts within the EU (except courts in Denmark and in the UK) will determine the applicable law using the 2007 Hague Protocol, whereas Swiss courts will apply the 1973 Hague Convention on the Applicable Law, and Norwegian and Icelandic courts will apply their internal private international law rules. As Norway has ratified the 2007 Hague Convention, as has the EU, that instrument replaces the 1956 New York Convention in relation to support by, and legal and administrative co-operation between, Central Authorities, as well as the previous Hague Conventions of 1973 and 1958 on recognition and enforcement, in line with Articles 48 and 49 of the 2007 Hague Convention. The older instruments are still relevant in relation to Iceland and Switzerland, the two countries not yet being parties to the 2007 Hague Convention.

As for other countries, either the 2007 Hague Convention (if the other state is party to it), or, again contingent on the other state being party to it, one of the older Hague conventions on recognition and enforcement of 1973 or 1958, together with the 1956 New York Convention, will have to be applied in the EU.

---

53 Cf text to (n 45) in section 4.2.

54 LIPP (n 12) Art 1 no 66.

55 LIPP (n 12) Art 44 no 20.

56 LIPP (n 12) Art 69 nos 9–14.

6. CONCLUDING OBSERVATIONS

National laws on family maintenance, maintenance proceedings and enforcement will remain different. In cross-border maintenance cases, accessibility, duration and effectiveness of proceedings and enforcement become paramount for maintenance creditors and their families.

The Hague Conference and the EU, as well as their Member States, have acknowledged the need for administrative and judicial co-operation in family maintenance and have acted upon this insight. The 2007 Hague Convention, together with the 2007 Hague Protocol and the Maintenance Regulation, may certainly have some shortcomings, but all in all they bring major improvements for families having to deal with maintenance issues in cross-border situations. Beyond these improvements on the practical level, the combined efforts on the EU level and within the Hague Conference have created a new system that integrates international and EU instruments in an innovative way.

The core idea is as striking as it is simple: a comprehensive and co-ordinated system for administrative and judicial co-operation should address citizens' needs in cross-border maintenance cases. It should cover all aspects of cross-border maintenance cases ranging from jurisdiction, recognition and enforcement, legal aid, support for parties by and legal and administrative co-operation between Central Authorities, to rules on applicable law. The 2007 Hague Convention should therefore apply in relation to states outside of the EU, and the Maintenance Regulation within the EU. In addition, the 2007 Hague Protocol should introduce a uniform set of rules to ascertain the law applicable to family maintenance obligations inside and outside of the EU. All these instruments should have the same material scope of application and cover maintenance based on any family relation.

These goals, however, have not completely become reality, neither on the international level nor on the EU or EEA level. This results from substantive as well as political differences. In several fields, negotiators could reach no consensus during the drafting processes of the new instruments. In addition, some states have remained outside the Maintenance Regulation, and/or have been reluctant to ratify the 2007 Hague Convention and the 2007 Hague Protocol. The major flaws of the new system are as follows.

First, the 2007 Hague Convention does not regulate direct jurisdiction.

Second, the 2007 Hague Convention regulates recognition and enforcement of maintenance judgments only for child and spousal support and limits the support by Central Authorities for spousal support to cases when it is claimed in connection with child support, leaving it to Member States to include other forms of family maintenance – as the EU is willing to do.

Third, the Maintenance Regulation has not brought about a uniform system for all EU Member States, since Denmark remains outside of all areas of harmonisation beyond jurisdiction, recognition and enforcement, and because there is a second track for recognition and enforcement of judgments, court settlements and authentic instruments from Denmark and the UK.

Fourth, the Maintenance Regulation and the Brussels I *bis* Regulation break the parallelism between the Brussels regime and the Lugano Convention, giving rise to many legal gaps, conflicts and difficulties. In principle, *vis-à-vis* Iceland and Switzerland, the old system of the Lugano Convention, the 1956 New York Convention and the Hague Conventions of 1973 and 1956 still applies, whereas in relation to Norway the Lugano Convention and the 2007 Hague Convention apply.

Fifth, the need for harmonisation of private international law rules on family maintenance is not acknowledged internationally, and only by a majority of European states inside and outside of the EU. Notably, Denmark, the UK, Norway, Switzerland and Iceland have remained outside the 2007 Hague Protocol.

Harmonising laws and establishing administrative and legal co-operation is always challenging, even more so when it is tackled on several levels at the same time. Multi-level harmonisation almost inevitably leads to multi-speed harmonisation, causing new divergences where uniform rules were instead intended. On the other hand, the experience of harmonising the rules for cross-border maintenance cases also tells us that multi-level harmonisation may still improve the situation for citizens considerably. Perhaps there could even be a lesson to be learned for Brexit?

FAMILY MAINTENANCE AND MULTI-SPEED INTEGRATION

A Norwegian Perspective

Anna NYLUND

1. FAMILY MAINTENANCE AND MULTI-LEVEL REGULATION

Globalisation, free movement of labour and migration affect regulations on judicial co-operation and cross-border proceedings in family matters, including family maintenance.[1] Since the turn of the millennium, EU (procedural) family law has emerged as a field of law. The EU Maintenance Regulation[2] was drafted concurrently with the 2007 Hague Convention on maintenance,[3] creating a direct link between EU law and international law. Before then, the Brussels regime[4] on the jurisdiction and the recognition and enforcement of civil and commercial matters had a few provisions regulating family mediation. So did its parallel instrument, the Lugano Convention,[5] which extends the free movement rulings to the entire single market, including European Free Trade Association (EFTA) states.[6] Despite the fact that the Agreement on the European Economic Area (EEA) widens the single market and the four freedoms to states outside the EU, the development of family law in the EEA or EFTA has stagnated. International law and EU law on family maintenance have taken a leap forward and formed a connection. Simultaneously, the connection between EU law and EFTA law has weakened: the Treaty of Amsterdam[7] has developed the competences of the EU, whereas EFTA law has maintained the *status quo*.

Currently, family maintenance is regulated on five levels: (1) on an international level through the Hague regime, (2) on an EU level, (3) on an EFTA level, (4) on a regional level, and finally (5) on a national level. The three first levels of law are interconnected and partially overlapping. However, a multi-level

---

1 Child maintenance was one of the first areas regulated by the Hague Conference on Private International Law in the 1956 Convention on the Law Applicable to Maintenance Obligations and the 1958 Convention on Recognition and Enforcement of Maintenance Obligations. Further, the New York Convention on the Recovery Abroad of Maintenance of 1956 underlines the importance of international co-operation in the field. See Volker Lipp, in this volume, for more detailed information.

2 Regulation (EC) 4/2009 on jurisdiction, applicable law, recognition and enforcement of decisions and co-operation in matters relating to maintenance obligations (Maintenance Regulation) [2009] OJ L7/1.

3 Convention of 23 November 2007 on the International Recovery of Child Support and other Forms of Family Maintenance.

4 The Brussels regime is used to refer collectively to the Convention on jurisdiction and the enforcement of civil and commercial matters of 27 September 1968 (the Brussels Convention); Regulation (EC) 44/2001 on jurisdiction and the recognition and enforcement of judgments in civil and commercial matters (Brussels I Regulation) [2001] OJ L12/1; and Regulation (EC) 1215/2012 on jurisdiction and the recognition and enforcement in civil and commercial matters (Brussels I *bis* Regulation) [2012] OJ L351/1.

5 Convention of 13 October 2007 on jurisdiction and the recognition and enforcement of judgments in civil and commercial matters (Lugano Convention) [2007] OJ L 339/3. The 2007 Lugano Convention repealed the Convention on jurisdiction and the enforcement of judgments in civil and commercial matters of 19 September 1988 (the 1988 Lugano Convention).

6 The term EFTA is used to demonstrate that the Lugano Convention extends beyond the EEA Agreement. Despite the close connection between the EEA Agreement and the Lugano Convention, Liechtenstein is not a party to the convention, but Switzerland is.

7 Treaty of Amsterdam amending the Treaty on European Union, the Treaties establishing the European Communities and certain related acts [1997] OJ C340/1.

approach may be beneficial for regulating family maintenance in a multi-speed Europe. A multi-level, multi-speed approach may also increase complexity and opacity, creating an intricate web of regulation.

This chapter examines the interplay between instruments at different levels and discusses whether the relationships are constructive or disruptive. The existence of several levels of regulation results in complexity, yet the levels are complementary, filling lacunae. This chapter explores how different levels of law could be used to enhance integration of civil procedure, including the advantages and disadvantages of each level. The focus is on managing multi-speed integration, where some countries are part of, or closely tied to, the single market, but do not participate in judicial co-operation.

The Nordic countries will be discussed in particular, in order to analyse the impact of EU membership and the EFTA law on cross-border maintenance. Nordic regional law will also be discussed in the context of a multi-level approach to regulation. This chapter concentrates primarily on jurisdiction and enforcement, but will also discuss the scope of application and administrative co-operation when relevant. The contents of each instrument will not be discussed in detail, since the aim is to discuss the interplay of the instruments and their role in multi-speed integration, not the instruments themselves.

First, some introductory remarks on family maintenance law will be made in section 2. Sections 3, 4 and 5 discuss and compare the regulation of jurisdiction and enforcement in the Lugano Convention and the 2007 Hague Convention from an EFTA law perspective. The choice between the conventions on the state level is also examined. Thereafter, in sections 6 and 7, the relationship between the instruments is discussed. Does the multi-level approach lead to coherence or complexity? Here, the Nordic regional level is introduced. The final section discusses the outlook for the multi-level regulation of family maintenance.

2. CROSS-BORDER FAMILY MAINTENANCE

Defining child and spousal maintenance is challenging. Family law maintenance is based on family law relationships, such as parentage, marriage or affinity. Depending on the country, other family relationships, such as cohabitation or same-sex partnerships, may also establish a duty to provide maintenance.[8] In some countries, maintenance for children above the age of 18 or 20 is rare; in others parents are expected to support their children until they finish

8 See *inter alia* Andrea Bonomi, *Explanatory Report Protocol of 23 November 2007 on the Law Applicable to Maintenance Obligations* (Hague Conference on Private International Law

university. Countries where welfare is provided on a highly individual basis tend to limit family maintenance, whereas countries with a family-centred welfare system extend maintenance. Family maintenance is delimited from maintenance obligations based on *inter alia* inheritance law and tort law. Maintenance can be paid in several ways: monthly, annually, as a lump sum, etc., and it can even be part of the division of marital property. A single transaction may include both division of marital property and maintenance. The Lugano and Hague Conventions skirt the problem by not defining maintenance or family maintenance.

Family law, including family maintenance, is deeply embedded in national culture and society. Differences concerning *inter alia* the status of cohabitation and same-sex partnerships result in hesitance towards recognising foreign maintenance decisions. Yet family maintenance is often pivotal for the children and parents concerned. Globalisation and the single European market increases the flow of people and consequently the need for uniform regulation ensuring efficient enforcement of maintenance obligations.[9] In the process, both liberal, 'divorce-friendly' countries and conservative countries must relinquish some of their principles.

Maintenance is decided in different settings and processes. A maintenance claim is often ancillary to divorce or child custody proceedings. It may be agreed upon in consensual proceedings or proceedings at administrative agencies. In many countries, such as the Nordic countries, a public body will pay the creditor (some) maintenance in the event that the debtor does not pay or pays late, which it then recovers from the debtor. Thus, the public body has a direct interest in having rights as a party in court and enforcement proceedings. Because maintenance often covers long periods, proceedings on amendment of maintenance are commonplace.

As for family law, in general, the parties in maintenance cases are individual citizens, often with limited knowledge of their legal rights and limited resources to enforce those rights. In cases involving maintenance of the child (and his/her residential parent), the best interest of the child requires expeditious proceedings. Due to the limited knowledge and resources of the parties and the pivotal role of family maintenance, international judicial co-operation generally proceeds through central authorities. Central authorities provide

---

2007) 27; Lara Walker, *Maintenance and Child Support in Private International Law* (Hart 2015) 38–39.

9 David Bradley, 'A Family Law for Europe? Sovereignty, Political Economy and Legitimation' in Katharina Boele-Woelki (ed), *Perspectives for the Unification and Harmonisation of Family Law in Europe* (Intersentia 2003); Erik Jayme, 'Cultural Dimensions of Maintenance Law from a Private International Law Perspective' in Paul Beaumont et al (eds), *The Recovery of Maintenance in the EU and Worldwide* (Hart 2014); Walker (n 8) 15–36.

information to the parties on the documents and forms needed, receive and process applications and exchange information. They reduce costs for the parties and ensure specialisation in cross-border family matters. The disadvantage of central authorities is that they add two extra steps in communication, since the national authorities communicate with the national central authority instead of directly with each other.

Although family law matters are often intertwined, the regulation of these matters is fragmented. Marriage, separation, divorce and matrimonial property are regulated in three different Hague Conventions,[10] maintenance in the 2007 Hague Convention and its Protocol and predecessors,[11] and parental responsibility in the 1996 Hague Convention.[12] Although questions on judicial co-operation and applicable law are interconnected, only the 1996 Hague Convention on parental responsibility has achieved the goal of regulating both aspects in a single instrument. The 2007 Hague Convention on maintenance has the rules of applicable law in a separate protocol.[13]

Since the turn of the millennium, EU family law has evolved and expanded rapidly. The Brussels II (*bis*) Regulation[14] on matrimonial matters and parental responsibility extended the EU regime of jurisdiction, recognition and enforcement to family law in 2001, and in 2009 the Maintenance Regulation was enacted to regulate cross-border family maintenance. The Rome III and IV Regulations (on divorce and succession respectively) followed suite.[15] With the exception of the Rome III Regulation, these regulations govern procedural co-operation, administrative co-operation and choice of law. The close connection between private international law and procedural law in

10 The 1970 Convention on the Recognition of Divorces and Legal Separations, the 1978 Convention on the Law Applicable to Matrimonial Property Regimes, and the 1978 Convention on Celebration and Recognition of the Validity of Marriages.

11 Protocol of 23 November 2007 on the Law Applicable to Maintenance Obligations.

12 1996 Hague Convention on Jurisdiction, Applicable Law, Recognition, Enforcement and Co-operation in Respect of Parental Responsibility and Measures for the Protection of Children.

13 For the background to the 2007 Hague Convention, see Paul Beaumont, 'International Family Law in Europe – The Maintenance Project, the Hague Conference and the EC: a triumph of reverse subsidiarity' [2009] *The Rabel Journal of Comparative and International Private Law* 509; and Volker Lipp, in this volume.

14 Regulation (EC) 1347/2000 on jurisdiction and the recognition and enforcement of judgments in matrimonial matters and in matters of parental responsibility for children of both spouses [2000] OJ L160/19 was repealed by Regulation (EC) 2201/2003 concerning jurisdiction and the recognition and enforcement of judgments in matrimonial matters and the matters of parental responsibility [2003] OJ L338/1. The latter entered into force 1 August 2004.

15 Regulation (EU) 1259/2010 implementing enhanced co-operation in the area of the law applicable to divorce and legal separation [2010] OJ L343/10; Regulation (EU) 650/2012 on jurisdiction, applicable law, recognition and enforcement of decisions and acceptance and enforcement of authentic instruments in matters of succession and on the creation of a European Certificate of Succession [2012] OJ L201/107.

these regulations should not be over-emphasised. The Brussels I (*bis*) Regulation is connected to the Rome Regulations[16] on applicable law and the European Court of Justice (ECJ) interprets the Brussels regime in light of the Rome regime.

3. THE LUGANO CONVENTION

The 1988 Lugano Convention[17] was established as a parallel to the 1968 Brussels Convention,[18] to create a single, coherent regulation of jurisdiction, recognition and enforcement in civil matters in the European Communities and the EFTA.[19] The single market requires uniform rules to ensure that the common substantial regulation can be enforced on an equal basis. Thus, the Lugano Convention is a necessary extension of the EEA Agreement, as it establishes free movement of civil judgments. The rules are to be interpreted uniformly with the Brussels regime; thus, the case law of the ECJ is key source for interpretation of the Convention.

The Brussels I Regulation repealed the Brussels Convention in 2001, and the Lugano Convention was revised in 2007 to re-establish parallelism. However, since entry into force of the Maintenance Regulation and the Brussels I *bis* Regulation, the Lugano Convention and the Brussels I *bis* Regulation have not been completely parallel. The revisions of EU instruments have so far not sparked a revision process for the Lugano Convention. Consequently, some of the rules, *inter alia* those on family maintenance, now differ.[20]

The Lugano Convention is applicable to civil and commercial law (Article 1(1)), but family matters are not covered (Article 1(2)(a)). Maintenance claims are, however, included almost irrespective of whether they arise from family relationships or other types of maintenance. The main distinction is between family law and inheritance law matters on the one hand, and maintenance on the other; distinctions between types of maintenance obligations

---

16 Regulation (EC) 593/2008 on the law applicable to contractual obligations [2008] OJ L177/6; Regulation (EC) 864/2007 on the law applicable to non-contractual obligations [2007] OJ L199/40.

17 Convention on jurisdiction and the enforcement of judgments in civil and commercial matters of 19 September 1988 (1988 Lugano Convention).

18 Convention on jurisdiction and the enforcement of civil and commercial matters of 27 September 1968.

19 Liechtenstein is not party to the Convention despite its EEA membership. Switzerland is a party to the Convention through its membership of the EFTA. However, Switzerland is not party to the EEA Agreement.

20 For a short background on the 2007 Lugano Convention, see e.g. Fausto Pocar, 'The New Lugano Convention on Jurisdiction and the Recognition and Enforcement of Judgments in Civil and Commercial Matters' (2008) 10 *Yearbook of Private International Law* 1; Despina Mavromati and Rodrigo Rodriguez, 'The Revised Lugano Convention from a Swiss Perspective' (2009) 20 *European Business L Rev* 579.

are normally of little relevance.[21] Family maintenance covers cohabitation and same-sex relationships.[22]

3.1. JURISDICTION AND ENFORCEMENT OF MAINTENANCE

In addition to the general rule in Article 2 of the Lugano Convention that a person must be sued in the state where they are domiciled, Article 5(2) sets out alternative fora for maintenance matters. To improve the position of the maintenance creditor as the weaker party, Article 5(2) allows the creditor to raise his/her claim before the courts where he/she is domiciled or habitually resident (*forum actoris*). A court hearing a divorce or child custody case may hear an ancillary maintenance claim when it has jurisdiction under its own law.[23] Jurisdiction in proceedings on amendment of maintenance is independent of the first proceedings. Thus, the court that first ruled on maintenance does not have jurisdiction in a subsequent case unless the defendant is domiciled in the state or the creditor is domiciled or habitually resident in that state, and the national rules point to that court. The Lugano Convention is, in principle, against rules where a court retains jurisdiction for subsequent cases, even when the rule protects the weaker party.[24] The general rule in Article 6 on multiple defendants and counterclaims is also applicable to maintenance. Article 23 on choice-of-court clauses applies in full to maintenance cases, giving the maintenance creditor, as the weaker party, limited protection from draconian clauses. Thus, a well-informed maintenance debtor may wish to have a choice-of-court clause in a maintenance agreement to avoid courts that are inconvenient for him/her.[25]

Although the Lugano Convention is limited to civil and commercial cases, the ECJ has held that it is *prima facie* also applicable when a public agency seeks to recover maintenance it has paid on behalf of the original debtor. This applies only as long as the claim for reimbursement is based on ordinary

---

21 Peter Mankowski, 'Article 5' in Ulrich Magnus and Peter Mankowski (eds), *Brussels I Regulation* (2nd rev edn, Sellier European Law Publishers 2012) 215–219.

22 It is assumed that the Convention classifies maintenance obligations arising from co-habitation as based in family law. See Mankowski (n 21) 217; Wolfgang Hau, 'Verfahren mit Auslandsbezug' in Hanns Prütting and Tobias Helms (eds), *FamFG Kommentar mit FamGKG* (Verlag Dr. Otto Schmidt 2013) 967.

23 When maintenance is ancillary to divorce or child custody proceedings, the court does not become competent for maintenance if it has assumed jurisdiction based solely on the nationality of one of the parties.

24 Paul Oberhammer, 'Art 5' in Felix Dasser and Paul Oberhammer (eds), *Lugano-Übereinkommen (LugÜ)* (2nd edn, Stämpfli Verlag 2011) 154.

25 Matthias Abendroth, 'Choice of Court in Matters Relating to Maintenance Obligations' in Paul Beaumont et al (eds), *The Recovery of Maintenance in the EU and Worldwide* (Hart 2014).

(private) law, and not in a situation where 'the legislature conferred on the public body a prerogative of its own' and the amount is the same as the obligation under statutory (private) law.[26] The public agency may not use the alternative forum provided in Article 5(2), because the rationale for the alternative forum is to protect the weaker party, the maintenance creditor.[27] It is assumed that the Convention is applicable when a private party, for instance a step-parent, claims reimbursement of maintenance paid. The private party is assumed to be allowed to benefit from the alternative fora listed in Article 5(2).[28] The rules on reimbursement exemplify the dynamic aspect of the Lugano Convention and the role of the ECJ in providing flexibility.

The Lugano Convention does not allow use of central authorities; all recognition and enforcement is by direct application to the competent court. Recognition and enforcement is under the same rules as other civil judgments.[29] Article 57(2) extends the scope of enforceable rulings to include maintenance obligations concluded with or authenticated by administrative authorities. The latter exception is important because in many countries administrative authorities have important roles in making decisions on maintenance.

3.2. THE LUGANO CONVENTION AND MAINTENANCE REGULATION

After the Maintenance Regulation entered into force in June 2011, the parallelism between the Lugano Convention and the Brussels I Regulation was broken for family law maintenance. The Maintenance Regulation does not have a counterpart in EFTA law, and the rules on maintenance were amended in the Brussels I *bis* Regulation to cover primarily non-family maintenance. The loss of parallelism results in different rules in the EU and in the EFTA states. Because the differences are subtle, one must be observant to spot the differences and not take similarity for granted. The relationship between the two instruments has been discussed. Some commentators maintain that the Maintenance Regulation cannot be classified as a successor to the Brussels I Regulation, but that it is rather an instrument regulating particular matters.[30] Others consider

---

26 Case C-271/00 *Steenbergen v Baten* ECLI:EU:C:2002:656, paras 32–37.

27 Case C-433/01 *Freistaat Bayern v Jan Blidjenstein* ECLI:EU:C:2004:21, para 30.

28 Hau (n 22) 1155.

29 Additionally, Art 50 has special rules for legal aid when the maintenance decision has been given by an administrative authority in Denmark, Iceland or Norway. Legal aid is not awarded for proceedings before the administrative authority, and, without the exception, the creditor would not qualify for legal aid at the enforcement stage.

30 See e.g. Jolante Kren Kostkiewicz and Michaela Eichenberger, 'International maintenance law in legal relations between Switzerland and the EU' [2015] *Comparative Law Review* 13;

it obvious that the Maintenance Regulation is a successor, and that the relationship between the instruments is clear.[31] If the Regulation is a successor, Article 64 of the Lugano Convention regulates the relationship between the two instruments; otherwise Protocol 3 regulates it. Ideally, a separate Protocol to the Lugano Convention would be draw up settle the matter.[32]

The Maintenance Regulation carries over the rules of the Brussels I Regulation and adapts them to the context of family maintenance. The rules on choice-of-court agreements (Article 4) and *forum necessitatis* (Article 7), and the detailed rules on public bodies as creditors (Article 46), are examples of such adaptations. Enforcement has been sped up, as the *exequatur* and most public policy and procedural defences have been abolished.[33] Some changes, however, such as use of habitual residence instead of domicile, have limited consequences in practice.

The long-term consequence of the lost parallelism is the lack of development of the Lugano Convention. As a parallel instrument to the Brussels I (*bis*) Regulation, the Lugano Convention relies in practice on the ECJ for authoritative interpretation and development. Although not formally binding, case law on the Brussels I (*bis*) Regulation ensures equal application and development of the law. Thus, the development of EFTA maintenance law has halted. Case law on the Maintenance Regulation is not directly applicable to the Lugano Convention and does not have persuasive authority;[34] however, it could serve as a non-binding source of arguments.

---

and Tanja Domej, 'Art 64' in Felix Dasser and Paul Oberhammer (eds), *Lugano-Übereinkommen* (Stämpfli Verlag 2011) 943–944.

31 Wolfgang Hau, 'Das Zuständigkeitssystem der Europäischen Unterhaltsverordnung – Überlegungen aus der Perspektive des deutschen Rechts' in Dagmar Coester-Waltjen, Volker Lipp, Eva Schumann and Barbara Veit (eds), *Europäisches Unterhaltsrecht* (Universitätsverlag Göttingen 2010).

32 For a discussion on the choice between the Brussels I (*bis*) Regulation and the Lugano Convention, see e.g. Axel Buhr, *Europäischer Justizraum und revidiertes Lugano-Übereinkommen* (Stämpfli Verlag 2010) 394–396; Andreas Furrer, 'The Brussels I Review Proposal: Challenges for the Lugano Convention?' in Eva Lein (ed), *The Brussels I Review Proposal Uncovered* (The British Institute of International and Comparative Law 2012) 174–176; and Trevor C. Hartley, *Choice-of-court agreements under the European and international instruments: the revised Brussels I Regulation, the Lugano Convention and the Hague Convention* (OUP 2013) 107–108.

33 Ilaria Viarengo, 'Enforcement of Maintenance Decisions in the EU: *Requiem* for Public Policy?' in Paul Beaumont et al (eds), *The Recovery of Maintenance in the EU and Worldwide* (Hart 2014).

34 When the Brussels regime and the Lugano Convention are parallel, the case law of the ECJ has persuasive authority, see Tanja Domej, 'Das EU-Zivilprozessrecht und die Schweiz' in *Jahrbuch Junger Zivilrechtswissenschaftler 2009: Europäische Methodik: Konvergenz und Diskkrepanz europäischen und nationalen Privatrechts* (Richard Boorberg Verlag 2009) 405–432.

4. THE 2007 HAGUE CONVENTION ON FAMILY MAINTENANCE

4.1. SCOPE OF THE 2007 HAGUE CONVENTION

The 2007 Hague Convention on family maintenance regulates recognition, enforcement and administrative co-operation, but not jurisdiction. Hence, it partially overlaps with the Lugano Convention. As at the end of 2018, it has entered into force in almost the whole Europe, and in Brazil, Honduras and the United States of America. The scope of application of the 2007 Hague Convention is vague. The Convention does not define the term 'family maintenance'. States may limit the Convention's scope of application to children under the age of 18 and associated spousal maintenance, or to expand the scope to cover maintenance obligations based on other family relationships (Articles 62 and 63). It is not entirely clear whether preliminary or ancillary issues determined in the same decision as the maintenance obligation itself are also included in the scope of application.[35]

The Hague Convention accepts public bodies as creditors and applicants when they are acting on behalf of an individual maintenance creditor or to claim reimbursement of maintenance the public body has paid to an individual creditor (Article 36). Maintenance decisions by administrative authorities are enforceable under the Convention. The optional Protocol to the 2007 Hague Convention governs the applicable law and helps to create coherent regulation of private international law and international procedural law.

The international character of the 2007 Hague Convention is an asset and an impediment. The scope of application is not standard. Each state determines whether cohabitation and same-sex partnerships are considered to be family relationships.[36] Vigilance is required to assess whether the Convention is applicable to the type of maintenance in question in all the countries involved in the claim.

4.2. JURISDICTIONAL RULES IN THE HAGUE CONVENTION

Although the 2007 Hague Convention does not govern jurisdiction directly, recognition and enforcement depend on the grounds on which the issuing court is seised. Rulings and decisions from courts and authorities whose jurisdiction is deemed exorbitant because the circumstances of the case have no significant

35 Walker (n 8) 47–51; Beaumont (n 13) 528.

36 Bonomi (n 8) 27.

connection to the place of the court do not deserve to be recognised and enforced. To ensure a common understanding of when a court or authority has assumed jurisdiction rightly, jurisdiction must be regulated at least indirectly by outlining some principles for acceptable or unacceptable grounds for jurisdiction (*competence indirecte*).

Article 20 enlists acceptable grounds for jurisdiction. Contracting states may issue reservations on some grounds of jurisdiction; thus, the list may not be applicable in all states.[37] States may also recognise rulings on the basis of other rules on jurisdiction. The list of acceptable grounds for jurisdiction leads to approximation, if not full harmonisation, of jurisdiction, because contracting states may wish to align their national rules with the Convention.

Article 18 regulates some aspects of jurisdiction in relation to amendment of maintenance decisions. When a court or an authority in the state where the creditor is habitually resident has made the first decision on maintenance, that state will retain jurisdiction in the event of amendment, provided that the creditor still lives there. There are exceptions to the rule when the parties have an agreement on jurisdiction, where the creditor submits his/her claim to another court, or when it is not possible to obtain a decision that is enforceable in practice from the original court. The rationale behind this is to avoid a change of jurisdiction that might come as a surprise to, and be to the detriment of, the creditor.[38]

Articles 18 and 20 illustrate the advantage of holistic regulation of jurisdiction, recognition and enforcement. Without rules on jurisdiction, a convention will inevitably be truncated.

4.3. RECOGNITION AND ENFORCEMENT: CHOICE OF TRACKS

The Hague Convention has two tracks for recognition and enforcement: a three-stage model and a two-stage model. The three-stage model laid out in Article 23 is the default. It follows the classical model whereby the competent authority first performs a *prima facie* review before declaring the decision enforceable. At the second stage, either party has a time limit of 30 or 60 days to lodge a challenge or an appeal, before a final decision on enforceability is then made. The third stage is enforcement. In the alternative model in Article 24, the declaration on enforceability at the first stage is based both on the grounds the respondent has raised and on a limited review *ex officio*.

37 Algeria Borrás and Jennifer Degeling, *Explanatory Report. Convention of 23 November 2007 on the International Recovery of Child Support and Other Forms of Family Maintenance* (Hague Conference on Private International Law 2013) 159–167.

38 Walker (n 8) 153–157.

The second stage consists of enforcement. The grounds for *ex officio* review differ slightly depending on the track.[39]

The 2007 Hague Convention requires child maintenance – and associated spousal support – to be channelled through central authorities. Other types of family maintenance are not required to pass through the central authority. States may extend proceedings before central authorities to all types of maintenance, but this is only available between countries that both do the same. Norway has declared that it will only accept applications filed through central authorities. Since both the EU and Norway have agreed to extend the use of central authorities to all kinds of spousal support, applications between EU Member States and Norway pass through central authorities. However, to take a non-EU example, Albania has not made the same declaration and recognises only direct applications for spousal maintenance unconnected to child support. An application from Albania is not recognised in Norway, as it cannot be filed through the central authority and direct applications to courts are not available. Although the 2007 Hague Convention covers spousal maintenance in both countries, the conflicting approaches to filing leads to non-recognition.

The two tracks for recognition and enforcement, the numerous opportunities for declarations to extend or limit the scope of application and the applicable rules, and the opportunity for states to issue reservations were necessary for the Convention to become a reality. However, the downsides to having so many exceptions are the incoherencies and the opaqueness of the rules. The grounds for non-recognition are also wider in the Hague Convention than under EU law and the Lugano Convention:[40] procedural fraud and ongoing proceedings on the same matter in the state where enforcement takes place are grounds for non-recognition in the Hague Convention, but not in the Lugano Convention.

5. THE LUGANO CONVENTION AND THE 2007 HAGUE CONVENTION

5.1. COMPARISON OF THE CONVENTIONS

The Lugano Convention has precise and comprehensive rules compared to the 2007 Hague Convention. Jurisdiction is regulated exhaustively and the processes of recognition and enforcement leave little room for discretion. The rules are applicable to all types of maintenance; enforcement cannot be

39 Walker (n 8) 165 et seq.
40 See also Walker (n 8) 173.

prevented on the grounds that the ruling is not based on a family relationship. However, unlike under the 2007 Hague Convention, enforcement is not expedited, and it may be difficult to navigate due to the absence of a central authority. Costs are likely to be higher and legal aid lower under the Lugano Convention. Nor are the rules tailored specifically to family maintenance.

The Hague Convention has tailored rules, but the rules vary depending on the type of family maintenance and the particular choices of each country. For instance, cohabiting and same-sex couples may or may not fall under the scope of the Convention. Child maintenance may be covered until the age of 18 or extend beyond the age of 21.[41] The Convention does not regulate jurisdiction, but limits jurisdiction indirectly. Extensions and limitations must often be mutual to apply. Recognition and enforcement are tailored to be simple for the creditor, but variation in proceedings makes the system complex.

Furthermore, the Hague Convention does not have a source for binding interpretation. Thus, states may interpret the provisions differently. Moreover, some provisions are ambiguous by design. Consequently, the Hague system is tailored to family maintenance, but is opaque.

Both conventions lack a direct mechanism for providing authoritative interpretation and development. In the case of the Lugano Convention, however, since it is linked to the Maintenance Regulation, it is at least possible to draw on case law on the Maintenance Regulation when interpreting the Lugano Convention.

5.2. CHOOSING BETWEEN THE 2007 HAGUE CONVENTION AND THE LUGANO CONVENTION

Both the 2007 Hague Convention and the Lugano Convention govern recognition and enforcement of maintenance decisions in family law cases. Hence, in matters concerning recognition and enforcement of maintenance awards, the question arises as to which Convention applies or whether the creditor is able to select the most effective rules.

For jurisdiction, the issue is simple, because the Hague Convention does not cover jurisdiction. Article 67 of the Lugano Convention sets out strict rules in relation to jurisdiction, because conflicting rules on jurisdiction reduce predictability and may result in parallel proceedings, which the Convention seeks to avoid. Formalism could solve the problem: the Hague Convention does not formally regulate jurisdiction, and thus the Lugano Convention prevails.

For the recognition and enforcement of maintenance decisions, the question is more complicated. The Lugano Convention supersedes conventions

[41] Bonomi (n 8) 27; Walker (n 8) 38–39.

'that cover the same matters', and states are precluded from entering into new agreements (Article 65). According to Article 67(1), the Lugano Convention does not affect the power of states to enter into agreements 'in relation to particular matters'. The question is whether the Hague Convention covers the same matters as the Lugano Convention or whether it covers 'particular matters'. Annex VII of the Lugano Convention lists the conventions it supersedes. Although the list is not exhaustive, it illustrates the type of conventions considered to cover the same matters. All conventions listed cover civil matters in general, and the previous Hague Conventions on maintenance are not included.

In *Tatry*,[42] the ECJ touched on the question of what a specialised convention is and recognised the Brussels Arrest Convention 1952 as such a convention. However, it did not indicate the grounds on which the convention was considered to be 'specialised'. Arrests are a specific type of protective interim measure, hence the outcome is hardly surprising. Family maintenance is a rather particular matter on the margins of civil law, which makes it similar to arrests. Furthermore, rules on family maintenance have been excluded from the Brussels I *bis* Regulation and added to the Maintenance Regulation. This underlines the special character of family maintenance. Thus, there are good arguments in favour of the Hague Convention prevailing as a particular regulation and superseding the Lugano Convention.

However, the Explanatory Report on the 2007 Hague Convention[43] clearly explains that the Lugano Convention supersedes the Hague Convention because it was concluded approximately one month before and thus falls under Article 51 of the Hague Convention. Consequently, both conventions seem to declare that the other convention supersedes it.

The 2007 Hague Convention has sped up proceedings specifically tailored to maintenance claims. However, it leaves more leeway to the enforcing state than does the Lugano Convention, which results in variations in coverage. Although the 2007 Hague Convention may be more expedient in general, in certain situations – for example, in claims arising from same-sex relationships – the Lugano Convention may be preferable. Article 52 of the Hague Convention gives parties the right to choose the most effective rules, such as the Lugano Convention. Furthermore, when an issue is not regulated in the 2007 Hague Convention, the Lugano Convention is applicable.[44] This is the case *inter alia*

---

42 Case C-406/92 *The owners of the cargo lately laden on board the ship 'Tatry' v the owners of the ship 'Maciej Rataj'* ECLI:EU:C:1994:400, paras 21–27.

43 Borrás and Degeling (n 37) 217.

44 Case C-533/08 *TNT Express Nederland BV v AXA Versicherung AG* ECLI:EU:C:2010:243, paras 54–56. We could ask whether this is applicable to the Lugano Convention as well. Considering the paramount goal of uniform application of the Brussels regime and the Lugano Convention, the answer should be in the affirmative.

for same-sex relationships, where the Lugano Convention applies but the Hague Convention may not. To reduce uncertainty, a party may prefer the former. The maintenance creditor can therefore choose the convention offering the best rules.

6. EUROPEAN LAW AND INTERNATIONAL LAW: A COMPLEMENTARY RELATIONSHIP?

6.1. THE LUGANO CONVENTION MAY FILL THE GAPS IN THE HAGUE CONVENTION

An immediate response to fragmented, partly overlapping legal regulation in the field of maintenance law is to claim that the law is opaque and (too) complex. However, in many respects, the opposite is true. European law reduces fragmentation, when used prudently.

The 2007 Hague Convention exposes some inherent weakness of international co-operation. It does not form a comprehensive regulation because it does not regulate jurisdiction. Additionally, it provides numerous opportunities for customisation, or a candy-shop approach, where states can pick and choose. The cost is loss of coherence, transparency and predictability in the form of 'rough patches' where law differs between the signatories.

In the absence of the Lugano Convention, jurisdiction would be determined based on national law and bilateral or regional treaties. The result would be unpredictable rules and probably an increased likelihood of non-recognition. The Lugano Convention creates a coherent system for jurisdiction. Relying on EU/EFTA law rather than national law has the advantage of coherence, both in terms of having to deal with only one set of rules regardless of the country in question, and because the Lugano Convention constitutes a coherent (at least comparably speaking) set of rules.[45] Thus, the Lugano Convention effectively fills many of the lacunae in the Hague Convention.

The Lugano Convention is also useful when a maintenance case is not covered by the 2007 Hague Convention. The Hague Convention covers cohabitation and same-sex partnerships only when the countries involved recognise these as spousal or family relationships. The Lugano Convention does not limit maintenance to child and spousal maintenance and is therefore applicable to maintenance for former co-habitants and same-sex couples too. Thus, these groups can rely on the Lugano Convention to enforce their rights. The Lugano Convention functions as a safety net that citizens can fall back on when the Hague Convention is not applicable.

---

45 See also Hau (n 31).

Iceland and Switzerland are parties to the Lugano Convention, but not to the 2007 Hague Convention. For Iceland, the Lugano Convention is the only European or international instrument available to secure recognition and enforcement. Switzerland is a party to the 1973 Hague Convention, but that convention does not regulate the procedures for recognition and enforcement in detail, instead leaving it to national law. Thus, the Lugano Convention is the more predictable option.

The Lugano Convention therefore fills many of the gaps in the Hague Convention, increasing coherence in the EFTA region.

6.2. THE HAGUE CONVENTION FILLS GAPS IN EUROPEAN LAW

The 2007 Hague Convention fills gaps in European (EFTA) family maintenance law by providing rules for recognition and enforcement that are specifically tailored to family maintenance. European countries could increase predictability by making uniform declarations. For instance, Norway and the EU have declared that they accept spousal support filed through central authorities. That said, the gaps are not completely filled, as EU has extended the convention to cover all types of family maintenance, but Norway has not. Nevertheless, despite some differences, deliberate, strategic use of mutual declarations is a strategy for filling gaps.

Furthermore, cross-pollination between private international law and international procedural law could be used to fill gaps. The Rome I and II Regulations serve as a source for interpretation for the Brussels I (*bis*) Regulation and the Lugano Convention. Although the Rome Regulations are not binding on Norway, Norwegian courts use them as a source of interpretation both for procedural law and private international law.[46] Norwegian private international law is mainly uncodified, which increases the role of foreign or non-binding international law as a source of legal arguments. Thus, the Hague Protocol could serve as a tool for interpreting the Lugano Convention and the 2007 Hague Convention, even though the protocol is not binding on Norway. A mindset favouring uniform interpretation of international conventions could therefore lead to approximation of the law.

Nevertheless, the EU approach has some downsides as well. First, exceptions, lacunae and overlaps are created through EU law – for example, Denmark and the United Kingdom have exceptions in relation to judicial co-operation. Therefore, EU instruments do not apply universally in the EU. Second, family

46 In HR-2016-1251-A and HR-2011-809-A, the Norwegian Supreme Court has confirmed the role of the Rome Regulations as a source of arguments.

procedure has taken a quantum leap within the EU, but a corresponding development in EFTA law has not yet occurred. These issues will be explored in the next part.

7. UNSOLVED ISSUES IN EUROPEAN FAMILY PROCEDURE

7.1. EXCEPTIONS, VOIDS AND OVERLAPS ORIGINATING FROM EU LAW

Exceptions, voids and overlaps emanating from EU law are tangible in the Nordic countries. Some of the voids are an inherent by-product of multi-speed integration, where Iceland and Norway are part of the EEA Agreement, but not the EU. Further complications arise from the Danish opt-out from co-operation in the area of civil justice, and from Denmark and Iceland not having signed the 2007 Hague Convention. In addition, co-operation between the Nordic countries still exists in the field of family law, adding a regional level of law.

The Maintenance Regulation does not *prima facie* apply in Denmark, but the rules in Chapter IV section 2 apply in relation to the enforcement and recognition of decisions from other Member States in Denmark and the UK. However, Denmark agreed in 2005 to implement the Brussels I Regulation and any amendments to it. Then, in 2009, it also declared it would apply the rules on jurisdiction, recognition and enforcement in the Maintenance Regulation,[47] though not the rules on administrative co-operation. Denmark is not a signatory to the 2007 Hague Convention and Protocol.

Within the Nordic EU states, the Maintenance Regulation and the 2007 Hague Protocol apply between Finland and Sweden, but in relations involving Denmark only part of the Maintenance Regulation applies and one has to fall back on the Brussels I *bis* Regulation and the 1973 Hague Convention on maintenance. Furthermore, the rules on recognition and enforcement are different for outgoing decisions from Denmark and the United Kingdom than from other EU Member States. The rules for incoming cases are the same as in the other European countries. In relations involving Iceland or Norway, the Lugano Convention applies. Thus, depending on which Nordic countries are involved, one of three sets of rules are applicable: The Maintenance Regulation,

---

47 Agreement between the European Community and the Kingdom of Denmark on jurisdiction and the recognition and enforcement of judgments in civil and commercial matters, letter from the Commission [2009] OJ L149/80. See also Agreement between the European Community and the Kingdom of Denmark on jurisdiction and the recognition and enforcement of judgments in civil and commercial matters [2005] OJ L299/62.

the Lugano Convention or, in case of Denmark, a combination of rules from different instruments.

On the international level, Finland and Sweden are parties to the 2007 Hague Convention and Protocol. Norway is a party to the 2007 Hague Convention, but not the Protocol. Denmark and Iceland are parties to neither. All Nordic countries, except Iceland, are parties to the 1973 Hague Convention. Thus, in situations where one needs to fall back on the international level of law, the safety net varies in coverage. The 1973 Hague Convention has few specific procedural rules and relies overwhelmingly on national law. It is unclear why Denmark has not signed the 2007 Hague Convention; it may be a question of a slight delay or a question of principle. Nevertheless, the restrictive Danish approach to judicial co-operation may have rubbed off on the 2007 Hague Convention due to Denmark's close relationship with EU law. Iceland, as a small country, often follows Denmark, and will probably wait for the Danish decision to sign the Convention.

Due to the requirement of unanimity in family law matters,[48] the Nordic Convention on Collection of Maintenance of 23 March 1962 has survived European integration.[49] The Nordic Convention is an example of an instrument that supersedes the Maintenance Regulation and the Lugano Convention in matters of child and spousal maintenance. Under it, rulings and decisions by authorities are directly enforceable without a declaration of recognition and enforceability as if the ruling were national. It is advantageous for the creditor; the majority of inter-Nordic maintenance claims are enforced under it. The Nordic Convention does not govern jurisdiction – therefore, the Maintenance Regulation and the Lugano Convention are applicable in that regard – nor are there rules on administrative co-operation. It bridges some of the gaps in enforcement created by multi-speed integration, but it simultaneously creates a new layer of law.

The Nordic countries throw into relief a patchwork of two regulations and four conventions regulating jurisdiction, recognition, enforcement and administrative co-operation in family maintenance law. The same also applies to EFTA law, as Switzerland is a party to the Lugano Convention and the 1973 Hague Convention. Brexit may increase the 'rough patches' and gaps in European family proceedings, because the United Kingdom will withdraw

48 See Art 81(3) of the consolidated version of the Treaty on the Functioning of the European Union [2008] OJ C326/47.

49 For an account of Nordic co-operation in family law and the 'back-seat driver' attitude of Finland and Sweden, see Maarit Jänterä-Jareborg, 'The Nordic Input on the EU's Cooperation in Family and Succession Law: Exporting Union Law Through "Nordic Exceptions"' in Burkhard Hess, Maria Bergström and Eva Storskrubb (eds), *EU Civil Justice Current Issues and Future Outlooks* (Hart 2015).

from the Maintenance Regulation and the Brussels I *bis* Regulation. It is also a signatory to the 2007 Hague Convention through its EU membership and so will have to sign the Convention as a non-member to maintain its status.

7.2. MAINTENANCE AND THE SINGLE MARKET: DO WE NEED EFTA LAW?

Extending the single market and free movement of labour to the EEA Member States augments the need for regulation of cross-border family relationships, including maintenance. Until the Maintenance Regulation entered into force, the Brussels and Lugano regimes combined served the purpose.

Today, the 2007 Hague Convention fulfils part of the need, but it requires measures to fill the gaps and ideally a mechanism to ensure uniform interpretation. Furthermore, using international law as a tool to create coherence in Europe requires political will imbued with a sense of pragmatism. Consequently, European law has an important role to play.

Currently, the main problem is the differences between the Lugano Convention and the Maintenance Regulation. One could argue that the Maintenance Regulation codifies developments in case law and indicates an organic development of particular rules for family maintenance. It builds on its predecessor, the Brussels I Regulation, and has been supplemented to increase access to justice in family maintenance. The Lugano Convention, and its EU counterparts, have been notably flexible instruments, amenable to development through teleological interpretation. Hence, it would be natural to interpret the Lugano Convention in line with that tradition and consequently align it with the Maintenance Regulation.

This approach has a significant weakness. Loss of parallelism between the Brussels I (*bis*) Regulation and the Lugano Convention has stripped the Lugano Convention of a mechanism for ensuring uniformity. Who will determine whether the Maintenance Regulation is used to interpret the Convention? Who will determine whether the Maintenance Regulation would *de facto* replace the rules on maintenance in the Lugano Convention by way of interpretation and which parts of the Lugano Convention would be replaced through interpretation, or whether the Maintenance Regulation should have a less marked impact on the interpretation of the Lugano Convention? Should the supreme court in one of the countries do so unilaterally, on the assumption that the other jurisdictions will follow its lead?

Alternatively, the Lugano Convention could be amended or a European Maintenance Convention could be drafted. Brexit could pose an obstacle to this solution, at least on a short- to mid-term basis. Resources are presently being channelled to Brexit, leaving little room for negotiations with EEA states. Depending on the outcome of Brexit, the EU may be unwilling to enter into such agreements to deter other countries from leaving the EU. The opposite may also be true: Brexit could underline the importance of European non-EU law and spark new development.

A fully parallel regulation is nevertheless unlikely. For one thing, EFTA states will probably oppose the rules requiring 'blind' mutual trust. The public policy aspect could also be a hindrance, as Norway prefers 'divorce-friendly' rules. Removal of safeguards for ensuring fair trial rights is perhaps a more serious obstacle still.[50] As a result, complete uniformity between the Maintenance Regulation and the Lugano Convention may not be feasible.

8. MULTI-LAYER MAINTENANCE LAW: FRAGILE AND ROBUST

European legislators are aware of, and have acted on, the need for judicial co-operation in family maintenance. Within the EU, the result is an innovative combination of EU and international instruments. Although the arrangements result in increased coherence for EU Member States, development of the EFTA aspects has stagnated. The loss of parallelism between the Lugano Convention and the Brussels I *bis* Regulation, and the Danish reluctance towards co-operation, expose the fragility of multi-level integration. Some challenges can be mitigated through interpretation and active use of other instruments, but interpretation alone cannot bridge the gaps.

A study of the Nordic countries demonstrates that legal coherence and approximation requires political will, along with courts committed to the goal of uniform interpretation. The price is to recognise and enforce rulings and decisions even when national law grants a different solution. The gain is transparency and foreseeability, and lessening the burdens on families with cross-border interests. Comparing the pragmatic Norwegian approach to the principled Danish approach shows the consequences of a political stance. The 2007 Hague Convention applies in Norway with largely the same limitations and extensions as for EU Member States. Therefore, Norway is part of a European regime which also applies to third countries that have signed the 2007 Hague Convention, while Denmark only participates partially in the intra-EU regime and not at all in the regime for third countries.

EFTA European family law is a question of managing multi-speed integration. The European and the international approach can be successfully combined, but it means developing EFTA law. Free movement of people requires free movement of family law judgments. Norway and Switzerland could

---

[50] For a criticism of the blind mutual trust required, see Viarengo (n 33); Walker (n 8) 105 et seq.

perhaps accept a revision of the Lugano Convention to include specific rules on maintenance, a new Lugano II Convention on family law, or both. However, Brexit has altered the landscape, creating complications and delaying development of a multi-speed approach. In the shadow of Brexit, the EU may not be willing to negotiate new instruments that allow for a 'pick-and-choose' approach to European integration. On the other hand, Brexit could in the end be the catalyst for a burgeoning of EFTA law.

CONCLUSIONS ON CIVIL PROCEDURE AND HARMONISATION OF LAW

Anna Nylund and Magne Strandberg

1. INTRODUCTION

As the book has provided us with a range of perspectives on the effect of European and international hard law, case law and soft law on national civil procedure law, it is now time to provide over-arching and comparative perspectives. Drawing on the earlier chapters, our aim is to shed light on some of the questions raised. Are some of the north-western European jurisdictions more affected by European rules than other jurisdictions? Are such effects also seen in national court practice? Are there discussions on the methods for implementing EU/EEA law in these jurisdictions?

Although these questions are general in the sense that they concern all types of European and international influence on national civil procedure, we will structure our discussion along the same lines as the structure elsewhere in the book. Most of the discussion will focus on comparisons within the topics found in the previous parts of the book (sections 2–5), but we will also compare the impact of each type of law and discuss selected over-arching issues (section 6).

2. HARD LAW INFLUENCE ON NATIONAL CIVIL PROCEDURE

During the last two decades or so, the list of EU regulations and directives concerning civil procedure law has become long and rich. The list includes a number of regulations and directives that primarily concern matters of civil procedure, especially for cross-border cases, and those that primarily concern a certain branch of substantive law but nonetheless include certain procedural rules for that law.[1] A characteristic feature of these directives and regulations is their fragmented nature – they either apply only to cross-border cases or only to certain substantive cases. Hence, the EU approach to civil procedure differs from the national approach, where civil procedure law is typically regulated in general codes providing rules for all sorts of civil cases.

As is noted by several authors in their chapters, it is challenging to incorporate fragmented EU hard law into a general national civil procedure law system. Incorporation is discussed in particular by Wolfgang Hau, who lists three possible kinds of voluntary over-implementation of EU hard law for the purpose of maintaining a coherent national regulation of procedural matters in general.[2] Hau suggests that a country could adopt entire legal instruments on civil procedure law in general, rather than only instruments on cross-border cases or a specific branch of substantive law. Further, he suggests making use of specific provisions outside the scope envisaged by the directive or regulation in question. Lastly, he suggests that a country could revise its own legal concepts and adopt concepts found in EU hard law. Such an approach would more often lead to one coherent set of concepts for all of civil procedure law – as opposed to one set of concepts applicable to civil cases in general and another set of concepts applicable for cases under the EU context. Interestingly, Hau notes that the German legislator has applied several types of voluntary over-implementation.

English civil procedure law seems to be far less affected by EU hard law than is German law. While the EU regulations and directives concerning civil procedure law have formally been implemented, they have not led to any real reform of English law and there has been no voluntary over-implementation.[3] In addition, their effect seems to be minimal in practice and is described by Sorabji as having been 'absorbed' into existing English civil procedure.

In both Finland and Sweden, the method of implementation seems somewhat haphazard. Most EU hard law on civil procedure seem to be regarded as 'technicalities' applicable only to cross-border litigation. The regulations and directives have most often been implemented in the form of a separate legal act on the international aspects of civil procedure, rather than integrated into the countries' general procedural codes.[4] The discussion in both countries

---

1 See Storskrubb, in this volume, section 2.
2 Hau, in this volume, section 4.
3 Sorabji, 'An Examination of the Influence of European Union Law on English Civil Procedure', in this volume, section 3.
4 Ervo, in this volume, section 4.

reflects scepticism towards harmonisation – and even approximation – of civil procedure law based on or derived from an EU law. Several commentators appear to question the need for many of the European instruments, and the results of those instruments seem modest: the European order for payment procedure and the small claims procedure[5] have turned out to be relative failures. While these EU rules have, of course, been implemented in both Sweden and Finland, they have not had any spill-over effect on the national systems, as such. For Sweden, this is hardly surprising, as there are already corresponding national proceedings. Interestingly, Finland has not over-implemented the European payment order procedure or small claims procedure, even though similar national procedures do not exist in Finland.[6] Thus, the existence of corresponding national proceedings seems to have limited influence on the over-implementation of EU law and use of European procedures.

Norway does not participate in the home and justice affairs, as these are not part of the EEA Agreement. Nonetheless, EU hard law has an impact on Norwegian civil procedure, through the Lugano Convention and through voluntary implementation of some parts of EU law. Regarding the modes of implementation, the Norwegian approach appears to be akin to the two other Nordic countries in this study, namely viewing EU/EEA civil procedural law as a 'technicality' rather than something with a potentially transformative power and an inspiration for the development of national law. As Maria Hjort explains, Norway's method of implementation reflects this attitude: haphazard and done with very limited national discussion.[7] However, an exception is the reform on security for costs, where the Norwegian legislator voluntarily over-implemented so that the rules became uniform for all cases concerning EU inhabitants. Voluntary over-implementation was a result of the intimate connection between substantive and procedural law, between rights and remedies.

To sum up, there seem to be some differences between the countries in this study in terms of how and to what extent EU hard law affects national civil procedure law. While several examples of over-implementation are found in Germany, no such thing is seen in England and only rare examples are found in the Nordic countries. We may wonder what the reasons are for such differences. EU membership could be one reason, but it does not seem to be the most important factor. The effect of EU hard law is limited in England, Sweden and Finland, even though all these countries are EU Member States.

---

5 Regulation (EC) 861/2007 establishing a European Small Claims Procedure [2007] OJ L199/22, Regulation (EC) No 1896/2006 of the European Parliament and of the Council of 12 December 2006 creating a European order for payment procedure [2006] OJ L399/1.

6 Ervo, in this volume, section 5.

7 Hjort, in this volume, section 6.

Norway, on the other hand, has voluntarily implemented some EU procedural rules and has over-implemented others.

One factor that could explain the differences may be the practical need for reform. As suggested by John Sorabji, there was no need for the Regulation establishing the small claims procedure because an effective and well-functioning small claims procedure had already been in existence since the 1970s.[8] Yet the example of the very low number of European small claims and payment order proceedings in Finland, where there are no corresponding national proceedings in place, seems to suggest the opposite. Another factor may be the dominant attitudes towards implementation of EU hard law. The more EU civil procedure is viewed only as 'technical' rules facilitating cross-border litigation, the less thought and effort is put into implementation, including selecting an appropriate method of implementation and using EU law as an impetus for national reforms. Moreover, if the main focus in a jurisdiction is the conceptual coherence of a set of rules, the pressure towards over-implementation may be greater than if the needs and outcomes in practice are the main focus. Acknowledging the risk of stereotyping, we may suggest that the typical systematic and coherency-seeking approach of German civil procedure law provides another approach to implementation of EU law than what is found in the more practice-oriented, instrument-based English and Nordic approach.

Even though some differences are found between the jurisdictions in this study, the overall impression is that EU hard law does not have a major role to play in the national civil justice systems. In the countries in this study, the impact seems to be rather peripheral and dependent primarily on the attitudes of the legislator and the practical need for reform. While EU hard law could serve as a source of inspiration, or even an impetus, for reforms of national civil procedure, or at least a tool for benchmarking, these effects are often absent. Successful harmonisation through hard law depends on many factors, including the quality of EU legislation, need, timing, attitudes and a willingness to evaluate national law based on European law.

3. *EX OFFICIO* APPLICATION OF EU CONSUMER LAW

The national courts' obligation to apply EU consumer law of their own motion, which has been developed by the ECJ in numerous cases from 2000 onwards, applies to both EU Member States and EEA states. As explained by Fredriksen and Strandberg, the principle of homogeneity and the EFTA Court practice on

8 Sorabji, 'An Examination of the Influence of European Union Law on English Civil Procedure', in this volume, section 2.1.

that principle make clear that the national courts' duty of *ex officio* application of consumer protection law under the EEA Agreement is equivalent to the same duty in the EU Member States.[9]

Even though courts in all of the north-western European jurisdictions must meet the very same obligation of applying consumer protection law of their motion, the obligation may be incorporated in different ways and the adjustments necessary in a jurisdiction may very well differ significantly from the adjustments necessary in another jurisdiction. For the jurisdictions included in this book, quite significant variations are found in terms of how this obligation is met, how it has affected the national system and the amount of attention the obligations have been paid by law-makers and national courts.

On one end of the scale, we find the Netherlands, where the obligation of *ex officio* application of consumer protection law has been taken very seriously. As underlined by Ancery and Krans, there are many judgments on the matter by Dutch courts, from both the Supreme Court and the lower courts.[10] The ECJ case law has also sparked a debate on the role of the courts in such cases. As early as 2000 – the very same year as the first ECJ judgment on the issue – a working group of Dutch judges wrote a report on how these matters should be dealt with. The report was updated in 2014. Furthermore, the topic has been the focus of several academic analyses, including a dissertation.

Norway is on the other end of the scale, as is shown by Fredriksen and Strandberg. Although the Norwegian Dispute Act is fairly new, the law-maker did not pay much attention to the obligations following from the EEA Agreement. The court's obligation to apply EU/EEA consumer law of its own motion was not on the agenda at all during the preparatory work for the Dispute Act in the late 1990s and early 2000s. Since then, these matters have not led to any official reports initiated by the courts or others, and no court judgments have dealt with this matter in Norway. The subject has been considered by academics, but that has not led to any practical effects (yet).

Germany also seems to have taken a rather passive approach to the obligation set up in ECJ case law. Although Ivo Bach emphasises that consumer protection law has been highly influenced by the EU,[11] the obligation of *ex officio* application of EU consumer law does not seem to have had a tangible influence on German procedural law. Bach further underlines that the well-established German rules on substantive guidance (*materielle Prozessleitung*) already provide a judge with the necessary tool for taking the positive actions required by the ECJ in consumer cases.

---

9 Fredriksen and Strandberg, in this volume, section 1.

10 Ancery and Krans, in this volume, section 1.

11 Bach, in this volume, section 2.

Based on Torbjörn Andersson's analysis, it seems that Sweden has also taken a rather passive approach to the obligations set out by the ECJ in consumer protection cases. Andersson does not mention any Swedish law reform dealing with these issues, and it seems the courts have not developed any specific criteria or guidelines either. As in Norway and Germany, the discussion of how to fulfil these obligations is based on the existing general principles of Swedish civil procedure.

It is hard to find a sound explanation for the differences between the very active Dutch approach and the rather passive approach taken by other jurisdictions in north-western Europe. The lack of court practice in Norway and Sweden may be explained by the fact that most consumer disputes are dealt with by complaints boards or in simplified debt-collection proceedings.[12] However, this alone does not explain the differences, because consumer ADR bodies hear the majority of consumer cases in both the Netherlands and the Nordic countries.[13] Furthermore, some of the cases reported from the Netherlands, for instance the *Froukje Faber* case, could just as easily have been a Norwegian case.

Another possible reason for the differences may be the established rules and ideas on the proper role of the judge and the division of powers between the court and parties. However, at the outset, it should be acknowledged that the four jurisdictions considered all rely on the same basic principles: the parties are responsible for bringing facts and evidence to the court; the court is responsible for the application of law; and the court has a well-established duty to clarify legal and factual issues.[14] There may nevertheless be some differences – possibly important ones – in relation to the court's right or duty to guide the parties on new matters of law or fact. Variation in the scope and methods of substantive guidance may, to some extent, explain why the obligation to apply consumer protection law has led to massive practical problems in the Netherlands, whereas no such thing is seen in the other countries studied. The Dutch questions about fulfilment of the obligations in appellate and cassation proceedings[15] would probably not be a problem in Norway, where appellate courts most often do a complete new examination of the issues being appealed, and where they have the same duties and powers as first instance courts.

---

[12] Andersson, in this volume, section 3.2; Fredriksen and Strandberg, in this volume, section 7.

[13] Ancery and Krans, in this volume, section 2.

[14] The idea that the judge must clarify issues is also found in the proposal of the European Parliament for common minimum standards of civil procedure, Article 9(2)(b), P(-TA-PROV(2017)0282 and the ELI/UNIDROIT Project on European Model Rules of Civil Procedure, Obligations Working Party's final report, rule 8(2); see Sorabji, 'The ELI-UNIDROIT Project', in this volume, sections 3.3 and 4.

[15] Ancery and Krans, in this volume, section 5.

A third possible reason for the differences is that the requirements of *ex officio* application of EU consumer law are not entirely clear. Each of the four contributions on consumer law discusses the extent of the duty of *ex officio* application. The essential questions are as follows:[16] How much information must the court have before a duty to clarify arises? In what ways may the judge intervene to retain impartiality? Does the court have a duty to examine the entire consumer contract or does examining the provision relevant for the issues in the dispute at hand suffice? Should self-represented parties be treated differently from parties with legal counsel? Given that all these aspects may be in doubt to a greater or lesser degree, the differences between active and passive approaches may result from differences in how leading ECJ cases are understood in the individual countries. The prevailing Dutch view seems to be that the ECJ has developed quite intense obligations for the national courts. While both Norwegian and German scholars argue in favour of dealing with EU obligations as matters of substantive guidance under domestic civil procedure law,[17] the Dutch approach seems to be that more than mere guidance is required to fulfil the obligation, at least under certain circumstances. If it is the case that mere guidance is not enough to fulfil the national courts' obligation, then another story may be told also in Germany and Norway.

Nonetheless, the policy of enhancing enforcement of consumer rights may potentially challenge prevailing understandings of the role of the judge and the division of duties and powers between the parties and the court. The issue, however, is complex because one must balance adversarial proceedings and impartiality on the one hand, with the goal of substantially correct judgments and efficient enforcement of consumer rights on the other hand. Even though some jurisdictions may handle the obligation to actively apply EU consumer law with well-established domestic rules, a balance must still be struck between conflicting interests or purposes in order to decide how and when these unclear or open-ended domestic rules should be applied. Therefore, the doctrine of *ex officio* application of EU consumer law is a potential source of turmoil that may alter existing doctrines and practices.

Since this kind of balancing of conflicting interests or purposes may also be at the heart of other cases, the incorporation of an obligation to apply EU consumer law may have a spill-over effect. From the perspective of national courts, the duty to apply EU consumer law *ex officio* is problematic in the absence of a corresponding obligation concerning consumer protection law of national origin. There may also be cases where consumer rules of EU and 'national' origin are mixed in one piece of legislation, or a national rule may simply extend EU law to new areas or give better protection. Therefore, there are good reasons to suggest that the procedural requirements set up by ECJ

[16] See Andersson, in this volume, section 2.

[17] Bach, in this volume, section 2.2.2; Fredriksen and Strandberg, in this volume, section 3.

for EU consumer law should be equally applied to other consumer protection rules. Although widening the scope of procedural requirements in this way is not at all necessary to fulfil EU/EEA obligations, it leads to more coherent national law.

As suggested by Ivo Bach, it can further be argued that the obligations developed by the ECJ should be taken as a vehicle for a broader widening of the court's duties to guide and in other ways help or assist a weaker party. A discussion of *ex officio* application of EU consumer law could spark a discussion of existing doctrines on the role of the parties and the role of the judge. Ivo Bach also ask why the court is not allowed to raise the question of limitation periods of its own motion.[18] As he notes, the reasoning behind the rule – that an honourable person may wish to pay a debt even after the limitation period has passed – is inconsistent, because a ruling would not prevent payment from being made anyway. Furthermore, the duty to apply consumer law *ex officio* may have spill-over effects on other areas with elements of public order and policy, and with mandatory rules, such as labour law, competition law and environmental law.

As to the scope of the EU/EEA obligation of *ex officio* application of consumer law, there are also some challenges relating to whether the obligation applies in other types of proceedings than ordinary court proceedings, for example where a consumer brings a case before a complaints board or a trader initiates simplified debt-collection proceedings. The issue arises as to whether, to what extent and how simplified proceedings and alternative consumer dispute resolution should be aligned with normal adversarial court proceedings to ensure equal and efficient protection of consumers. As Torbjörn Andersson explains, a passive consumer unaware of his/her rights may suffer a loss, which, in turn, reduces the efficiency of consumer law. Currently, the level of consumer protection varies depending on the type of proceedings chosen and whether the consumer or trader initiates the proceedings. The current situation presents an obstacle to the policy that the ECJ has promoted through its case law.

4. INTERNATIONAL LAW COMBINED WITH EU LAW

The Maintenance Regulation[19] demonstrates the fruitfulness of a multi-layered approach to harmonisation. By linking international law, the 2007 Hague Convention[20] and EU law, it achieves coherent rules for cross-border cases both

---

18 Bach, in this volume, section 3.

19 Council Regulation (EC) 4/2009 on jurisdiction, applicable law, recognition and enforcement of decisions and cooperation in matters relating to maintenance obligations (Maintenance Regulation) [2008] OJ L7/1.

20 Convention of 23 November 2007 on the International Recovery of Child Support and other Forms of Family Maintenance.

within and outside the EU. Although the 2007 Hague Convention does not regulate jurisdiction, the Maintenance Regulation does so by providing a set of jurisdictional rules aligned with the rules on recognition in the Convention, thus creating coherent regulation of maintenance in the EU and retaining conformity of intra-EU and international rules. Simultaneously, it enables multi-speed integration, ultimately letting the 2007 Hague Protocol[21] govern choice of law. As a result, Denmark and the United Kingdom were able to harmonise the procedural aspects of cross-border maintenance, without having to accept a harmonisation of the choice-of-law rules. The EU Member States form a uniform entity for third countries, which facilitates recognition and enforcement of family maintenance.

From the perspective of EEA/EFTA countries, connecting international law and EU law is as such welcome, but it has one crucial shortcoming: the Lugano Convention was not included in the development. The Lugano Convention and the Brussels I Regulation[22] were parallel instruments ensuring uniform rules for jurisdiction, recognition and enforcement. Now the rules on family maintenance have been transferred from the Brussels I *bis* Regulation to the Maintenance Regulation, disrupting the uniformity and causing some problems for implementation. Despite some negative effects, the 2007 Hague Convention and the Lugano Convention also complement each other by filling lacunae. Therefore, the 2007 Hague Convention helps with harmonising law across the EU–EEA divide.

The diversity of the rules on cross-border family maintenance in the Nordic countries illustrates the multifaceted character of multi-speed integration. The willingness to harmonise national law with EU and international law to increase coherence and facilitate cross-border proceedings may be more important than EU membership *per se*. Gaps and 'rough patches' may be unavoidable, but pragmatic interpretation and a deliberate quest for coherence smooth the way. Using a combination of international law and EU law may provide a strategy for solving the EU's relationship with the UK post-Brexit.

5. SOFT LAW

Soft law measures may be an essential component of harmonisation. Indeed, hard law and case law-based harmonisation may turn out to be futile if not accompanied by soft law. European civil procedure is founded on mutual trust

---

21 Protocol of 23 November 2007 on the Law Applicable to Maintenance Obligations.

22 Council Regulation (EC) 44/2001 on jurisdiction and the recognition and enforcement of judgments in civil and commercial matters (Brussels I Regulation) [2001] OJ L12/1.

and the rule of law, which necessitate both a well-functioning national civil procedure system and knowledge of the civil justice systems in other Member States. Various soft law approaches – such as judicial training networks, benchmarking in the EU Justice Scoreboard and development of common standards – extend stakeholders' understanding of comparative aspects, and thus contribute to mutual trust and the quality of national legal systems.

As Storskrubb suggests, a narrow focus on procedural rules is insufficient. The scope of harmonisation and chosen measures must be far wider to include a range of various issues, *inter alia* the independence of the judiciary, administrative co-operation and increased transparency. Judicial training is essential to ensuring equal and efficient application of European procedural law. Further, harmonisation calls for approximation of terminology and concepts. The ELI-UNIDROIT project is a key step in achieving these goals.

As explained by John Sorabji, the ongoing ELI-UNIDROIT project pursues the European rules on civil procedure as a coherent set of best practices.[23] By abandoning minimum standards and the lowest common denominator approach, the project aims at creating rules bridging – or at least narrowing – differences in national systems and to provide impetus for reform of national law. The project on European model rules has already had some success – many of the rules are implemented in the European Parliament's suggestion for an EU directive on common minimum standards for civil procedure.[24] Additionally, the reform of civil procedure in Hungary draws on the project.[25] The model rules approach elucidates how best principles rather than minimum standards may provide for more efficient harmonisation by encouraging countries across Europe to critically assess their current rules and practices, as Sorabji explains. Instead of conforming to the lowest common denominator, model rules invite European countries to rethink their litigation systems and cultures and to be innovative. The soft law approach engages countries regardless of their affiliation to the EU, extending 'European' civil procedure beyond the borders of the EU.

Despite the ambitions of using general soft law as a powerful tool for harmonising civil procedure across Europe, the soft law approach requires that countries are willing to engage in benchmarking and in re-evaluating current ideas, principles and practices. Conflicting policy goals may, however, be a further obstacle to adopting best practices, as Storskrubb notes.[26]

---

23 Sorabji, 'The ELI-UNIDROIT Project', in this volume, section 3.2.

24 European Parliament resolution of 4 July 2017 with recommendations to the Commission on common minimum standards of civil procedure in the European Union (2015/2084(INL)).

25 Sorabji, 'The ELI-UNIDROIT Project', in this volume, section 4.

26 Storskrubb, in this volume, section 4.2.

6. HARMONISATION OF LAW: OUTCOMES AND CHALLENGES

Across Europe, civil procedure is undergoing harmonisation, or at least approximation, through various mechanisms connected to EU hard law, international law and soft law. The level of harmonisation depends on many factors, including the type and quality of the European mechanism, the intended outcome, whether there is a need for reforms nationally, and the national attitude and traditional approach to the procedural issue at stake. Hard law mechanisms may not, perhaps somewhat surprisingly, be the most efficient method of approximation of laws. This may be the case because their aim is sometimes to facilitate cross-border proceedings rather than harmonisation *per se*, and because some of the EU Member States consider such mechanisms to be mere technicalities.

The national approach seems to be a vital factor when explaining whether and how different instruments influence national law. The Nordic countries consider much EU hard law to be 'technical', which may explain why it has had very limited impact on national law in the region. An unsystematic approach to implementation of *inter alia* sector-based rules may also hamper harmonisation and cause fragmentation. Interestingly, the requirements on *ex officio* application of EU consumer law have been subject to very limited debate in the Nordic countries considered in this study. The underlying reasons for this limited interest in the interrelation of EU law and national civil procedure remain unclear. Perhaps lack of awareness is self-perpetuating. The contrast to the Netherlands is striking, where Dutch courts and scholars have repeatedly addressed the issue of *ex officio* application of EU consumer law, constantly uncovering new issues. Similarly, the German discussion partly reflects the extensive academic interest in the field of European civil procedure. Academic writings trickle down to courts and legal counsel, *inter alia* through handbooks and scholarly texts.

Harmonisation is also a matter of politics and policies. The Maintenance Regulation, Lugano Convention and 2007 Hague Convention serve as examples. On the one hand, Denmark and the United Kingdom have opted out of parts of the EU regime. On the other hand, from its outside position, Norway has – in the main – made corresponding reservations and declarations to those of the EU so as to achieve parallel rules. Voluntary (over-)implementation and the application of soft law also necessitate political will – and perhaps even a culture inclined to use foreign law actively – to achieve harmonisation of law and develop national law.[27]

Family maintenance illustrates how international law may be a successful tool for harmonisation, both within the EU and in Europe more generally.

[27] Sorabji, 'The ELI-UNIDROIT Project', in this volume, section 5.

Similarly, soft law is an important avenue to coherence in the wider European context. Moreover, both methods also create options for managing multi-speed integration. Norwegian law demonstrates how the EEA Agreement has a semi-permeable character: procedural rules are intimately connected to enforcement of substantive law, such as consumer law and intellectual property rights, and pass through the filter into Norwegian law.[28]

All four types of law discussed in this volume have the potential to produce harmonisation, but also to increase the quality of the national civil justice system. All of them may serve as a source of inspiration for improving the national system and as an impetus for reforms. However, they may also induce lawyers to reconsider current structures, concepts and ideas. The idea of using EU law, international law or soft law to rethink current national law is echoed in most contributions in this book.

In sum, a multi-level approach to harmonisation or approximation of civil procedure may prove best. However, we should not underestimate the manifold obstacles to harmonisation, *inter alia* lack of understanding of the character of EU procedural law and the potential benefits of using international instruments in developing national law. If both national and international actors understand the benefits and potential adverse effects of EU, international and soft law influences on national civil procedure, and act accordingly, the interaction between different domains of law may be smoother and the most advantageous method of implementation may be selected.

Although each of the four aspects of harmonisation discussed in this book result in enhanced coherence and quality of proceedings, they may also have adverse effects particularly from the national perspective. Fragmentation of national civil procedure is a palpable threat. *Inter alia*, the piecemeal sectoral approach, special proceedings, rules or requirements only applicable to some cases, and inadequate co-ordination of proceedings may result in increased complexity, unpredictability and opacity, by challenging the coherence of the system. Why should the judge have a duty to intervene actively in consumer cases but not in labour cases? Why should enforcement of consumer claims focus on the courts, when courts hear only a fraction of the alleged infringements? Why should one implement a national version of the small claims procedure when the EU procedure hinges on national law?

The quality of the measures and the approaches chosen may also be decisive in terms of their impact on national law. The better European instruments complement international instruments, and the more the instruments offer best practices, the more likely they will be to induce harmonisation and provide an impetus for national measures. Poor quality minimum standards and overly complex rules may lead to 'technical' implementation.

---

28 Hjort, in this volume, sections 4 and 6.

ABOUT THE EDITORS

Anna Nylund is Professor of Law at the University of Tromsø – The Arctic University of Norway, specialising in civil procedure and alternative dispute resolution. She is Head of the Research group for procedural law and dispute resolution. She is a member of *inter alia* the International Academy of Comparative Law, the International Association of Procedural Law and a board member of the Nordic Association of Procedural Law.

Magne Strandberg is Professor of Law at the University of Bergen, Norway, and specialises in civil procedure law, theories of evidence and tort law. He is Co-chair of the Research Group for civil procedure law. He takes part in two working groups under the ELI-UNIDROIT project entitled 'From Transnational Principles to European Rules of Civil Procedure' and is a member of the Nordic Association of Procedural Law.

www.ingramcontent.com/pod-product-compliance
Ingram Content Group UK Ltd.
Pitfield, Milton Keynes, MK11 3LW, UK
UKHW051922100926
8556IPUK00021B/1318

9 781780 686936